The Sociology of
Community Connections

The Sociology of Community Connections

John G. Bruhn

New Mexico State University
Las Cruces, New Mexico

 Springer

Library of Congress Cataloging-in-Publication Data

Bruhn, John G., 1934–
    The sociology of community connections / by John G. Bruhn.
        p. cm.
    Includes bibliographical references and index.
    ISBN 0-306-48615-6 (hardbound) – ISBN 0-306-48617-2 (ebook) – ISBN
    0-306-48616-4 (paperback)
    1. Community.   2. Social networks.   3. Neighborliness.   I. Title.

HM756.B78 2004
307—dc22   2004054829

ISBN-10: 0-306-48616-4   e-ISBN 0-306-48617-2
ISBN-13: 978-0306-48616-6

Printed on acid-free paper.

Printed in the United States of America.   (TB/BM)

9 8 7 6 5 4 3 2 1

springeronline.com

To my Nebraska hometown, Norfolk,
where I experienced the love of community

Preface

People seem to have less time for one another and the nature of the time they do spend with others is changing. How and why we connect with people seems to be increasingly related to their usefulness in helping us to achieve individual goals and meet individual needs. While pursuing the credo of the survival of the fittest is not new, it has usually been balanced by a concern for the common good.

While there are many people who experience healthy, long-lasting, mutually beneficial relationships in our society, the values and ethics that sustain them lack the societal support evident in previous decades. In our society, indeed, in the world, there seem to be more broken and fragmented relationships than in the past, an absence of connections where they appear to be needed, an uncertainty and lack of trust in relationships we have sustained, and a tendency to select, restrict, and even plan, those connections which promote self-interest.

Depending upon their disciplinary vantage point, scholars differ in their attributions of causes for the changing and weakening of social connections in our country. These causes include technology, rapid social change, the ineffectiveness of social institutions in meeting new needs, greed and selfishness, greater ethnic diversity, the loss of community as a "place," generational differences, changing values, and fear. It is likely that all of these factors have contributed to the new ways in which we connect with each other.

Psychiatrist Anthony Storr (1988) pointed out that earlier generations would not have rated human relationships as highly as we do now. They were too preoccupied with merely staying alive and earning a living to have much time to devote to the subtleties of personal relations. Extending Storr's comments, Ernest Gellner (1996), a psychoanalyst, suggested that our present preoccupation with, and anxiety about, human relationships has replaced former anxieties about the unpredictability and precarious-ness of the natural world. He argued that, in modern affluent societies, most of us are protected from disease, poverty, hunger, and natural catas-trophes to an extent undreamed of in previous generations. But modern societies are unstable and lack flexible structures to respond to change. Increased mobility and social change have altered the institutions of fam-ily, religion, and education, which provided stability and guideposts in the past. Because we have more choice as to where we live, what groups we should join, and what we should make of our lives, our relations with other people are no longer defined by age-old rules and have, therefore, become matters of increasing concern and anxiety. As Gellner expressed it, "Our environment is now made up basically of relationships with others" (p. 34).

In recent years social scientists have attempted to understand what has happened to create the superficiality of connectedness we now observe and experience in our relationships with one another. A current concept used to interpret the changing character of American society is "social capital." Social capital refers to connections among individuals—their networks of connections that generate trust and reciprocity. A society that is character-ized by dense networks of reciprocity and trust is more efficient and stable. As Putnam (2000) said, "Trust lubricates social life" (p. 21). Trust is a form of social capital. It is essential to the willingness to cooperate voluntarily and therefore encourages behaviors that facilitate productive social inter-action (Tyler, 2001). Tyler suggests that the potential value of trust is that it encourages people to invest themselves in groups and institutions. To the extent to which people intertwine their identities with others social capital is created and facilitates the functioning of groups and institutions. Tyler warns that the basis of trust can change and the scope of trust can decrease in a society. When trust shatters or wears away, institutions collapse (Bok, 1978).

Brehony (2003) describes how rapidly trust and a sense of community can change. According to surveys immediately after September 11, 2001, 60 percent of Americans attended some kind of memorial service and Bible sales rose by more than 27 percent. There was a new respect for firefighters, police, and the military, and people rediscovered family, friends, and neigh-bors. But a Gallup poll conducted on September 21–22, just a week and a half after the tragedy, showed that church and synagogue attendance rose by only six percent. Compared to poll results conducted immediately after the terrorist attacks, Americans six months later were doing less praying, crying, and flag waving. A September 14, 2001 poll showed that 77 per-cent of Americans said they were showing more affection for loved ones than usual. By March 2002, that number had dropped to 48 percent and most of the people surveyed said they were back to life as usual (Brehony, 2003). There is no evidence that the tragedy of September 11 has had any impact on increasing attendance at religious services or on the importance of religion in the lives of Americans.

Americans have a tradition of rallying to help each other in times of crisis and then returning to life as usual. Life as usual seems to fit Messick and Kramer's (2001) description of "shallow trust," the type of trust associated with the interactions we have with strangers and acquaintances. Shallow trust evokes fast, mindless, shallow responses, like looking around before crossing a road or counting your change after a purchase. Messick and Kramer point out that shallow trust provides for shallow relationships, temporary groups and unstable organizations. Temporary systems of trust function as if trust were present without traditional sources of trust, such as shared experience, fulfilled promises, reciprocal disclosure, and familiarity being present. Trust has become quick, automatic, taken for granted, and shallow (Meyerson, Weick, & Kramer, 1996).

As human beings we reach out to create systems of relationships. We form various kinds of communities that embrace our diversity and uniqueness as well as our membership. We need social connections in order to survive. We continuously seek out relationships and change them as we age and our needs change. As our collective needs change we modify our culture and its social institutions, which, in turn, shape our individual lives.

This is a book about how we interact and connect with each other as individuals and groups in a variety of social situations. We interact out of necessity; we connect as a consequence of choice. Our connections are what create community. Networks of communities that are interdependent, diverse, and responsive to change, yet cohesive, provide the infrastructure for a healthy society. In today's world our societal infrastructure is continuously being tested by forces and demands that attempt to alter it, and thereby to change the nature of how we connect within our various communities. We need to analyze these forces and demands and understand the impact they have on our connectedness so that individually and collectively we can create more social capital than we use.

Acknowledgments

This book has evolved from the lectures and discussions in my class "The Sociology of Community" over the past four years. I am grateful for the constructive criticism from the many students who, through their questions, critiques of readings, topics chosen for term papers, personal experiences, and service learning projects have helped me in shaping a course, and a book, that incorporates theory, problem-solving, and application in useful ways.

I appreciate the time that Nate Brewer and Chuck Gerken gave me in obtaining their views and information related to the chapter on religious connections. Marty Tousley graciously gave me an interview and information on self-help and professional groups. Beverley Cuthbertson-Johnson provided many insights and suggestions for several chapters and words of encouragement. Christine Shinn's technical and professional expertise was invaluable in preparing the graphics and tables. The photographs of Roseto, Pennsylvania were taken by a friend, the late Remsen Wolff. Tracy Grindle typed several drafts of the manuscript with great care and helpful suggestions.

JOHN G. BRUHN

Contents

The Sociology of
Community Connections

There can be hope only for a society which acts as one big family, and not as many separate ones.

ANWAR SADAT

Chapter 1

Social Connections

INTRODUCTION

Humans are social beings who require the support and companionship of others throughout their lives. Social cooperation has played an essential part in man's survival as a species, just as it has in the survival of sub-human primates. Ethologist Konrad Lorenz (1965) pointed out that man is neither fleet of foot nor equipped by nature with a tough hide, powerful tusks, claws, or other natural weapons. Primitive man had to learn cooperation in order to protect himself from more powerful species and in order to succeed in hunting large animals; his survival depended upon it. Modern man has moved a long way from the social condition of the hunter-gatherer, but his need for social interaction and positive ties with others has persisted. Group living is an adaptation that provides protection, cooperation, competition, and communication to improve the chances for survival.

Some social scientists doubt whether the individual possesses significance when considered apart from the family and social groups of which he is a member. They consider that it is close social ties that give individual lives significance. Relationships act as points of reference that help us make sense of our experiences (Marris, 1982). We are embedded in networks of unique relationships which give our lives meaning, provide social support, and create opportunities. In the course of daily life we encounter many people who contribute to our sense of self. In essence we invest ourselves in each other. When people disappear and are replaced by others, we feel a sense of loss, however transient the relationship (Levin, 1980; Bruhn, 1991). After a loss we seek new connections, which is essential to our adaptation and integration with the external world.

It is well documented that social relationships are important for health and well-being (Berkman & Syme, 1979; Reynolds & Kaplan, 1990; Cohen &

Syme, 1995). Relationships are a major source of daily stress, but they also protect against the effects of stress. Deficiencies in social relationships such as social isolation and lack of social support are associated with physical and mental health problems (Bolger & Kelleher, 1993). Behavioral patholo- gies, ranging from eating disorders to suicide, are more common among people who are unattached (Baumeister & Leary, 1995). The need to belong is mysterious—no one knows why a healthy person will deteriorate if de- prived of human contact. We do know that most people find relationships necessary for survival and, when social interaction is limited or absent, the social and psychological scars are lifelong and irreversible. Modern societies use prisons, and prisons use solitary confinement, to punish peo- ple, which illustrate the principle that depriving people of close, primary relationships is aversive.

The effects of different kinds of relationships on social and psycho- logical well-being are mediated through recurrent patterns of support and conflict in daily life. It appears that it is our continuous learning from pos- itive and negative life experiences that provides the resilience for us to continually grow to meet life's challenges. When individuals become so- cially disconnected they are deprived of one of the key elements necessary to continue to grow and develop, that is, to benefit from the feedback from others and one's environment (Glantz & Johnson, 1999). Whether our so- cial connections are successful or unsuccessful, we learn how to connect with other people early in life.

OUR EARLIEST CONNECTIONS

The tendency to form interpersonal attachments is a fundamental characteristic of human biology (Bowlby, 1982a). When there is frequent, face-to-face interaction social bonds form easily. People want to be loved, recognized and have their dignity respected. The process of attachment seems to be involved in significant human relationships at all life stages, although the reasons for attachment and the way in which it is expressed vary with different ages and social contexts (Baumeister & Leary, 1995).

Social Bonds

Babies become interested in one another as early as two months. Bowlby (1982a, b), in his studies of the mental health of homeless chil- dren, noted that human infants began to develop specific attachments to particular people around the third quarter of their first year of life. When attachment in infancy is secure it is associated with social competence in toddlers. When attachment is not secure lower social competence in the form of heightened aggression has been noted in preschool and beyond (Shonkoff & Phillips, 2000). Before their first birthday infants show preferences for, and responsiveness to, certain adults. Attachments reduce a child's fear in novel and challenging situations and enable the child to explore and manage stress. In addition, attachments strengthen a child's sense of competence and efficacy.

Early studies of attachment behavior focused on mother-infant interactions (Bowlby, 1982a, b; Ainsworth, 1979). In recent decades more attention has been given to father-infant bonding and to the ecology of the family environment as it influences children's attachment behavior. The father's participation in the birth, and his attitude toward it, has been found to be a significant factor in predicting father-infant attachment (Peterson, Mehl & Leiderman, 1979). Whether the family is a single or dual earner household has been shown to affect father bonding with infants from four to thirteen months; boys from dual earner families were more likely to have insecure attachments with their fathers, but not with their mothers (Braumgart, Julia, Courtney & Garwod, 1999). Father-preschooler attachment has been found to be related to attitudes and behavior surrounding play. Fathers of more securely attached children gave more direction to their children and in turn, their children made more suggestions and positive responses (Kerns & Barth, 1995). Furthermore, fathers of secure infants were more extroverted and agreeable than fathers of insecure infants, they also tended to have more positive marriages and experienced more positive emotional spillover between work and home (Belsky, 1996).[1]

Children use their parents as a secure base. When the base becomes insecure, bonding also becomes insecure. Parents have been observed repeatedly in their homes during family discussions and play with their children as early as six months postpartum. Interpersonal hostility during family play predicted less secure preschooler-mother attachment, whereas at three years, greater marital conflict was associated with a less secure attachment with both the mother and father (Frosch, Mangelsdorf & McHale, 2000). Owen and Cox (1977) found that chronic marital conflict produced disorganized attachment behavior that could not be mediated by ego development or sensitive parenting. For example, eating disturbances have been found to be associated with the child's perception of the father as unreliable and undependable (McCarthy, 1998). McGarvey's (1999) research team studied the bonding styles of the parents of incarcerated youth and found that youth whose parents had a bonding style of affectionless control reported greater distress (feelings of low self-esteem, hopelessness, and suicidal attempts and thoughts), than youth whose parents had an optimal (satisfactory) bonding style.

A frequent key finding in the literature is that attachment to one parent compensates for, or buffers against, an insecure attachment in the other (Fox, Kimmerly & Schafer, 1991; Verschueren & Marcoen, 1999). As Belsky (1996) pointed out, the more infant, parent, and social-contextual assets a family has, the greater the probability that the child will have a secure attachment.

Studies suggest that early attachments set the stage for other relationships. Companion animals are a vital part of the healthy emotional development of children. As children develop, animals play different roles for the child at each stage of development. In laboratory experiments, it has been found that people of all ages, including children, use animals to feel safe and create a sense of intimacy (Robin & ten Bensel, 1985). It is widely accepted that the key factor in the relationship between children and companion animals is the unconditional love and acceptance of the animal for the child, who accepts the child "as is" and does not offer feedback or criticism (Beck & Katcher, 1983). Securely attached young children, compared with insecurely attached peers, have an easier time developing positive, supportive relationships with teachers, friends, and others. Securely attached children have a more balanced self-concept, a more sophisticated grasp of emotion, a more positive understanding of friendship, and they show greater conscience development, and more advanced memory processes than insecurely attached children. By the age of three, children in all societies have developed friendship patterns (DuBois, 1974). Establishing friendships with other children is one of the major developmental tasks of early childhood. Friendship is an important way we become integrated into society. Friends play an important part in the creation and maintenance of social reality (Jerrome, 1984). Social skills are important in the formation of children's friendships. Children in grades three and four who had good social skills had more friends and interacted more positively with peers than children with poor social skills (Fehr, 1996). Popular children were judged to be more socially competent than unpopular children. Children who do not have actual peer relationships often compensate with fantasy friends. Studies have shown that the lack of satisfactory peer relationships in early childhood can create deficits that cannot be reversed by later experience. The specific experiences of children without friends influence the ways in which these children will experience separation and loss as adults. Children who learn to equate being alone with being lonely and rejected will carry a fear of loneliness with them as they grow up. Lonely adults have much in common with children without friends (Rubin, 1982).

Parent belief systems and modes of parent-child interaction provide important ways in which culture is transmitted to children. The kind of interactions parents have with larger society affects the child's socialization. Children are very susceptible to the positive effects of social connectedness. The best predictor of children avoiding behavioral and emotional problems was the degree to which they and their parents were enmeshed in a supportive social network, lived in a supportive neighborhood, and attended church regularly. Even in preschool years parent's social capital confers benefits on their children, just as the children benefit from their parent's financial and human capital. Social capital is especially crucial for families who have fewer financial and educational resources (Runyan, Hunter, Socolar, et al., 1998). The ways in which parents talk with their children is one of culture's most powerful symbol systems (Shronkoff & Phillips, 2000). Ainsworth (1979) noted that it is the way the infant organizes his or her behavior towards the mother that also affects the way in which the infant organizes behavior toward other animate and inanimate aspects of the environment.

Tizard and Joseph (1970) found that it was not only attachment, but the social context in which young children spent significant time that influenced their cognitive development. Children in nursery schools, compared to those cared for at home, were found to be less friendly, less willing to stay alone, more shy, less verbally adept, had fewer neighborhood social experiences, and significantly fewer experiences in the adult world. The consistency of the environment and caregivers is key to developing secure and trusting relationships in children.

An adult's capacity for creating good relationships with other adults depends upon the person's positive experience with significant adults as a child. However, attachment varies in quality and quantity. Not every human being has the same need for attachments. Storr (1988) emphasized that intimate attachments are *a* hub around which a person's life revolves, not necessarily *the* hub. Some people choose to live their lives with superficial or limited relationships, or monastic lives of silence, e.g. Trappist monks. Storr pointed out that the development of the capacity to be alone is necessary if the brain is to function at its best and, if the individual is to fulfill his highest potential. Sarason, Pierce and Sarason, (1990) question whether close attachments in childhood always equate with a need for closeness in adulthood. Perhaps it is sufficient for some adults to know how to access, and use, available socially supportive ties on an "as needed" basis.[2] But, a network of supportive ties needs to be established and held in reserve until needed, so even seemingly perfunctory social ties take time to establish.

Thomas (1974) described how all animals are social, but with different degrees of commitment. He wrote:

In some species, the members are so tied to each other and interdependent as to seem the loosely conjoined cells of a tissue. The social insects are like this; they move, and live all of their lives, in a mass; a beehive is a spherical animal. In other species, less compulsively social, the members make their homes together, pool resources, travel in packs or schools, and share the food, but any one can survive solitary, detached from the rest. Others are social only in the sense of being more or less congenial, meeting from time to time in committees, using social gatherings as ad hoc occasions for feeding and breeding. Some animals simply nod at each other in passing, never reaching even a first-name relationship. (p. 102)

Social bonds are nonetheless the basic building blocks of the larger world. While these bonds begin in the family, they are not limited to it. Of available agents of socialization, the family has the greatest impact. Until children begin school the family has the responsibility of teaching children skills, values, and beliefs. Overall, research suggests that nothing is more likely to produce a happy, well-adjusted child than being in a loving family. All learning does not result from intentional teaching by parents. Children also learn from the kind of environment that adults create and the modeling they do, knowingly or unknowingly. Whether children see the world as trustworthy or hostile, depends largely upon their early connections with adults.

Schooling also enlarges children's social worlds to include people with social backgrounds different than their own. In addition to formal knowledge, children also receive informal lessons about society's way of life. Among peers, children learn to form social relationships on their own. The mass media has become an increasingly important influence in teaching children values. A national survey by the Henry J. Kaiser Family Foundation (Roberts, Foehr, Rideout & Brodie, 1999) found that children between the ages of two and eighteen averaged five and a half hours per day watching television and video tapes, playing video games, and inter-acting with computers, as many hours as they spent in school or interacting with their parents. The majority of children and older youth have their own media in their rooms, and view it alone or with other children absent adult presence. Media influence the attitudes and behavior children and youth develop regarding all kinds of relationships.

The early years of socialization are key in helping to shape an individ-ual's personality, beliefs, and values, including attitudes toward social con-nections. Culture helps us understand differences in human interactions—what is valued and what is not valued. We do not choose the individual worlds in which we are born; therefore, we learn to understand people and their cultures through their interactions. People do not simply interact in a context; they join with others to *create* a context and to determine what kind of behavior is called for (Schwalbe, 1998). Schwalbe has said that while behavior in many social situations is fairly predictable, it is "interactional surprises" that provide the most effective contexts for learning about each other. Learning through interactional surprises continues throughout life. It is through the early stages of socialization that we learn to trust others and ourselves, and begin to internalize our experiences with community. Interactional surprises always test, and either strengthen or weaken, our earliest learning about social trust (Erickson, 1963).

WHEN EARLY CONNECTIONS FAIL

One of the ways we have learned to understand normal attachment between parents and child is by observing children who have a deficiency. A certain degree of attachment has to occur for survival, but there are all kinds and degrees of attachment. Some mothers will try to never leave their babies, while there are mothers who leave their children alone too much. Both extremes create their own difficulties in maturation. Sometimes the need to belong and the fear of being alone helps the child defend and even protect an abusive parent. On the other hand, attachment to the mother fails when children are left alone for extended periods of time in environments where there is inadequate stimulation and emotional contact, resulting in their failure to thrive socially and intellectually (Ordway, Leonard & Ingles, 1969). There are autistic children from birth, who are unable to become attached to any object. These children often fail to smile and cannot adequately differentiate themselves from animate or inanimate objects. There are also disturbances which occur when a child is suddenly deprived of contact with its mother through a serious illness, and when a child is not able to separate from its mother properly.

Parental behaviors such as anxiety, agitation, ignoring, or support, during early childhood illness can also influence children's attitudes toward illness which may become part of their adult behavior when ill (Melamed & Bush, 1985). We know that very young children are capable of empathetic behavior, and in combination with physical symptoms, mothers' minor illnesses become an important learning resource for child socialization (Tinsley, 1997). Children see different levels of attachment modeled among family members during times of illness and other crises. For example, they may see a parent "use" illness as a way of eliciting love and attention, or they may see a parent deny pain or illness to assert their independence and resist support from spouse and family.

Researchers have found that the early experience with an attachment figure contributes to a person's experience with future relationships and feelings of self-worth, self-efficacy, and a capacity to enjoy intimacy. The attachment experience itself helps to form a child's personality, but it is the interactions between the mother and the child that are of critical importance. Close relationships high in intimacy give the mother and child a feeling of being understood, validated, and cared for (Sarason, Pierce & Sarason, 1990). On the other hand, some individuals develop an "attachment hunger," and become so attached to, or dependent upon, another person that they become disabled and dysfunctional.[3]

Several studies have linked attachment failures in early life with particular health effects in adulthood. Thomas and Duszynski (1974) followed 1,185 medical students who had attended The Johns Hopkins Medical School between 1948 and 1964. When the study first began all of the students were in good health. While students they were questioned about certain aspects of their early lives. The investigators then followed the students for many years after their graduation, returning to the questions they answered as students to ascertain any connections between their early childhood attachments and their health status as an adult. The researchers found that the physicians who developed cancer, mental illness, or who later committed suicide were more likely to have described the lack of close family relationships, particularly with their fathers, early in their lives. These physicians also described themselves as suffering from loneliness and experienced more disruptions of close relationships throughout their adult lives (Thomas & Greenstreet, 1973).

Paffenbarger and his colleagues (1966; 1969) examined the incidence of suicide in a population of 40,000 students, and found that 225 of former University of Pennsylvania students had committed suicide in the years following graduation. They compared these suicide cases with a large number of randomly selected students. The researchers found that those students who later committed suicide were likely to have come from homes where the parents had separated or divorced, or the father died early. Other distinguishing characteristics were the same as for death from coronary heart disease: nonparticipation in sports, secretiveness, and social isolation. The early loss of a parent, social isolation, and loneliness were highly predictive of both suicide and premature death from heart disease.

In a related study, Russek and his colleagues (1990) randomly chose 125 men from the Harvard University classes of 1952–1954, and asked them to rank their parents on a four-point scale of emotional closeness. Thirty-five years later, the researchers examined the medical histories of these volunteers and found that those who had ranked their relations with parents as strained and cold experienced significant poor health. Ninety-one percent of the men who reported that they did not have a close relationship with their mothers suffered serious medical crises by mid-life, including coronary heart disease, hypertension, duodenal ulcer, and alcoholism. This is in contrast to the forty-five percent of such illnesses among the men who reported that they had warm relationships with their mothers. More striking was the finding that all of the men who reported that both parents were cold and aloof had serious health problems by mid-life.

The results from these studies illustrate how important the earliest interpersonal interactions between a child and its parents are in developing successful connections later in life. A key aspect of early childhood interactions is that the child acquires a sense of stability and continuity about social interactions (Cohen & Syme, 1985). A longitudinal study of 216 "ordinary" people, who were interviewed periodically and given several psychological scales and surveys over twelve years, revealed that not all effects of childhood deprivation in adulthood were negative. Some participants in the study who had deprived childhoods became resourceful and optimistic adults, finding a mate and friends that they lacked as a child (Fisk & Chiriboga, 1990). The researchers found that, while most of the deprived young people tended to be pessimistic and continued to harbor ill feelings about their parents in adulthood, there were exceptions. Participants who were creative and curious, had a capacity for intimacy, mutuality, made friends, and who coped with stress adequately, were more likely to overcome their deficits in early life attachments.

Further evidence that the relationship between childhood deprivation and adult attachments comes from a thirty-five year prospective study of ninety-five men who were first interviewed as college sophomores (Vaillant, 1978). Findings suggested that a poor childhood environment leads to poor object relations in adulthood, but does not affect the quality of marital relations. Vaillant concluded that marriage served as a means of mastering unhappy childhoods for many of the men.

René Dubos (1968) pointed out that as human beings we experience the world through our senses. An infant senses the quality of its physical and social environment through how it is treated, and learns to reciprocate accordingly. Reciprocation can be a stimulus to the development of a close affective and protective bond, from which the infant, and later the child, can generalize to other close relationships and chosen ties (Pilisuk & Parks, 1986).

We generalize our experiences regarding attachments to others. We develop an attitude towards fellowship (or community) or, as Alexis de Tocqueville called it, "an art of association." And, we modify our attitudes about the type and extent of the social ties we want with others on the basis of our memories of, and experiences with, previous attachments (Lynch, 2000).

Relationships are good for us. People who are happier, and in better physical and mental health, tend to have good relationships of all kinds. The kinds of relationships found to be most beneficial are marriage and

Table 1.1. Benefits Derived from Social Connections

- Recognition of others; feedback from others about ourselves
- Acknowledgement and reciprocation of emotion and feelings
- Provides safety net or social support
- Enhances health and well-being, recovery from illness, longevity
- Expands friendships and creates new social networks
- Connectedness gives life meaning and happiness
- Connections are necessary to meet basic needs of survival
- Connections are the way we learn the rules for living in a particular culture
- Connections link the past and present
- Through connections we identify with others, share ideas, and talents that may benefit larger groups of people

cohabitation, family and kinship, friends, work relationships, neighbors, and memberships in organizations (Argyle & Henderson, 1985). Relationships offer a variety of direct and indirect benefits including caring, trust, sympathy, affirmation, tangible and informational help, and social support. Other benefits are summarized in Table 1.1.

Personal Attachments across the Lifecycle

The nature of personal attachments and social networks affects the ease with which people make life stage transitions and their well-being at each stage. Stueve and Gerson (1977) used data from a survey on men's best friends conducted among 985 men living in the urban areas of metropolitan Detroit, to explore how personal relationships change over the life course. Lifecycle stages provide both opportunities and constraints regarding friendship choice. A particular life stage influences the pool of friends available in any particular setting as well as the costs and benefits of any given friendship. The researchers found that marriage, parenthood, and aging all influenced men's social networks. Of the life transitions examined the most pronounced break occurred on entry into young adulthood, when married men became fathers for the first time. They left intimate childhood friends behind and formed new relationships with adults who shared the responsibilities of family life. Socializing with friends became more home-centered and less frequent. As needs and situations change people reevaluate and reconstruct their social networks.

Lifecycle patterns in social behavior are typically caused by the demands of family, the slackening of energy, and the shape of careers. Time with friends peaks in one's early twenties, declines with marriage and children, rebounds in one's sixties with retirement and widowhood, and gradually declines with the death of friends. According to Putnam (2000), civic engagement also follows a lifecycle pattern, rising from early adulthood to a plateau in middle age, from which it gradually declines. By examining the arc of life's civic engagement in the United States from the 1950s to the latter 1990s, Putnam found an overall decline in civic engagement in all age groups in the United States. Since the 1950s each generation that has reached adulthood has been less engaged in community affairs than its immediate predecessor. This has been evident in a national decline in social capital. Putnam concluded that much of the decline in civic engagement in the United States during the last third of the twentieth century is attributable to the replacement of an unusually civic generation by several generations that are less embedded in community life. The context in which the majority of our connections are played out occurs in communities of various kinds.

COMMUNITY ATTACHMENTS

Community: A Definition

There is no single agreed upon definition of community, but generally community implies that there are relationships between a group of people, usually in a certain locale, that go beyond casual acknowledgment.[4] These relationships are closer than casual relationships because the group shares some common goals, values, and, perhaps a way of life that reinforce each other, creates positive feelings, and results in a degree of mutual commitment and responsibility. Communities vary, as do the individuals who are members of them, but community also implies a degree of constancy in fellowship and belongingness among members. Members choose to associate with, or connect to, each other.

> Scott Peck (1987) has expressed the meaning of community as follows: If we are going to use the word "community" meaningfully we must restrict it to a group of individuals who have learned how to communicate honestly with each other, whose relationships go deeper than their masks of composure, and who have developed some sufficient commitment to rejoice together, mourn together, and to delight in each other, make others' conditions our own. (p. 59)

Loewy (1993) adds an additional perspective to Peck's concept of community. He said, "in true communities members share a common belief in community itself as a uniting value. In such communities suffering is held to a minimum, solidarity is firm, and purpose is strong" (p. 234). Peck's and Loewy's definitions describe social units we might call "tight," "strong," or "closed." Not all communities exclude outsiders, but most watch their boundaries carefully so that the uniqueness of the culture and solidarity of its members can be retained, e.g. religious and ethnic communities.[5] On the other hand, community members who violate norms may be ostracized, e.g. members of religious orders who violate vows. In the process of socialization we learn the value of close attachments as well as the value of broadening those attachments to others outside of our family.

It is what we learn about relationships in our families that encourages or discourages us from broadening our connections to neighbors, organizations, and beyond. Extending our connections involves crossing social and cultural boundaries. The experiences we had with trust in our families will also affect the degree of comfort we have with extending ourselves to trust others.

Sense of Place

We become socially and emotionally attached to places as well as to persons. Place attachment involves the emotions, attitudes, beliefs, and behaviors associated with a specific physical place. Places create emotion and feeling in us because they reflect the values and beliefs we learned and experienced in that setting (Humnon, 1992). For example, "the pub" is an institution unique to England . . . despite honorable efforts, the pub has not been successfully transplanted into other countries, because it is an organic part of the growth of English community life (Hunt & Satterlee, 1986). Similarly, Oldenberg (1997) laments the loss of "the third place" in America . . . an informal public place that was essential to good towns and great cities in the past, when conversation was the main activity. The third place was the place where Americans spent their time besides home and work, a place Oldenberg calls "neutral ground," "a leveler," which he says has been replaced almost entirely by relaxation, entertainment, and companionship in the privacy of one's home.

There was a great deal of concern among early social theorists that, as American society became more urbanized, the increasing size, density, and heterogeneity of urban life would weaken the primary ties of urbanites to neighbors and kin, which, in turn, would sap the strength of emotional attachments to place (Wirth, 1938). Studies have shown that sense of place is not strongly related to size, density, or heterogeneity, but these factors do alter our "sense of community."

Sense of Community

A sense of community is positively related to a subjective sense of well-being (Davidson & Cotter, 1989). People are looking for relationships that can be characterized as kind and understanding, but it is growing harder to find open and expressive relationships. People's ties with each other are fragile, and their bonds with others are disrupted as friends move or change jobs. There is a basic need to belong, which includes the need for frequent personal contacts and for bonds with others that provide stability and emotional concern (Baumeister & Leary, 1995). Unfortunately, an increasing number of people do not have bonds with others (Jason, 1997), and also report being unhappy whether they live in the suburbs or in cities (Adams, 1992).

Sarason (1974) said that almost everyone knows what a sense of community is. It is "feeling," "knowing," or the "degree of comfort" that everyone is working together toward a common goal, or participating in an activity or event that depends upon everyone's cooperation. Researchers have described four aspects of the sense of community (McMillan & Chavis, 1986). The first aspect is the *sense of membership*, that is being a part of a team. The second aspect is *influence*, that is, believing as a member of a team that a person has some degree of power and can make a difference to the outcome. Third, is the *integration and fulfillment of needs*, namely that a person can "round out" the team through their individual skills and abilities. Last is the aspect of a *shared emotional connection*, where a person feels good about participating in a joint effort and enjoys the acceptance of other team members.

A sense of community can be limited to a specific task or action such as a group effort to obtain a sufficient number of signatures to get a local candidate's place on a ballot, or a "neighborhood watch" effort to reduce crime, or a united voice from parents to make local schools safer (Colombo, Mosso & DePiccoli, 2001). A sense of community is often the result of a community disaster where individual and group differences that might separate people during normal times are overlooked in a community's pulling together to help survivors or victims. A sense of community is also evident among ethnic groups, especially newly arrived immigrants, who "stick together" often settling with others from their ethnic group who preceded them in an effort to survive in a strange and new country. A sense of community can also indicate the degree of bondedness between people who live in a small community where everyone knows one another and their level of trustfulness.

Prezzo and his colleagues (2001) found that the strongest predictor of a sense of community was the degree of neighboring. Neighboring can be an important complement to family support systems, especially for adults with no, or limited, family support. Neighboring can enhance the safety of older people, improve their access to critical goods and services, and promote their independence, positive feelings about themselves, and enhance their general psychological well-being and social involvement (Wethington & Kavey, 2000). The help most likely to be exchanged in neighboring is passive, short-term, and problem-focused.

Community attachment and ties are lowest in neighborhoods with high residential mobility. The length of one's residence in a community is the strongest predictor of neighboring activities and community attachment (Jeffres, 2002). It is not uncommon that people living in adjacent units in an apartment complex or near to each other in single family homes, have not had a conversation with their neighbors, do not know their names, or have no interest in even a cursory connection with them. Many young couples both work, single persons usually have social connections with people other than where they live, and the elderly and single women are reluctant to initiate conversations with strangers. With frequent job transfers and travel, short-term job commitments, and complex personal and family dynamics, most urban neighborhoods are not places to expect to establish meaningful social ties. One's residence has become a stopping off place between work and a social life that is found elsewhere.

A sense of community is also related to the degree of responsibility we feel when our help might be needed in a community crisis. Milgram (1970) found striking deficiencies in social responsibility in crisis situations in cities. He provided as an illustration the Genovese murder in Kew Gardens, a staid, middle class area in Queens, New York on March 14, 1964 (Milgram & Hollander, 1964). Catherine Genovese, coming home from a night job in the early hours, drove into a parking lot at Kew Gardens railroad station and parked. Noticing a man in the lot she became nervous and headed toward a police telephone box. The man caught and stabbed her in three separate attacks over a half hour. Twice the voices and glow of bedroom lights from 37 of her neighbors, many of whom witnessed the stabbings from their apartment windows, frightened him off. One witness called police after Genovese was dead. In attempting to explain their actions most of the witnesses said that they didn't want to get involved (Gansberg, 1964; Mohr, 1964). When the sense of community dissipates, events like the "Kitty Genovese syndrome" continue to occur.

In 1995, another tragic death occurred on a bridge in downtown Detroit. Deletha Wood hit another car driven by Martell Welch. With dozens of other cars stopped on the bridge, Welch pulled Wood out of her car, ripped off some of her clothes, and pushed her down on the car hood to beat her. One of Welch's friends then held her down while Welch retrieved a jack that he used to smash her car. Wood broke free and ran to the bridge railing, where she threatened to kill herself. Welch's friends yelled, "Jump, bitch, jump!" as she dropped off the bridge. Two men jumped off the bridge to save her, but it was too late. Wood's body was recovered downstream minus a leg, which had been severed by a passing boat. Several motorists called 911 on their cellular phones, and 26 people came forward to help police track down the suspect (Stokes & Zeman, 1995).

There is a part of citizenship that is not explicitly taught in our culture and that is, decisions about when and where to not become involved. At some time in each of our lives we will experience a situation where the personal risks to our safety or that of our family, legal liability, or other consequences dissuade us from becoming involved in saving a life or calling for help. Learning about the consequences of not connecting with others is as important in our socialization as learning the benefits of connecting with others. A sense of community involves reciprocity in caring, sometimes at great personal risk.

Milgram (1972) pointed out that one's close friends do not necessarily live in close physical proximity, but even Genovese's general cries for help caused no one to help or call for help. Milgram explains that such a lack of involvement and sense of responsibility may be people's way of coping with urban overload or it may illustrate the limits of the Good Samaritan principle in cities where there is continual evidence of the hardness of life. Etzioni (1993) said that people help one another and sustain the spirit of community because they sense it is the right thing to do. A sense of community implies a sense of reciprocity or acceptance of the principle of the Golden Rule (Etzioni, 1996b).

We know what the sense of community is at its two extremes, when it is present and when it is absent. When it is absent we experience it as a lost sense of meaning and decrease in the quality of life (Prezza & Constantini, 1998). When it is present we experience it as genuineness and caring. Between these two extremes we create many different kinds of illusionary and temporary ties with each other, often referred to as *pseudo communities* (Levin, 1980). As a district manager of Starbuck's Coffee recently said, "We don't just sell coffee. We sell community. We offer a culture. We create a place that isn't work, isn't home, is a little escape where you can read a book, visit with a friend, and have your favorite espresso drink" (Hermann, 2001). Moe and Wilkie, (1997) expressed it differently. They said, "today community is any rootless collection of interests rather than people rooted in a place."

What makes a community important and meaningful is an individual's feeling that he or she is valued, and that his or her safety and protection is provided for, and that there is access to resources outside the community (Sarason, 1974). The kind of community that each individual believes fosters healthy connections for them is what is key. This has been called the *competent* community (Iscoe, 1974). Not all communities are competent, some are incompetent, and others are destructive. Individuals choose the environments they think will be the best for them, physically, socially, and psychologically. Individuals differ in their tolerance of social spacing, and hence, their tolerance of community, as illustrated by the following German fable told by ethologist (animal behaviorist) Paul Leyhausen (Wilson, 1975):

> One very cold night a group of porcupines were huddled together for warmth. However, their spines made proximity uncomfortable, so they moved apart again and got cold. After shuffling repeatedly in and out, they eventually found a distance at which they could still be comfortably warm without getting pricked. This distance they herewith called decency and good manners. (p. 257)

No one residential environment can satisfy every person's needs. Indeed, people's needs change. Communities differ in their ability and willingness to adapt to meet the changing needs of their members. Overall, only about nine percent of the United States population has not moved during the last thirty years. States and counties with a high proportion of "long-termers" have experienced less change, have an older population and have limited opportunities for economic growth.[6] Substantial, sustained geographical mobility has measurable impacts on communities and individual and family attachments to them.

When a community is no longer a vital part of each person's interest, solidarity is lost, and community easily falls apart (Loewy, 1993). Community dies when it no longer seeks to reach a common ground to meet the needs of its members, when its members no longer work toward collective solutions to common problems, and when there is no longer enjoyment in solidarity and its obligations. Community dies when the sense of community dissipates. It is often replaced by temporary experiences of togetherness purposely planned or created by tragedy.

Community: Present or Missing?

The word "community" carries a degree of emotionalism almost equivalent to that of the American flag; it represents unity, affirms our belief in civility, causes us to assess our belongingness, and reminds us of the irreversibility of social change. Community can usually only be described, not defined, and experienced, not generalized. A call for community is often heard in difficult times and situations because it is a positive word which implies togetherness. Some observers have lamented the loss of community, while others say that community is still present but in different forms.

One journalist wrote, " 'community' is one of those words that could use a nice vacation but probably won't be getting one. For centuries,

American moralists have fretted about the fragmenting of community" (Lears, 1997). Sociologist Dennis Wrong (1976) has pointed out that the concern over the loss of community in modern society is over a century old. According to Young (2001), communities lost their Gemeinschaft in the 19th century and continued to lose their virtue in the 20th century. Some writers go back to primitive societies to discover models of "true" community, others locate community in their childhoods, in rural villages and small towns, and in communes, but one thing is certain about community, it is always gone (Wrong, 1976). The reasons for the loss or lack of community are numerous. Frequently named contributors to the erosion of community in earlier decades are consumerism, bureaucracy, competitiveness under capitalism, the overriding goal of success, and changes in the structure of the economy. In the 1950s social critics complained that there was too much community, too much conformity, and too much participation in collective tasks. In the 1990s there was concern that individualism had gone too far, and with continuing urbanization that community as a 'place' had almost disappeared. José y Gasset once pointed out that "people do not live together merely to be together. They live together to do something together" (Wrong, 1976, p. 78). The error, according to Wrong, lies in conceiving of community as an end in itself, apart from the activities and functions that bind people together, and apart from those values that constitute a shared vision of life. The achievement of community, he said, cannot come from pursuing it directly, but only as a by-product of the shared pursuit of more tangible goals and activities (Wrong, 1976).

There is considerable evidence that "the" community has been attenuated by time, technology, and shifting values (Starr, 1995). Some business entrepreneurs, who believe community is missing, have attempted to reestablish it as a place. For example, the Agritopia Project in Gilbert, Arizona is an effort to design and build a neighborly community around an organic farm. There will be historic looking houses with porches, basements, backyards, home-based businesses, community gardens, and a town square. Driven by principle rather than economics alone, the project attempts to solve several problems common in current development neighborhoods lacking character and livability (Jensen, 2002). On the other hand, those who believe that community is present but in new forms, point to the computer which has created new electronic connections and communities. It is not only a decrease in connectedness that is an issue in debates about whether or not community has been lost. People continue to connect, but what seems to be missing is the loyalty and trust we experienced in earlier decades. Loyalty and trust are intricately related to what people value. There is evidence that a significant shift in values is the major reason for the decreased loyalty, trust, and sense of community that is being observed and experienced today.

SHIFTING VALUES, CHANGING CONNECTIONS

Fukuyama (1999) points to a worldwide shift in values over the past four decades that he calls The Great Disruption. He has found that this significant shift in values has occurred in all developed countries except Japan and Korea, which have strong familialistic traditions. The conditions that were the major causes of the value shift were the transition from an industrial to an information age economy and the birth control pill. These factors have led to the rise of individualism and diminution of community. Indicators of this value shift are increased crime, diminished importance of the family, kinship, and social cohesion, and decreased trust in public institutions. (See Table 1.2.) The effects of this value shift are a decrease in society's social capital and civility. This shift has taken different forms and progressed at different speeds in different countries, but trust has declined in most all developed countries.[7] Trust, according to Fukuyama, is the key by-product of the cooperative social norms that constitute social capital. While public or institutional trust has eroded, private or personal trust has declined as well (Fukuyama, 1995). The decline of trust has a direct effect on the ability of individuals to not only perform the responsibilities of citizenship with credibility, but on the ability to relate to one another with integrity and accountability.

Putnam (1996; 2000) and Fukuyama came to similar conclusions. Examining a number of different surveys of Americans from 1965 through 1985, Putnam found evidence of a continuous decline in social networks, trust, and people's connectedness to the life of their communities. He noted that there were important differences among generations. Americans during the Depression and World War II were more deeply engaged in the life of their communities than the generations that have followed them. The passing of this "long civic generation" appeared to be an important cause of the current decline in our civic life. Yet, generational differences did not seem sufficient in itself to explain the sharp decline in social capital and civic engagement. Why, Putnam, asked, beginning in the 1960s and accelerating in the 1970s and 1980s, did the fabric of American community life begin to fray? Why are more Americans bowling alone instead of in bowling leagues as in earlier years? (Putnam, 2000).[8]

Many possible answers have been suggested for this puzzle including time pressure, mobility, suburbanization, disruption of family and marital ties, the civil rights revolution, growth of the welfare state, Vietnam, Watergate, changes in the economy, movement of women into the labor force, and as Fukuyama suggests, the information age and the birth control pill. Putnam systematically examines data that indicates some, if not all, of these factors have contributed to a shift in our values. But, the largest

Table 1.2. Institutional Changes and Value Shifts in the United States Circa
1960 to 2004

Social institutions involved	Key values involved	Indicators of shifts in values
Family	• autonomy • commitment • responsibility • rights	• alternative forms of family • new reproductive technology • "Wider" families (rights and obligations)
Education	• bureaucracy • accountability • choices • standards • discipline • achievement	• increase in home schooling • safety concerns • violence • mainstreaming
Religion	• integrity • trust • ethics • accountability	• electronic church • decreased membership • leaders held legally accountable
Politics and government	• trust • accountability • responsibility • honesty	• voter apathy • cynicism • skepticism • terrorism
Economy and work	• opportunity • diversity • independence • loyalty • ethics	• globalization • mergers • downsizing • CEO indictments
Health and medicine	• rights • ethics • responsibility • autonomy • trust • money	• ethical issues • loss of physician's autonomy • increasing inequalities in affordability of care

culprit, Putnam says, is television. Controlling for education, income, age, race, place of residence, work status, and gender, television is strongly related to social trust and group membership. He points out there is direct evidence about the causal connection between television usage and a decrease in civic engagement from surveys conducted in several communities just before and just after television was introduced. A major effect of television's arrival was a reduction in participation in social, recreational, and community activities among people of all ages. In addition, television increases aggressiveness, reduces school achievement, and is associated with psychosocial problems among heavy watchers. Television privatizes leisure time and anchors people at home. Heavy users are isolated, passive, and detached from their communities, although we cannot be certain that they would be more active in their communities in the absence of television (Putnam, 2000).

Over the past four decades Americans have changed their attitudes toward, and connections with, several traditional social institutions, especially religion, family, government, and school. The effects of weakened support and the pressures of social change have caused these institutions to stretch their resources and accountability in attempts to meet the diverse and changing needs of society.

Wuthnow (1998) believed that most Americans still care deeply about their communities and make efforts to connect with other people. But these efforts do not take the same forms as they had in the past because of increased diversity, fluidity, interdependence, and the specialization of contemporary life. As a result our social institutions have become fragmented and porous with less rigid boundaries, which, in turn influences how we carry out our responsibilities. We observe a looseness in the way we are connected in society, and porousness allows some people to slip through the cracks and become isolated and disconnected. What we had previously experienced as tightly-knit communities have become "on call" types of connections that meet people's needs at various times. Indeed, the mobility and fluidity of our society increases the chance that the members of communities change before we can get to know them as persons.

Naroll (1983) said that the "moral nets" that tie people together have weakened. Communities exist, but they are less likely to be warm and fuzzy places, and what holds them together are the common interests of their members and not their deep emotional ties. There is less opportunity for people to demonstrate their trustworthiness or to experience the reciprocity of trust. It is not only trust, but the friends of trust, namely, integrity, commitment, professionalism, and what Purdy (1999) has called "the common things" (responsibility, commitment, and dignity), that have changed. These are some of the unintended consequences of social change (Handy, 1994).

Trust, Community, and Social Capital

Trust is the glue that holds communities together. Cohesive communities, in turn, build social capital. Trust is the expectation that people will interact honestly and cooperatively to benefit each other. Trust helps community members reach a consensus about assigning value to its resources. These resources exist in friendships, organizations, subcultures, and institutions, and are used to accomplish certain tasks, for example, the socialization of children (Coleman, 1994). These networked resources, the reciprocities that result from them, and the achievement of mutual goals through shared resources, is what is known as social capital (Field, Schuller & Baron, 2000). Social capital is about networking; those persons who have strong relationships with others will be more likely to share and exchange resources than those who have weak relationships. But, close relationships do not necessarily indicate high trust, and high trust can sometimes be dysfunctional, so people with weak ties can also generate social cohesion and trust (Granovetter, 1973).

Trust is key to the debate about the state of our country's connectedness. Figure 1.1 shows how trust mediates the relationship between social networks and social capital. Misztal (1996) said that trust promotes social stability (community), social cohesion (friendships and associations), and collaborations (networks). Some authors argue that changes in attitudes and behavior, including trust, can be attributed to generational differences, and strongly assert that our core values as a country have not changed (Ladd, 1999; Lin, 2001; Skocpol, 1997; Samuelson, 1996).[9] Turiel (2002), stated that the decreased trust observed may be related to the ways moral goals are being attained in our society. In a recent national study, Wolfe (2001), found that the traditional moral virtues of loyalty, honesty, self-restraint, and forgiveness, are alive and well although they don't resemble the ideals of previous generations. Wolfe found that Americans want to lead a good life, but they are determined to decide for themselves what a good life means.

Singer (1995) would say that this personal search for virtue in a world of choice is one of the major reasons for the loss of community.[10] In Singer's words, ". . . the collective impact that each of us has in pursuing our individual self-interest will ensure the failure of all our attempts to advance those interests" (p. 22). Myers (2000) agreed, stating, "Another potential price we pay for radical individualism is its corrosion of communal well-being. Several of the problems that threaten our human future . . . arise as various parties pursue their self-interest but do so, ironically, to their collective detriment" (p. 185).

The Right to Disconnect

Howard (1994) pointed to the Right's Revolution, beginning in the early 1950s with civil rights law, as the origin of a massive value shift in

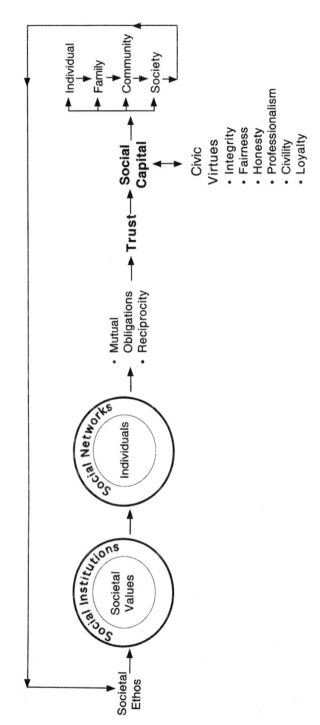

Figure 1.1. Interrelationships between Societal Values, Social Networks, Trust, and Social Capital in Society

the United States when reformers began to advocate a change in the way law worked. Rights became a way to eliminate all inequalities. He noted that today even ordinary human encounters involve lawyers. Rights have become a fad. Handing out rights was supposed to provide justice in a fragmented society. But rights have ended up dividing society. Rights have become a wedge that has split the common good (Howard, 2001).

We have become a society where everyone has the right to disconnect. It is believed that freedom for all would be enhanced if each person could use law to preserve his own freedom (Howard, 2001). We see institutions as the enemy, whereas in reality we create institutions and are their members. When institutions no longer meet our needs we should reframe them, or abolish them, not act as if we are their victims and attempt to control them.

The Rights Revolution has gained momentum over the past forty years, eroding the connectedness between people that Putnam claimed is necessary to create social capital. Instead, the Rights Revolution has fostered suspicion, cautiousness, anger, fear, and defiance among all citizens. There is no incentive to know one's neighbor, to become engaged with social and civic groups other than those that are concerned with protecting a personal right and to vote only to oppose an initiative that threatens one's own property or lifestyle. There is such disbelief that citizens can collectively help in curbing crime that many citizens feel more secure in purchasing their own weapon to be certain of their own protection.

PURPOSEFUL CONNECTIONS

Networked Connections

Wellman (1999) affirmed that large scale social change has not destroyed communities. Community has rarely disappeared from societies, rather it has been transformed. The transformation we have experienced in our society is treating community as networks of personal relationships rather than as a place. The defining criterion of community, according to Wellman, is what people do for each other, not where they live. We connect for a purpose. Communities are about types of social relationships that are personally meaningful. Neighborhood is, for example, only one form of a personal community. People can maintain meaningful and supportive connections without common residence and even without frequent face-to-face contact, or as Webber (1970) has suggested there can be "community without propinquity."

Most people affect their society through personal influences on those around them. We each construct and choose our own social connections.

We tend to build networks of relationships composed of other people like ourselves and associate with people like ourselves (Fischer, 1982). Community is a person's set of ties with friends, relatives, neighbors, and work associates. But we also have ties with persons whom we may not like or with whom we voluntarily choose to associate. Often our connections are neither egalitarian nor reciprocal, but they may be important (Wellman, 1982). In this way, community can be conceived of as a "community of limited liability," where individuals may demand more from their community than they are willing to invest and when the community fails to meet their needs they leave (Janowitz, 1967). It is likely that individuals with these expectations will not invest the time to get to know their neighbors unless there is a specific reason to do so. Indeed, it is more the norm that, except for family and small clusters of friends, most members of a community do not know each other (Wellman & Gulia, 1999).

Social network analysts have found that communities today are usually loosely bounded, sparsely knit networks of specialized and privatized ties. There are several elements that make personal communities unique such as their range or extensiveness, frequency and type of contact, degree of intimacy, and the type of relationship between network members, i.e. kin, friends, and work associates. Personal communities change as the relationships among these elements change, therefore, people must maintain different portfolios of network ties (Wellman & Gulia, 1999; Wellman & Potter, 1999). Putnam (2000), said more of our social connections are one shot, special purpose, and self-oriented. Most of the personal community ties that people use to transact their daily lives today are short-term and do not require reciprocity, nor is it expected.

Multiple Communities

Most people are connected to numerous networks in different types of personal communities, which, if both virtual and real-life interactions are included, could easily number in the hundreds or more. Some people may cast a wide net in an effort to explore which connections are most beneficial or useful to them at a given point in time. Others may carefully select their network choices opting for membership in fewer, but more densely knit communities. Still others may purposefully mix and match their network choices blending risk-taking and stability. There are good reasons to carefully weigh one's decisions about joining networks. Not all social networks provide the same accessibility, accountability, availability, intimacy, confidentiality, or rewards. The advantage of being tied to multiple networks is that one can gain access to a wider range of resources through network linkages. Multiple network links provide a great deal of flexibility in the duration of different links, their strengths, availability and accessibility, and benefits (Craven & Wellman, 1973).

The epitomé of an expert networker and member of multiple communities is Paul Revere. Everyone knows about Paul Revere and his midnight ride. American legend is that of Revere as a solitary messenger who rode horseback throughout the Lexington-Concord area randomly awakening people announcing that the British were coming. Fischer (1994), in his recent book, dispels this legend describing how Revere was an organizer and promoter of the common effort. Many other riders helped Revere carry the alarm. Revere was a strong character and had a vibrant personality. He had a reputation for getting things done. He served as clerk of the Boston Market, was health officer of Boston, founded a fire insurance company, organized a charitable association, served as jury foreman, was coroner of Suffolk County, a Mason, active in several political organizations, and a silversmith. He supplied evidence for the Boston Massacre and made five revolutionary rides to visit towns to justify the Boston Tea Party. Revere was gregarious, always a joiner, known as "an associating type of man," a zealot for freedom, who at his funeral had troops of friends. He was a doer and others trusted him.

As Fischer explains:

> [Revere's] astonishing speed did not occur by accident. It was the result of careful preparation. Paul Revere and other messengers did not spread the alarm merely by knocking on individual farm house doors. They also awakened the institutions of New England. The midnight riders went systematically about the task of engaging town leaders and military commanders of their region. They enlisted its church and ministers, its physicians and lawyers, its family networks, and voluntary associations (p. 139) . . . much of what happened that night was cloaked in secrecy, but repeated evidence indicates that Paul Revere played a unique role. From long association he was acquainted with leaders throughout the province. He knew who they were and where to find them even in towns that he had not expected to visit. (p. 141)

Revere was a "generalist" whose self-interest was the community. While there are many citizens today who are members of multiple communities, most of the communities are carefully selected, and added and dropped, as they meet the needs of individuals. Perhaps the only aspect of multiple community membership today that is shared with Revere is the skill in developing linkages between communities. Networking helped Revere promote the common good. Today networking is used to promote the specialized interests and goals of individuals and groups. Etzioni (1993) aptly showed how the networking of special interest lobbyists craft and promote policies that do not represent the community at large. Paul Reveres are rare today. When they exist they are solitary advocates who are characterized as alarmists. Others cautiously listen to their message but resist joining their network because of the ambivalent personal rewards of working for the common good in an age where individual achievement is rewarded whether or not there are societal benefits.

SUMMARY

One of the first things we learn in the process of socialization is that social connections shape the quality of our lives. We require the support and companionship of others throughout our lives. When we are deprived of human contact, or are unsuccessful in our connections with other people we can experience a variety of physical and mental health problems.

Early attachments set the stage for adult relationships. Children use their parents as a secure base. When parental relationships become insecure bonding between parents and child also becomes insecure. The greater the child, parent, and social-contextual assets a family has, the greater the probability that the child will have a secure attachment.

Friendship patterns for children are an extension of their parental experiences. Social skills are important in the formation of children's friendships. Children with social skills have more friends than children with poor social skills. The lack of satisfactory peer relationships in early childhood can create deficits that cannot be reversed by later experience. Children are very susceptible to the positive effects of their parent's social connectedness. Social connections are especially important for families who have few financial and educational resources because they provide an entré into vital social networks.

School, in addition to the family, enlarges children's social worlds to include people with social backgrounds different than their own. We generalize our experiences regarding attachments to others and develop an attitude towards fellowship and community. Community implies a degree of constancy in fellowship and belongingness among members. Members choose to associate with, or connect to, each other.

Communities vary, as do the persons who are members of them. We are members of many different kinds of communities as we move through the lifecycle. We become attached to physical places as communities because physical features reflect the values and beliefs we learned and experienced in that setting. We also know whether community is present or absent by our "sense" of the degree of comfort we feel. A sense of community usually is associated with the degree to which people know and trust one another. What makes a community important and meaningful is a person's feeling that he or she is valued, and that his or her safety and protection is provided for, and that there is access to resources outside of the community. What is key is the kind of community that each person believes fosters healthy connections for them.

When community is no longer a vital part of each person's interest, solidarity is lost, and communities fall apart. There is concern on the part of many scholars of the world scene that community is declining. The concern over the loss of community is not new. The concern has a long history, but its revival is usually associated with heightened urbanization, residential mobility, and rapid social change.

The erosion of "the" community as a place particularly, has been said to have gained impetus around the 1960s when the world began to experience significant shifts in values, especially in family values. In addition, the transition from an industrial to an information age economy and the birth control pill led to the rise of individualism, a decline of community, decreased trust in public institutions, and in society's social capital. Scholars and researchers have vigorously debated whether there is a decline in community, or whether the observed shifts in attitudes and behavior are due primarily to generational differences. For example, a recent, large survey conducted in different geographical regions of the United States found that the traditional moral values of loyalty, honesty, self-restraint, and forgiveness are alive and well although they don't resemble the ideals of previous generations. Individuals want to decide for themselves what a good life means for them. We have become a society where the Rights Revolution gives individuals the right to disconnect. Howard (2001) believes the Rights Revolution has gained momentum over the past forty years, eroding the connectedness between people that is necessary to create societal social capital.

Social network analysts argue that large scale social change has not destroyed communities, rather communities have been transformed. This transformation is treating community as networks of personal relationships rather than a place. The defining criterion of community, the analysts state, is what people do for each other, not where they live. We each construct and choose our social connections and build networks of relationships composed of other people like ourselves.

Communities today are usually loosely bounded, sparsely knit networks of specialized and privatized ties. These personal networks change as the elements comprising them change so people must maintain different portfolios of network ties. More of our social connections are one shot, special purpose, and self-oriented. Most people are connected to numerous networks in different types of personal communities ranging from virtual encounters to real-life interactions.

Networking helped Paul Revere promote the common good. Today networking is used to promote the specialized interests and goals of individuals and groups. Paul Revere "generalists," whose self-interest is the community, are rare today.

QUESTIONS FOR DISCUSSION

1. Is it possible for adults to overcome the effects of social isolation or broken social bonds in their early childhoods? How might a person's early experiences with attachments and connections influence the values and beliefs they teach to their own children?
2. Is it possible to learn to trust others in a distrustful society?
3. What are some of the ways individuals can disengage or distance themselves from connections they do not want to make?
4. What are some of the factors that cause us to re-evaluate our connections and social networks as we age?
5. What are the communities you are currently a member of and what needs or purposes does each serve? Are there gaps in your social connections and networks now? If so, why? Are these gaps important enough to fill? How do these gaps affect your other connections and networks?
6. Have you observed or experienced the limits of the Good Samaritan principle? What are the social, legal, and personal limits of your willingness to help another person in need?
7. What are your limits in trusting others—how many people would you ask to collect your mail while you were out-of-town? How many people would you let store items in your garage? How many people would you ask to borrow money from? How many people would you lend your cell phone to? What are the various factors or conditions you would consider in these situations of varying degrees of trust?
8. Why do many people today feel that they are victims?
9. What does "the common good" mean to you personally? How do you contribute to the common good? How do we learn about the common good in our society?
10. Do you believe the United States has lost (or is losing) social capital? Explain.
11. How connected are you to your community? To larger society? Do you do volunteer work? Are you active in organizations? Did you vote in the last election?

Chapter 2

Conceptions of Community
Past and Present

INTRODUCTION

The concept of community in sociology has its origin in Ferdinand F. Tönnies' theory of Gemeinschaft and Gesellschaft (Community and Society) in 1887 (Sorokin, 1940; Loomis, 1957). But the idea of community was evident much earlier in Confucius' theory of the five fundamental relationships (Bahm, 1992). Confucius contrasted Small Tranquility with Great Similarity in the same way Tönnies compared the mentality of Gemeinschaft with its opposite Gesellschaft. Contrasting societal typologies were evident in the work of Plato (the Ideal Republic versus the Oligarchic Society), Aristotle and Cicero's ideas of true and false friendship, St. Augustine's concepts of the City of God versus the Society of Man, and many other social thinkers before and after Tönnies.

The word "community," much like the word "culture," has been used so freely in the lay and scientific literature that it is often assumed that everyone understands it and is in agreement about its importance. Yet, while the definitions of both words can vary substantially, they seem to be protected as if they were totems.

Since its origin in sociology, community has been contrasted with society, an equally variably defined and broad concept. According to Berger (1998) the contrast between community and society is part of the conservative political tradition of sociological ideas. Even as social change has greatly eroded the traditional conceptions of community, emotional debates about the loss of community persists among both laymen and social scientists. Berger (1998, p. 324) describes the contrast—"community is tradition; society is change. Community is feeling; society is rationality.

Community is female; society is male. Community is warm and wet and intimate; society is cold and dry and formal. Community is love; society is business." The word community and its variable meanings has continued throughout the centuries because it is an emotional attachment to place and it offers ideal guidelines for human relationships. The early theorists of community were influenced by the cultural and societal changes they experienced while developing their theories. Where and when people experienced community has influenced their conceptions of it.

EUROPEAN CONCEPTIONS OF COMMUNITY

Karl Marx (1848) was one of the first sociologists to analyze the effects of industrialization and urbanization on communities in Europe. He, and his colleague, Fredrich Engels, believed that the growth of the city was liberating in that specialization enabled people to act on their own. In cities people could assume a political role, planning their environment using new scientific skills. Marx and Engels (1844) saw the emergence of the city as an evolution from the tribe to the state. But, not every city was liberating; some remained attached to the bonds of their primitive community—with a limited division of labor, common property, and lack of individualism. As a result, some cities were dependent upon agriculture and lacked the drive of a dynamic economy. The further complete, and worldwide evolution of cities, they believed, would only occur when workers became aware of the real cause of their problems, (which was capitalism), united, and acted to transform their society.

"Community" in Europe, had its roots in Teutonic culture. It was proposed by Ferdinand Tönnies in his classic work in which he described two contrasting kinds of social life: Gemeinschaft (village or community) and Gesellschaft (association or society; Tönnies, 1887; 1940; Sorokin, 1940). These two prototypes occupied the opposite ends of a continuum; societies evolved from their childhood (Gemeinschaft) to their maturity (Gesellschaft). Tönnies favored Gemeinschaft as the ideal type of community with its simple, familialistic, intimate, private way of life where members were bound together by common traditions and a common language, and villagers experienced a sense of "we-ness." At the other extreme, Gesellschaft, represented a lifestyle of self-interest, competitiveness, and formal relationships. Tönnies was concerned, as he observed the effects of the Industrial Revolution and rapid urbanization in Europe, that Gemeinschaft would be lost as these social changes altered social relationships and humanity became more mature.[1] He romanticized Gemeinschaft and intellectually resisted its further evolution.

**Table 2.1. Milestones in the Evolution of the Concept of Community
in Europe, 1840–1925**

Karl Marx (1848) and Friedrich Engels (1844)
- Human condition of cities is the result of economic structure.
- Changing the economic structure would create a different city with different social interaction patterns.

Ferdinand Tönnies (1887)
- People united by family ties, work for the common good (Gemeinschaft) in contrast to individualism and disunity of cities (Gesellschaft).
- Gemeinschaft is superior. City as a threat to human values.

Emilé Durkheim (1893)
- Mechanical solidarity based on social bonds; Organic solidarity based on individual differences.
- Organic solidarity is superior. City creates new cohesion based on mutual interdependence.

Georg Simmel (1905)
- City life can cultivate indifference.
- People can adapt by aloofness.
- Freedom in the city can help develop individuality.

Max Weber (1921)
- Cities could be positive liberating forces.
- Need to develop full urban community based on model of medieval communities.
- Historical and cultural conditions would produce different types of urban adaptation.

A contemporary of Tönnies, Emilé Durkheim, also observed the industrialization of Europe and developed a theory of community based on two contrasting types, *mechanical solidarity* and *organic solidarity*. Durkheim believed that people who lived in small towns and in family units were united because they shared customs, rituals, and beliefs, and were able to subsist without dependence on outside groups. These people had *mechanical solidarity* because their social bonds resulted from their likeness—they were united automatically. On the other hand, societies that were based on differences, especially occupational specializations, were more dependent upon each other to meet various needs. This was typical of cities. Durkheim called this form of social order *organic solidarity*.

In contrast to Tönnies, Durkheim (1893) believed that urbanization was a positive force as it enabled people to have greater freedom and choice. While Durkheim acknowledged that city life would be more complex and have more problems, he also saw that urban life would provide for greater individual development and new forms of social involvement. Durkheim's conceptualization of community gained more creditability because he saw community as more than its context or setting and proceeded to define a set of Gemeinschaft-like characteristics that could be found in both villages and cities. Tönnies romanticized a type of place and saw social change as destroying a good thing, whereas Durkheim emphasized the importance of the characteristics of relationships and how social change shapes and reshapes them in different contexts and times.

Georg Simmel (1905) also a contemporary of Tönnies and Durkheim, was an astute observer of social conflict and became concerned about the social psychology of the city. In particular, Simmel feared that people would react to increasing population density by developing psychological disorders and antisocial behavior. Like Tönnies and Durkheim, Simmel was concerned about the effects of urbanization on human values. He wondered how an individual could maintain a spirit of freedom and creativity in an urban environment. In the city some people could maintain their individuality by being different or acting different in order to call attention to their presence. He believed, optimistically, that people could transcend the pettiness of city life by adopting a blasé attitude or detachment so that they could reach a new level of spiritual and personal development. According to Maciones and Parrillo (2001), much of the current evidence fails to support many of the fears of classic theorists like Tönnies and Simmel in particular, about the pathology of urban living.

Tönnies, Durkheim, and Simmel developed their theories of the city by reading about and experiencing the cities they knew. Max Weber (1921) sharply disagreed with this approach, believing that any theory that focused on cities in only one part of the world at one point in time was of limited value. His approach was to survey cities in several countries. On the basis of his research Weber developed a concept of an ideal type of city, which he called the "full urban community." While he believed that not all cities would contain all of the elements of an ideal city Weber proposed that a full urban community would be characterized by: 1) trade or commercial relations; 2) a distinct mechanism of exchange or market; 3) a court and some degree of legal autonomy; 4) social relationships and organizations; and 5) some degree of political autonomy. Weber, like Durkheim, believed that cities could be positive forces, but he was pessimistic about 20th century cities. He thought that medieval cities were the only ones that met his definition of a full urban community. Weber, nonetheless, hoped that the "good life" of medieval cities might reemerge.

Weber disagreed with his contemporaries who saw cities as creating social and psychological qualities that made urban life distinct. Instead, Weber suggested that economy and politics gave cities their uniqueness. Therefore, different societies would create different types of cities.

The major contributions of four of the six European theorists (Marx, Engels, Tönnies and Durkheim) were their analyses of the contrasts between rural and urban life and, in addition, they established the city as an important concept to study. Simmel and Weber contributed theories about how cities worked. Simmel, Weber and Tönnies saw the city as a threat to the erosion of human values. Durkheim acknowledged urban problems but was optimistic about an individual's ability to cope with them. Finally, Marx and Engels saw the solution to urban problems as the replacement of the capitalistic system (Maciones & Parrillo, 2001).

AMERICAN CONCEPTIONS OF COMMUNITY

Human Ecology

Continued urbanization and a steady flow of immigrants, many of whom settled in cities, contributed to the development of urban sociology in the United States. It was not surprising that Chicago, which had grown to a population of nearly three million by the beginning of the 20th century, would become the site of the first urban studies center in the sociology department at the University of Chicago. Robert Ezra Park, an energetic journalist, who was influenced by a book written by a fellow journalist describing urban problems (Steffens, 1904), was recruited to develop the center. The center flourished as many other outstanding sociologists joined the department and became actively involved in studying city life.

Park (1952) was convinced that all parts and processes of the city were linked and that the city was a moral as well as a physical organization. He said, "Human ecology is... not man, but the community; not man's relation to the earth which he inhabits, but his relations with other men, that concerns us most" (p. 165). Park's image of the city centered around three principles. One image was that of city life as a complex division of labor driven by industrial competition. He was concerned that commercialism would result in the erosion of traditional ways of life. A second image Park had of the city was that formal, large-scale bureaucracies would replace informal face-to-face interaction. The third image was an emphasis on the social and psychological aspects of urban life. Park believed that city life would become increasingly rational, that is, social connections based on likeness would be replaced by those based on self-interest or necessity (Maciones & Parrillo, 2001).

Park's concept of human ecology was an application of the biologist's concept of the "web of life," where all things form a system of interdependence. Park was interested in the social processes by which cities maintained their balance or equilibrium and the processes that disturbed that equilibrium (Park, 1936). In Park's view, the city was a living laboratory

Table 2.2. Milestones in the Evolution of the Concept of Community in the United States, 1915–1950

Robert Park (1915)
- Saw city as a moral and physical organization.
- City as a system and living laboratory.
- Saw possibilities of freedom and balance in the city.
- First formal urban studies program in U.S.

Robert and Helen Lynd (1929)
- Studied a representative American community.
- Identified division of population into social classes.
- Conducted follow-up focused on economic and political power and social class.

E. Franklin Frazier (1932)
- Emphasized the importance of the ecology of black communities.
- Analyzed class distinctions among blacks.

Louis Wirth (1938)
- Developed first theory of the city—size, density and heterogeneity of population interact to create a way of life termed "urbanism."
- Was pessimistic about urbanism as a way of life—saw the positive aspects compromised by disorganization he observed in Chicago.

Robert Redfield (1930s)
- Developed a theory of a folk-urban continuum based on his observations of four communities in the Yucatan. Population increases cause folk communities to move along the continuum to become cities.

Carl Withers (1940)
- Studied small village in the Ozarks to find conformity in lifestyles, consensus on issues, similar values, and hostility to outsiders.

William Foote Whyte (1940)
- A study of the social structure of an Italian slum.
- Deals with the structure and leadership of informal groups of "corner boys" and their relationships with racket, police, and political organizations.

W. Lloyd Warner (1941)
- Studied the social class structure of a New England city.
- Detailed social class with economic, geographic, and ethnic factors.

St. Clair Drake and H. R. Clayton (1945)
- Studied the social class system of blacks in Chicago; delineated three social classes.

A. B. Hollingshead (1949)
- Analyzed the social system of a small mid-western town and the socialization of high schoolers.
- Identified five social classses.

in which one could study natural areas, their structures, processes, patterns, and relationships to other areas of the city. For example, a study of Chicago's spatial patterns showed that there were five concentric zones which radiated out from the center of the city to the suburbs. The zones were differentiated from each other by how land was used. This pattern of urban development was thought to be applicable to other cities in the United States.

In 1938, Louis Wirth published an essay titled "Urbanism as a Way of Life," which gained much notoriety and acceptance. His contribution to urban sociology was to identify factors that he believed were universal social characteristics of the city. He defined the city as a large, dense, permanent settlement with socially and culturally heterogeneous people. The three dimensions of Wirth's paradigm of the city: size, density, and heterogeneity, interacted to create what he called "urbanism." Like Park, Wirth saw the freedom cities could bring, but was critical of the possible effects of urbanism, namely a dissolution of traditional values and meaningful relationships. He warned that the positive aspects of urbanism would be overtaken by the problems of city life. A more positive urban environment could only be created by deliberate urban planning.

Robert Redfield (1941), an anthropologist, proposed a theory of the evolution of different types of communities. Redfield drew upon archeological and ethnographical evidence to conclude that there was a folk-urban continuum—a broad and subtly shifting range of communities extending from the folk village at one extreme to the city at the other. He believed this pattern existed throughout the world. Small communities are isolated, religious, closely knit and insular, while cities are diversified, secular, loosely knit, and fluid. He found four communities in the Yucatan Peninsula that enabled him to study the folk-urban continuum in the 1930s. As Redfield studied the communities he observed a subtle shifting of behavior as the communities moved along the continuum. Causes of the movement along the continuum were an increase in population, which, in turn, created density and more formal, impersonal relationships. The differences observed by Redfield could be detected in a single community as it moved through its lifecycle. It is noteworthy that the dimensions of Louis Wirth's paradigm of urbanism, namely size, density and heterogeneity are also important components of Redfield's conception of the evolution of the city. Both Wirth and Redfield were concerned that the costs of urbanism were the personal values found in simpler communities.

Anthropologist Carl Withers (pseudonym James West, 1945), observed the folk end of the continuum in his study of Plainville, a small Missouri village of 275 families in the Ozarks. The community's exposure to the outside world was a highway running through town. Plainvillers were cautious, isolated, showed similar lifestyles, beliefs and values, and had a tolerance for nonconformists, but not for outsiders. While the villagers "knew" they were "behind the times," they relished their slow movement toward "modernity." Plainville would be on the folk end of Redfield's continuum, but the highway through town would eventually be an intrusion on the town's isolation and move it further down the continuum towards modernity.

The ecological school of sociology of doing studies in the community was very different from the abstract theorizing about community of European sociologists. The studies carried out in the 1920s and 1930s in Chicago were descriptions of the real life conditions and behavior in "natural communities." There was a special interest in the disconnectedness of individuals and groups such as hobos, prostitutes, slums, juvenile delinquents and gangs, professional thieves, and dance hall workers.

In the late 1930s and early 1940s William Foote Whyte (1943/1955) lived in Cornerville, a slum district inhabited almost exclusively by Italian immigrants and their children for three and a half years, eighteen of those months were with an Italian family to obtain an intimate view of family life and to establish contacts with the community. Whyte learned Italian to be able to talk with the older generation, and joined in local activities to win friendship and confidence with the community. Cornerville was known as a problem area and was at odds with the larger community. Whyte believed that only when the structure of a society and its patterns of behavior have been identified, can solutions be provided for real and perceived problems. This classic work was typical of the Chicago School of Human Ecology.

In the tradition of the Chicago School, Eliot Liebow (1967), an anthropologist, studied a small group of anchorless adult Negro males who came together regularly on Tally's Corner in a blighted section of Washington, DC's inner city in the early 1960s. Liebow, much like William Foote Whyte, attempted to understand the survival and resiliency of these men in the face of the anti-community forces that operate within the contemporary urban slum. The men fell back on their primary group and used friendship and the buddy system as a resource and buffer to cope with failure when necessary. Liebow (1993) later in his career became a participant observer in a study of an emergency shelter for homeless women in a small city near Washington, DC. He detailed the life histories of several women and followed their progression after they left the shelter. Liebow concluded that people are not homeless because they are physically disabled, mentally ill, abusers of alcohol or other drugs, or unemployed. These conditions do not explain homelessness. Homeless people are homeless because they do not have a place to live.

However, criticisms of the generalizability and replicability of the studies along with the availability of new sources of census data and sociological research methods, and increased suburbanization and geographical mobility, caused the ecological model to lose its appeal in sociology (Bernard, 1973; Brint, 2001). While the ecological studies of Chicago faded, community studies with different approaches and objectives were conducted in other small towns in the United States. Some studies focused on describing the power and social class structures of small communities and attempted to identify measurable characteristics of social class.

Among the first of such studies was that conducted by Robert and Helen Lynd (1929) in the mid-1920s in what they called a representative American community, Middletown, later identified as Muncie, Indiana. They were interested in finding out how basic needs were met in a relatively closed social system. They used a blend of ethnographic methods and statistical data. The Lynds found that the ways needs were satisfied was through a social structure that divided the population into business and working classes, each of which performed essential social functions differently. The researchers followed-up the community ten years later focusing on its class and political power structures. They described the power that certain persons acquired as a result of their social position in Middletown.

An Australian anthropologist, W. Lloyd Warner (1941), applied some of the same techniques he had used in Australia to study communities in the United States. He was primarily interested in how communities maintained stability and achieved social integration. Warner used strict criteria to select a New England town, which he studied in the 1930s and named Yankee City. In a series of reports Warner described the class and status structure of Yankee City, its ethnic patterns and industrial system. He found that the various social structures were highly integrated around the structure of social class. He identified six social classes and their differing lifestyles.

In the late 1940s Warner studied Jonesville, a small community in the Midwest, to better understand structural factors that explained community integration. Instead, he gained insights into the divisiveness of social class and factors that would mitigate it such as upward social mobility. Later, other studies validated the importance Warner attached to upward social mobility as a method of reducing the resentment of inequalities in social rank (Bernard, 1973).

Three studies of the social class structure of black communities have been conducted. The earliest was that carried out by W. E. B. DuBois in 1899 in Philadelphia. DuBois distinguished four social classes on the basis of income. Deploring the chasms that separated the classes, he was dedicated to organizing the community to achieve unity and cohesion to benefit the masses. In a study completed in 1932, E. Franklin Frazier (1937), showed that the organization and disorganization of black family life in Chicago were closely tied to the economic and social structure of the black community. As a result of segregation the black community had assumed a definite spatial pattern. Frazier identified seven zones radiating outward from Chicago's central business district. He noticed that family disorganization diminished and community life was more stable in the zones that were more distant from the city's center. Another study of the class structure of the black community in Chicago was carried out by St. Clair Drake and Horace R. Clayton (1945) in the early 1940s. The study analyzed the ecological, institutional, and cultural patterns of the community. Color, occupation, income, standard of living, and proper public behavior were criteria used in delineating a system of three social classes.

In the mid 1940s A. B. Hollingshead (1949) studied a small town in the Midwest with an interest in the socialization process of adolescents, especially how social class influenced this process. Hollingshead identified five social classes in his study of Elmtown which led to the subsequent development of a quantifiable approach to placing individuals in a social class on the basis of their achieved educational level, usual occupation, and place of residence. This method, known as the Index of Social Position, was later applied by Hollingshead and a psychiatrist, Fredrick Redlich (1958), in a study of the interrelationship between social class and mental illness in New Haven, Connecticut. They found a relationship between social class and the distribution of types of mental illness. Moreover, each class reacted to mental illness in different ways, and psychiatric patients in the various social classes received different kinds of treatment. For example, patients in the upper social classes were more likely to receive psychotherapy, while patients in the lower social classes were more likely to receive pills, electric shock, or become hospitalized.

Community Power

Floyd Hunter (1953) was interested in community power and how it was used. He intensively interviewed forty men who were in decision-making positions in Regional City, a southern city in the United States of about half a million people. The forty men were selected from a larger list of men who had reputations for their power. Hunter's goal was to describe the people who were regarded as powerful. He found that decision-makers made up several power pyramids. They were understated as persons and appeared to be conservative, hard-nosed, fearful of change, and somewhat guilty about being powerful.

Table 2.3. Milestones in the Evolution of the Concept of Community in the United States, 1950–2000

Floyd Hunter (1953)
- Studied community power focusing on key decision-makers and their interactions.

C. Wright Mills (1956)
- Tied power to social class.
- Conceived of "power elite"—those in charge of complex institutions.

Arthur Vidich and Joseph Bensman (1958)
- Studied the small town of Springdale in upstate New York to analyze progress toward urbanism.
- Found no rigid social classes; simple small town life was influenced by outside forces.

Robert Dahl (1961)
- Study of New Haven, CT showed that political resources were limited to social class.
- Community leaders had influences on decisions depending on their use of political resources.

Herbert Gans (1962)
- Studied five different urban lifestyles.
- Argued that urbanism is not a single, distinctive lifestyle.

Eliot Liebow (1963)
- Participant observation of 24 Negro men who shared a corner in Washington, D.C.
- Understanding the lifestyle, group dynamics, and routines of the hard-to-reach in the city.

Barry Wellman and Paul Craven (1973)
- Communities are social networks and not local solidarities.
- The city is a network of networks.

Amitai Etzioni (1991)
- Organized communitarian movement.
- Free individuals require a community that is a middle ground between libertarian and authoritarian.
- Need a reaffirmation of moral values and enhancement of social responsibilities.

Barry Wellman and Milena Gulia (1999)
- Social networks can exist among people who do not live in the same neighborhood.
- Internet offers specialized interactions (virtual communities).

C. Wright Mills (1956) tied power to conceptions of social class. He viewed power as related to community by emphasizing the power gap between the lower-upper and upper-upper social classes, thus conceiving of a "power elite"—people who were in charge of a complex of institutions.

Mills saw that power and status at the community level could be incorporated into a national system of power and status, i.e. the military-industrial complex.

Robert Dahl (1961), a political scientist, introduced the concept of political resources during the late 1950s. To Dahl, what mattered was not one's reputation as being powerful, but the use of political resources in the actual participation in decision-making. In his study, carried out in New Haven, Connecticut, Dahl found that leaders and constituents had varying degrees of influence on decisions. Political resources were unequally distributed and linked to social class. Some people used their resources more skillfully than others. Age, interest in specific issues, and vested interests were among the factors that determined how and when political resources were used. He found that the use of political resources ranged along a continuum of elitism to pluralism.

Research into the power structure of communities yielded the consistent finding that there is no single power structure of a community. Power and its use varies depending on the nature of the community, the characteristics of the persons holding key positions in the community, the community's stage in its lifecycle, and the resources available in the community to be used (controlled).

Lifestyles

Similarly, Herbert Gans (1962) found that urbanism is not a single distinctive lifestyle. He divided the population of a typical post industrial American city into five different groups, each with a distinctive lifestyle. One group was labeled *cosmopolites*. They were the professionals and white collar workers with a broad range of interests. They valued the city's culture more than the social life of their own neighborhood. A second group included the *unmarried, and the married and childless*, who were footloose. Like the cosmopolites they sought companionship outside of their neighborhood. The third group were the *ethnic villagers*, who were immigrants to the United States. They followed a way of life much like they knew previously. The two remaining groups were the *deprived*, and the *trapped and downwardly mobile*. The trapped were enveloped by the slum and were unable to leave. The deprived were handicapped by poverty, emotional and racial problems. Of these groups the ethnic villagers and slum dwellers had the strongest bonds of community because their interdependence was based on family ties, kinship, and shared culture.

An intensive attempt was made to analyze the progress of a small New York town (Springdale) toward urbanism by a team of Cornell University sociologists headed by Arthur Vidich and Joseph Bensman (1958) in the late 1950s. The team searched for rigid social classes, but found none. Instead, they found that the supposed simplicity of small town life was enormously complex and influenced greatly by forces outside of the community, in contrast to the townspeople's self-image of being "just plain folks." Springdalers were very displeased when they learned that the researchers portrayed them as being shaped by outside forces.

Networks as Communities

Barry Wellman and his colleagues at the University of Toronto have taken a network or "community liberated" approach to urban studies. They pointed out that when cities are studied as networks or structures of interpersonal linkages the diversity of the city becomes a source of strength rather than of chaos (Craven & Wellman, 1973). They defined a network as a specific set of linkages among a set of persons or larger social units such as families, organizations, or corporations. These linkages can be used to interpret the social behavior of the people involved in them.

Wellman found that urbanites are members of many networks, some of which are tightly knit and others loosely knit. Networks characterized by a high density of ties which are directly tied to each other are communities. Communities, therefore, are the kinds and qualities of interpersonal ties between people. Some ties are unique and personal, e.g. a neighborhood (Wellman & Potter, 1999), but the majority of ties are diverse and can be far reaching. Most people are members of multiple communities.

In a random sample survey of adults living in a Toronto suburb Wellman (1968) found that a variety of intimate ties potentially provided access to a more diverse set of resources, while heavy involvement with kin retained connections to a solitary system. Furthermore, he found that the strong primary ties of his respondents were extended beyond Toronto. Only a small minority of intimates resided in the same neighborhoods as the respondents. These distant ties were maintained by telephone more frequently than person-to-person contact. Wellman found that the great majority of respondents were not encapsulated within the bounds of one solitary group, but were linked to multiple, not strongly connected, social networks. When help was needed it was always available from at least one intimate. Wellman pointed out that intimacy is not a unidimensional construct. Thus, when intimates are lost from a network they can be replaced by friends and co-workers.

Wellman emphasized that intimate networks are only one kind of personal network. Each person is a member of networks of all of the people with whom one is linked. This complexity of network clusters provides persons with more resources than only one network limited to a specific locale. Studying how people connect and use their strong and weak ties provides the opportunity to understand how micro and macro community levels are linked (Granovetter, 1973).

THE NEW URBAN SOCIOLOGY

Many of the early theories of communities and cities have not stood the test of time and the basic assumptions of others have been shown to be erroneous. Certainly the early theorists had their limitations as futurists. Yet, they drew attention to the effects of rapid social change, especially urbanization, on the quality of life and nature of social relationships. As urbanization has continued, and now engulfs the majority of the population in the United States, many urban sociologists have turned their attention to the study of the political economy of cities.[2] The "new urban sociology" (Walton, 1981), which focuses on social conflict and inequalities, is considered a reaction by some sociologists to the conventional, natural ecological studies of the Chicago School. On the other hand, Smith (1995) argued that the work of two of the Chicago ecological theorists, particularly Amos Hawley and Roderick McKenzie showed an affinity to the new urban sociology.

Gottdiener (1994) discussed several concepts that are the hallmarks of the new urban sociology including a shift to a global perspective on capitalism and the metropolis; the inclusion of factors such as social class exploitation, racism, gender, and space in the analysis of metropolitan development; an attempt to integrate economic, political, and cultural factors of analysis; and a multicentered regional approach to cities and suburbs. In addition to changes in perspective, the new urban sociology involves changes in the way human environments are analyzed.

Most of the new ideas in urban sociology have their origin in the work of Max Weber, Karl Marx and Friedrich Engels. Marx and Weber believed societies were organized around integrated systems of economics, politics, and culture. Engels observed several aspects of capitalism at work in urban space. He noticed that social problems were created by the breakdown of traditional society and the dynamics of capitalism. New urban sociologists have followed this "political economy" approach.

There are two perspectives that emerge in the new urban sociology: *the growth machine and the sociospatial approach.* The *growth machine* is associated with the work of John Logan and Harvey Molotch (1988), who were dissatisfied with the traditional ecological approach to urban development. These theorists, influenced by the work of Henri Lefebvre and other French urbanists, believed that urban change involves the activities of a group of real estate developers who represent a separate class (rentiers). This class prepares land for new development and pushes the public agenda to pursue growth. Growth is often blocked or tempered by divisions in a community supported by groups that oppose growth. The *sociospatial perspective* is inspired by the work of the French philosopher, Henri Lefebvre (1991), who considered real estate development the major focus of change in metropolitan areas. The sociospatial perspective considers government intervention and the interests of politicians as a principal factor in metropolitan change. This perspective also considers the role of culture as critical in understanding metropolitan life. Finally, the sociospatial approach takes a global view of metropolitan development such as the influence of global economic changes and how these interrelate with national and local levels of organization. Perhaps the most distinguishing characteristics of the sociospatial approach is that it utilizes a number of different facts that account for urban development and change and seeks to provide a balanced view of both push and pull factors in urban and regional growth (Gottdiener, 1994).

SOCIAL MOVEMENTS AND CONCEPTIONS OF COMMUNITY

Communitarianism

In the United States a new communitarian movement emerged in the 1980s. According to Selznick (2002) this was in response to three developments. It began as a controversy among philosophers, initiated by MacIntyre's book *After Virtue* (1984) and Michael Sandel's book, *Liberalism and the Limits of Justice* (1998), the first editions of which came out at the same time. These writings criticized the premises of liberalism, especially political and economic individualism and the notion that people can readily free themselves from unchosen attachments and obligations. These critics were called "communitarians" and a communitarian–liberal debate ensued. A second source of the new communitarianism was a response to the Reagan/Thatcher era in the United States and Great Britain. These leaders strongly supported capitalism, encouraging the distrust of government, resistance to taxation, and a preference for market solutions to societal problems. This thinking created a retreat from social responsibility. A third source of communitarianism was a growing uneasiness about the welfare state especially that it made Americans dependent on handouts and thus unable to participate in sharing the essential values of democracy (Selznick, 2002, pp. 5–7).

In the 1980s the profound shift in societal values written about by Fukuyama, and the progressive loss of social capital documented by Putnam, were well underway in the United States. These significant social changes, along with the factors pointed out by Selznick (2002), contributed to the advocacy of communitarian ideals (more responsibilities, fewer rights) and communitarian public policies (national service, campaign finance reform, welfare reform) by some sociologists. Amitai Etzioni (1993; 1996a), a sociologist, has assumed the key leadership role in this social movement in the United States. He defined the communitarian movement as working to bring about the changes in values, habits, and public policies that will allow us to do for society what the environmental movement seeks to do for nature: to safeguard and enhance our future (Etzioni, 1993, pp. 2–3). Communitarians seek a renewed commitment to public purposes and social institutions. Selznick (1995) pointed out that while community depends on personal virtues such as commitment, caring, discipline, and self-transcendence, we cannot let these personal responsibilities take care of themselves. They require the collective intelligence and sacrifice of all citizens to nurture personal virtue and serve the common good by limiting personal gain (p. 37).

Etzioni (1995) explained that communities are not aggregates of persons acting as free agents, but also collectives that have identities and purposes of their own and can act as a unit. It is the challenge of communitarians to pull people together from the extremes of autonomy and antagonism to a middle zone of mutuality by relying on community pressure and individual morality.

Communitarian thinking basically involves a return to "we-ness" in our society, in our social institutions, and in our social relationships. A return to the spirit, but not the time, of the 1950s. As Etzioni (1993) has put it, "a shoring up of our moral and civic order" (p. 249). This is a complex agenda involving sufficient consensus among the public, and the politicians who represent it, to make significant changes in public policy that will change mind-sets, lifestyles, and social responsibilities.

There are two key factors in social movements—who is to be changed and how much? Communitarianism is a progressive and reformative social movement aimed at promoting new social patterns in our society (and perhaps in other democratic countries). As such it appeals to a huge population to change (or fine tune) its values. This first step is key. Is there enough widespread dissatisfaction with the moral and civic environment in our society that a reformation is regarded as necessary? There may be agreement among many people that our sense of community or "we-ness" has been replaced by "what's right for me," but modifying or compromising individual gestalts to accommodate a greater sense of community may be asking too much.

The communitarian movement, therefore, is not only an attempt to revive the spirit of community, but it is also a civic and democratic movement as well; in a sense it is a call for a national community.

The Communities Movement

Across the United States there are a number of community-based movements and local groups that share complementary visions and approaches to community transformation. Some, but not all, of these movements include: Healthy Communities, Sustainable Communities, Community Building, Civic Democracy, Livable Communities, Safe Communities, and Smart Growth. In 2000, the National Civic League and the Coalition for Healthier Cities and Communities received a grant from the W. K. Kellogg Foundation to evaluate the potential for the convergence of these movements into a single "communities movement" (Kesler & O'Connor, 2001). This Communities Movement Project carried out dialogues in several locations in the United States, convened an advisory council, and conducted a survey, to frame common themes.

A shared *sense of community* was the most frequently cited area of agreement among the community movements. The second most common theme among the groups was *social justice*. The third content theme that emerged was *process as substance*, that is, the support of dialogue, feedback, and collaboration. What also emerged from the meeting of the various groups was the little awareness some people had of the presence of other movements in their own communities even those movements that shared common goals. Despite major agreement in goals, there was not much enthusiasm among the various groups for merging their interests or identities. Paradoxically, there was unanimous support for creating yet another integrative movement that would link the existing groups!

Kesler and O'Connor (2001) heard in several of the group dialogues that nationally based movements don't really matter at the local level. People care about issues, not movements. The energy that Americans once exercised to address shared community concerns is now being used to address issue-specific debates at the local level (O'Connor & Gates, 2000). While it is important to create grass roots participation in issues, people often come to "own" issues and create personal communities, which often become competitive and divisive.

Communities that spend the majority of time debating and little time to uncovering the shared value of different groups risk chipping away at their civic infrastructure and damage their foundation for community decision-making (O'Connor & Gates, 2000). Citrin (1998) discusses his concern about the ways community can be expressed in the Healthy Communities movement. On the one hand, his concern is whether groups will broker with each other for health services and functions, as if the market place were a community, or on the other hand, whether groups will become community partners providing health services and functions. In the first instance health is regarded as a commodity or product. In the second instance health is considered as an expression of the total community environment (Wilcox & Knapp, 2000).

LOOSE CONNECTIONS: MOVING TO THE CENTER OF THE CONTINUUM

The conservative right has been critical of the community movement in that they feel the emphasis on moral transformation represents a threat to their religious beliefs. For example, some criticize the communitarians of planning a moral revival involving the family and school but paying little attention to religion. The liberal left has been critical of the movement because they regard the consensus-oriented communitarian approach as antiliberal. Both conservatives and liberals are concerned that someone might try to impose their values on someone else (Kesler, 2000). Brint (2001) offers his moderating views to understanding the future of community. While retaining some of the virtues of community and eliminating its myths he argues that loosely connected communities of place, loosely connected friendship networks, activity-based elective communities, and nonideological imagined and virtual communities provide a measure of connectedness with few constraints on individual freedoms. These looser, sporadic, ad hoc connections are the forms of community that seem to be developing in contemporary industrial societies (Wuthnow, 1998). Communitarians see themselves as a centrist alternative to the extremes of libertarianism and collectivism (Myers, 2000).

The commonality of loose connections acknowledges that communities of place are largely passé except in isolated and rural areas and that people are involved in numerous, complex and changing social networks which they call upon on as-needed. Communities are not the same as they were in the past (Gemeinschaft) but they are not lost in our world of rapid change (Gesellschaft), rather they have become a blend of the characteristics of both extremes. As a result no single theory portrays the middle of the community continuum.

The word community continues to possess a positive image. Despite varying definitions most people know what it is, some value it, and few have become emotionally attached to it. Whether the revival of modified Gemeinschaft type communities by some architects and planners has lasting appeal has yet to be seen.

SUMMARY

Early European and American sociologists were concerned with the impact of urbanization on community as "a place" and created a legacy for the concept. Sociologists and other social scientists have continued to debate the meaning and relevance of the concept of community. Some laymen and social scientists lament the loss of community as a place, but more are concerned with the shift in values and loss of social capital that have created fragmented social institutions and decreased social cohesion in our society and in most countries in the Western world. Efforts are not being directed at correcting the complex causes of why and how community has faded, since the causes are tied up with the interdependencies and progression of social change over several centuries. Rather several social movements, such as communitarianism, are attempting to abate the further unraveling of our social connectedness by affirming, through collective actions, personal virtues and responsibilities that serve the common good.

In academia, new urban sociologists have focused their attention on the distribution of wealth and power in the city. They explain the structure of the city by the pursuit of profit, which is the basis of capitalist society. The ideas of Karl Marx form the basis for contemporary urban sociology. What is new is the application of political economic theory to urban life, namely how social structures and the processes of social change benefits some groups in the city at the expense of others.

Perhaps the most significant change and contribution to understanding community today is the conceptualization of it as a series of networks of varying sizes, density, and purpose that extend beyond a physical location.

The characteristics of the networks can be used to interpret the social behavior of the people involved. Communities, therefore, are the kinds and qualities of interpersonal ties between people. Some ties are unique and personal while others are diverse and extensive. People have portfolios of networks that can be used to connect them with others for various reasons at various times. The concept of community as a group of natural, changing, mobile networks that meet a variety of changing needs makes community personally meaningful in a society in which 'place' is less permanent and meaningful.

QUESTIONS FOR DISCUSSION

1. Do you know of Gemeinschaft-type of communities that exist today? Where are they and why do you think that they continue to exist?
2. Explain why early European sociologists were concerned about the effects of industrialization and urbanization on communities and American sociologists focused on power and social class.
3. How can social class be determined; what are the factors or characteristics that determine class? Why is social class of importance to sociologists?
4. Are any or all of the various attempts to revitalize "community" likely to be successful? Does the concept of "community," like the "family," have practical value today or are these concepts ideals of the past?
5. Why is there no theory of community in sociology? Should "community" be limited to the disciplinary boundaries of sociology?
6. What are the limitations, if any, in studying social networks as communities?
7. Why have studies of "natural communities" lost their appeal in research in urban sociology today?

Chapter 3

Common Ties
Immigrant and Ethnic Communities

INTRODUCTION

T. S. Eliot (1949) wrote, "A people should be neither too united nor too divided if its culture is to flourish" (p. 49). This statement emphasizes the dilemma of multiethnic societies. "Under assimilative pressure, cultures may be lost that contain common elements needed for adaptation to a changing world—the loss of a kind of cultural gene pool. Under pluralistic and separatist pressures, cultural forms may be preserved that are maladaptive and unjust—sexist, racist, harshly stratified, and militarized" (Yinger, 1985, p. 173). With such a broad perspective of possible definitions and interpretations it is not surprising that "ethnicity" is variously seen as ways to: preserve a precarious cultural heritage; soften class distinctions; protect or win economic and political advantages for disadvantaged groups; furnish a more intimate and flavorful connection with large, impersonal societies; and retard the shift of overwhelming power to the state (Yinger, 1985).

Ethnicity is also about how individuals and groups of different cultural backgrounds interact, or do not interact, with each other, and how racial and ethnic groups fit into larger society. Ethnicity is about the personal choices people make about connections and networks with others, and how choices about associations affect the ability to experience American ideals. Sanders (2002) said, "ethnic boundaries are better understood as social mediums through which association transpires rather than as territorial demarcations" (p. 327). This will be the focus of this chapter.

49

Transitions in Social Ties

The history of the United States for over four centuries has been molded by successive waves of immigrants.[1] The population of the United States today, except for 2.3 million Native Americans and Alaska Natives, consists almost entirely of immigrants and descendants of immigrants (Jones, 1992). Today there are more people of Irish ancestry in the United States than in Ireland, more Jews than in Israel, more blacks than in most African countries. There are more people of Polish ancestry in Detroit than in most of the major cities in Poland, and more than twice as many people of Italian ancestry in New York than in Venice (Sowell, 1981).

While the first immigration wave to the new world began early in the 17th century, the United States government did not require masters of arriving immigrant ships to hand in lists of passengers to customs until 1820 (Bouvier, 1992; Jones, 1960). But the census of 1860 revealed that out of a total population of almost 31.5 million, the United States had 4.1 million foreign-born inhabitants. The greatest bulk lived north of the Mason and Dixon line and east of the Mississippi. The three great immigration waves, the first two covering the years 1815–1860 and 1860–1890, came from the same general areas of Europe. Both groups were predominately from the British Isles, Germany, Scandinavia, Switzerland and Holland. During the third great wave the majority of immigrants were from Austria, Hungary, Italy, Russia, Greece, Rumania and Turkey (Jones, 1960).

There is now a fourth generation, comprised of the great grandchildren of immigrants who were part of the last great wave of immigration that ended with the imposition of quotas in 1924. What makes this generation unique is that its members have no direct ancestral memories that reach back to their countries of origin (Steinberg, 1989). The culture that is being preserved is the residue of cultures that immigrants carried over with them generations earlier, and often does not exist any longer even in home countries, which have also undergone processes of modernization and change (Glazer and Moynihan, 1963). Ethnic groups, even after distinctive language, customs, and culture are lost are continually being recreated by their new experiences in America.

Ellis Island was abandoned as a landing depot for immigrants in 1954 confirming the belief of many Americans that mass immigration was a closed chapter in United States history (Jones, 1992). But again, America entered a period of rapid ethnic change. Immigration to the United States in the 1980s reached almost 10 million, the highest peak in United States history (Fix & Passel, 1994). More than 10 million legal and illegal immigrants entered the United States in the 1990s, in part as a result of the 1990 Immigration Act, which permitted up to 700,000 legal immigrants to enter the United States yearly. After three years this number would decrease to 675,000. This total did not include refugees or those legalized under the Immigration Reform and Control Act (Cose, 1992). In 2001, a total of 1,064,318 persons legally immigrated to the United States. In addition, estimates in the average growth rate of illegal residents from the Immigration and Naturalization Service (INS) in 2001 ranged from 275,000 to 300,000 per year. Five countries accounted for 40 percent of the legal immigrants, Mexico, India, The People's Republic of China, Philippines, and Vietnam. The majority of illegal residents came from Mexico, El Salvador, Guatemala, Canada, and Haiti.[2] Within the next decade (by 2010), nearly one-third of the United States will be classified as a race other than white (Junn, 2000). That proportion is projected to rise to 47 percent by 2050.

There has not been a national consensus regarding how the United States should respond to the reality of ethnic group prejudice and racial and ethnic group differences. Public policy debates wax and wane according to the number and resources of new immigrants. This is reflected in the range of metaphors used to describe ethnic America—the melting pot, the ethnic mosaic, the tapestry, the salad bowl, and the symphonic orchestra (Kivisto, 1989).

The term "melting pot" is popularly used because it connotes the positive aspects of equality, freedom and acceptance. Yet the melting pot has not been a reality for all racial and ethnic groups, as "melting pot" implies that all groups can be or choose to be assimilated into the dominant culture. Anne Fadiman, in her book *The Spirit Catches You and You Fall Down* (1997), pointed out that Hmong refugees who came to the United States from Laos in the 1980s did so to save their Hmong ethnicity. Had they been safe in Laos they would have stayed there. They were what sociologists call "involuntary migrants." Fadiman said, "It is well known that involuntary migrants, no matter what pot they are thrown into, tend not to melt" (p. 183). Fadiman described how the Hmong wanted to be left alone to be Hmong, clustered in all Hmong enclaves in cities. However, some families were resettled by the United States government to isolated rural areas where, disconnected from traditional supports, families experienced high levels of anxiety, depression, and paranoia. Many Hmong were overwhelmed. Between 1982 and 1984 three quarters of the Hmong population of Philadelphia left town and joined relatives in other cities. During the same time, a third of all Hmong in the United States moved from one city to another, often without their sponsor's knowledge (Fadiman, 1997). Although "partial" Americanization may have brought certain benefits, many Hmong have viewed assimilation as an insult and a threat. The Hmong immigrated to be themselves in a culture that did not know and understand them, a culture they did not choose to join, and a culture in which they had no connections before the post Vietnam War.

Somalian refugees who fled clan warfare in East Africa and came to the United States in 2000 had different expectations than the Hmong. Somalis wanted to become fully engaged in the United States culture. The United States government located the Somalis in Atlanta, but, since February, 2001 about 1,100 have migrated to Lewiston, Maine, a community of 36,000 with a strong Roman Catholic and Franco-American heritage, because of its cheaper housing, low crime rate and more access to public services. As the influx of Somalis continued the Mayor of Lewiston published an open letter in the local newspaper stating, "Please pass the word: we have been overwhelmed and have responded valiantly. Now we need breathing room. Our city is maxed out financially, physically, and emotionally." City officials say the Somalis have strained social services, including welfare, job training and English-as-a-second-language programs. The Somalis cried bigotry, the Governor appointed a task force on immigration and refugee issues and the local Methodist Church organized a march to support the Somalis, but the Mayor has many defenders. "The mayor could have done it a different way, but with them people you almost have to be blunt like that," said one supporter. "They think this is a great opportunity for them, this prejudice thing. If you look at them the wrong way or they don't have enough money, they say it's prejudice." One Somali woman said, "Just like everybody else, I want my kids to do well and be safe. Just like everyone else I want to have a house by the beach one day" (Belluck, 2002). Sometimes "the melting pot" doesn't melt, but the Somalis, unlike the Hmong, put the ideal to a test.

The melting pot has been a reality for European immigrants as reflected in the high rates of marriage outside of one's religious or ethnic group. Blacks have been excluded from the melting pot (Van den Berghe, 1981). Some groups such as the Pennsylvania Amish and Hasidic Jews have actively resisted both acculturation and assimilation and managed to retain their separate identities.

Despite the ideal of a pluralistic society, it is an expectation on the part of many, if not most, Americans that immigrants will acculturate to and assimilate into the dominant culture. Indeed, since ethnic areas often tend to look different, some of the native-born populations will see immigrant neighborhoods as evidence that new immigrants are not adapting to United States society (Smith & Edmonston, 1997). While the ideal of cultural pluralism is a society that allows for a maximum of ethnic diversity, practicing one's ethnicity is not entirely an easy choice. It can extract heavy personal and social costs such as exclusion and isolation, rejection, harassment, and even hate. Ethnicity is permissible to many people if it is "mainstream ethnicity" subordinate to American identity (Kivisto, 1989). On the other hand, some advocates of cultural pluralism argue that racial and ethnic minorities should not only maintain their identities, languages, and cultures, but remain separate from mainstream society (Bouvier, 1992). Advocates for group rights demand special privileges for their followers. The movement to honor diversity through multiculturalism was originally undertaken to promote tolerance, but some ethnic groups have insisted on asserting group rights over individual rights which emphasizes their differences rather than their commonalities with the dominant culture. As a result, diversity, in some places, has become divisive (Mallet, 1997).

T. S. Eliot implied that moderating the ideal of equality might have its difficulties. The equality continuum ranges from the expectation, at one extreme, that ethnic groups will relinquish their cultural characteristics to become completely blended into a larger, dominant, homogenous American culture, to the opposite extreme of the refusal of some ethnic groups to join the dominant culture while enjoying the benefits of being different but equal.[3] Societies do exist that are predominately ethnically homogeneous or that are segregated, yet they cannot flourish when their practice of equality is so limited. This is perhaps why some writers have suggested that the ideal of ethnicity in the United States is more analogous to a "vegetable stew" where all ingredients contribute to a desired outcome, yet each ingredient retains some of its individual distinctiveness. Novak (1972) advocated "unmeltable ethnics" lest America become a tasteless homogenized soup.

NEWCOMERS WITH OLD CONNECTIONS

Finding the Familiar

Immigrants tend to cluster in certain geographic areas and occupations. Since they usually depend on the assistance of kin and others from their culture, ethnic neighborhoods are often essential stepping stones for their social and economic adaptation. Even when government policy tries to disperse new arrivals as with the case of Cuban refugees in the 1960s and Vietnamese refugees in the 1970s, secondary migration has led to a reconcentration of immigrants with others from their culture who preceded them (Smith & Edmonston, 1997).

The tendency of first arrivals to cluster in central locations dominated by their own ethnic group is no different in 2003 than it was in 1908, although it appears to be true for the poorest immigrant groups, while those with some resources locate near their friends and relatives in more dispersed locations. Such centrally located enclaves provided then, and still provide today, a social support system that includes housing, a sense of community, and jobs. Although individual migrants make personal decisions regarding the opportunities and liabilities they perceive, and although they use the networks and contacts established by earlier migrant groups, their decisions are set in a larger context of changing national policies that may facilitate or impede their actions. Migrants are not a unified group, they come at different times for different reasons (Clark, 1998). For example, the war in the Balkans has resulted in the most recent large-scale immigration of refugees in the United States. By 2000, approximately 107,000 Bosnian Muslims had arrived in the United States for permanent resettlement after fleeing war in the former Republic of Yugoslavia. New York State is now home to over 12,000 Bosnians the majority of whom live in six counties in the state (United States Department of State, 2002).

Ethnic residential concentrations and ethnic economies are initial efforts by the first generation to get a foothold in a new culture. Zhou (1992) pointed out that New York's Chinatown is primarily an economic enclave[4] where economic behavior is closely embedded in the structure of social relations. Ethnic solidarity endows group members with social resources that compensate for their disadvantages as minorities. Social capital such as family and kinship networks, loyalty, mutual trust and obligation, facilitates entrepreneurial success. Indeed, community networks and social capital are major resources for achieving social and economic goals in New York's Chinatown. These resources are so important that Chinese families maintain links to the enclave even while they are enjoying upward social mobility and when they live outside of Chinatown. Social capital helps produce human capital. Lin (1999) has noted the importance of the relationship of social capital to human capital. Well-connected relatives and social ties can enhance the opportunities for individuals to obtain better education, training, and skill and knowledge credentials. Better trained and educated individuals tend to associate in social networks rich in resources and "give back" to their communities, so human capital, in turn, strengthens social capital. Indeed, most newcomers are not completely isolated from American society. They work, live in neighborhoods and attend school in proximity to the dominant culture. For example, a study of Orthodox Jews in Toronto, Canada found that the Orthodox Jewish community there maintains a strong traditionalist orientation yet is integrated into the consumerist materialistic culture of Toronto (Diamond, 2000). Connections at the neighborhood level feed into metropolitan and national levels to create a continentally connected but locally rooted religious community.

Diamond pointed out the importance of being able to practice one's values in determining where one lives. Orthodox Jews immigrating to

Toronto make a deliberate choice to live within walking distance of the synagogue. When Orthodox Jews move to a new suburban neighborhood they organize a congregation as soon as possible. Families then live in "a place." "A place" means having many families living within walking distance of one another and engaging in the same rituals and practices according to the same calendar. This community provides social capital through a range of formal and informal social services and networks such as sending children to the same school, providing meals for women during the birth of a child, inviting friends to a Sabbath meal, and sharing various rites of passage.

The concept of neighborhood is fundamentally bound by a sense of place. Neighborhoods are communities of place. Neighborhoods need not be "ethnic," they can be identified by certain types of housing, an income group, a limited geographic area perhaps with unique physical attributes such as a bay, or mountains, or by the self-definition of the people living there, for example non-traditional or non-conformist groups. Although ethnic communities may be based upon residence in the same locality, they essentially center on the shared attitudes and behaviors that bind together the people themselves (Godfrey, 1988). The stereotype of the immigrant is often that of an individual transplanted from a familiar to a strange environment and being disoriented and isolated. The reality is that the majority of immigrants are connected with networks at the time of their arrival that they can use to construct their own personal world and livelihood. The internal social cohesion and cultural coherence that social networks provide enable the immigrant to be separate and maintain an ethnic identity in a pluralistic society (Godfrey, 1988).

Recent immigrants to the United States seem more inclined to settle outside of urban enclaves than were immigrants in previous eras. Suburbanization is strongly determined by socio-economic status and the financial ability to enter the suburban housing market. Now there are fewer barriers to suburban residence for recent immigrants even when they speak English with difficulty. As the percentage of immigrants in the suburbs increases it is easier for new arrivals to settle there as the networks and infrastructure established by predecessors is already there (Alba, Logan, Stults, Marzan & Zhang, 1999). Increasing ethnic minority presence in the suburbs has also created new political alliances and enabled new strategies for immigrants to connect regionally in the United States. The place where immigrants first settle when they arrive in the United States matters. As Americans have abandoned central cities for suburbia social and economic resources and voters[5] have followed, leaving the city core as a generally unhelpful and unhealthy place to begin a new life in a new culture.

There is some evidence that the connections some immigrants make in the United States inhibit their upward mobility in American society. Glazer (2000) has noted that New York's blacks now include, as a result of 30 years of immigration, a large percentage of immigrants from the Caribbean and their children. They are often better educated, and they have a strong drive to home ownership and entrepreneurship. But it is not clear that these advantages are maintained in the second generation. Many children of the Caribbean immigrants are pulled into the debilitating street and school culture of black adolescents and teenagers. By the second or third generations, the Caribbean's advantage may not be much. Rather than raising the group they may lose the distinctive characteristics which aid social mobility, and become indistinguishable from native African Americans (Waters, 1990). Thus, not all immigrants are able to use connections in their new environment to continue the progress of their predecessors.

ADAPTATION

How immigrant groups adapt to their new culture will depend on the nature and extent of the ties that bind members to each other. The nature and extent of ties will influence their expectations. Do they wish to retain their separate ethnic identity, fully or partially, or integrate with the dominant culture? These are often not conscious decisions made at a specific point in time, rather decisions change as the experiences of immigrants change. Indeed, immigrants to the United States who have no old connections or predecessors to assist in their adaptation may make only those changes that are necessary to maintain their daily survival in their new culture, carefully protecting their cultural boundaries. Their adaptation is geared to the circumstances of necessity. Cornell (1996) pointed out that circumstances variously encourage and discourage immigrant's expectations. But the basis of group cohesion determines to some degree the extent of the group's vulnerability to circumstances. Circumstances create ethnic groups, but equally important are the various kinds of group ties that determine a group's encounters with circumstance.

Immigration involves challenges to social identities and a sense of community. Sonn (2002) saw immigrant adaptation as a process of community–making that first involves developing a meaningful social identity and second, establishing ties and social networks that will lead to a sense of belonging. Community-making is, of course, easiest when there are predecessors to join, and difficult when an ethnic group is the first to come to the United States. When there are predecessors, the basic element of community-building, namely networks, is present. When there are no predecessors it is the boundaries of the group, a common culture and history that provide social cohesion and ethnic integrity in a new setting.

Boundaries Bind, Networks Connect

Ethnicity is like a social womb. The ethnic community functions as a refuge against the alienation of a different society. Ethnic communities provide a safety net where one's own kind can experience a sense of belonging. Ethnic communities or areas, therefore, maintain physical and social boundaries. There are social pressures on ethnics to conform to habits, beliefs and values, even those who may visit, but not live in the community of their fellows. For example, a young Korean professional woman who immigrated to the United States to complete a degree in higher education visited a Korean church in the Korean area of the large city in which she was living. Upon meeting the minister he asked her how many children she had. She was not married and in Korean culture it was expected that she would be married. The woman did not wish to be in a situation where she would be quizzed about why she was not married so she only returned to the Korean area to buy groceries. Even in the grocery store she was identified as new to the area and asked by several Korean women, "Is your husband an American?" The unmarried woman apparently looked shocked and embarrassed and the Korean women then followed with the statement and question, "Don't feel embarrassed, our husbands are Americans. Your husband must be Korean?"

Ethnic boundaries exert powerful pressures on people of a given ethnicity to conform. Fellow ethnics who do not fit the mold are quickly identified. In this way boundaries bind members of an ethnic group to their culture and to each other. Some ethnics commute between ethnicities, presenting an acculturated front in one situation and a traditional one in another. A decision to assimilate is the result of circumstances occurring over a long period of time. People usually do not choose to assimilate unless there are advantages to do so. In the case of the unmarried Korean professional woman she maintains contact with her family in Korea and lives and works in the United States where she experiences greater freedom in being herself. However, when she encounters Korean men on the faculty of universities she is often asked by them, "How many children do you have?" even before they ask what part of Korea she came from. Consequently, she avoids social situations where she might have to explain her marital status.

Ethnic boundaries are constructed by members of an ethnic group for purposes of deciding who will be included and boundaries are constructed by members of the dominant culture to keep an ethnic group "in its place," for example to prohibit the association with an ethnic group member and prevent their possible assimilation. People tend to assimilate when their ethnic group is geographically dispersed; when they constitute a numerical minority living among strangers; when they are in a subordinate position; and when they are allowed to assimilate by dominant groups (Van den Berghe, 1981). The more territorially compact an ethnic group the more solidarity it can show, and therefore the less incentive to assimilate. Broadly speaking, assimilation has been the easiest and fastest for northwestern Europeans mostly of Protestant faiths. The more similar socially and culturally immigrants are to the dominant culture the more options they will have in their new environment.

Some groups, usually religious conservatives, like the Hasidic Jews of Brooklyn, New York, the Amish of Ohio, Indiana, Pennsylvania and Michigan, the Hutterites of Montana, the Shaker's of Maine and New Hampshire, and the Mennonites of Virginia and Upper Canada, have managed to retain their separate ethnic identities and to resist both acculturation and assimilation. They live together separate from the dominant society, maintain strict discipline within their group, enforce endogamy, minimize and stigmatize contacts with the dominant culture, and cultivate a sense of their own rightness, objecting to "modernism," war, and technology.

Boundaries also limit communication with members of the dominant culture. In her study of intercultural friendships Gareis (1995) found that people who had out-going personalities, high self-esteem, and were not enmeshed with their cultural identification were more likely to establish friendships with people from other cultural groups. Establishing cross-cultural friendships was influenced by one's personality, but competence in communication and willingness to communicate were essential in crossing ethnic boundaries.

Even the groups that choose to be socially isolated from dominant society must sometimes interact with it. For example, Hmong living in Section 8 housing may have neighbors who are not Hmong (Miyares, 1997). Amish are being asked to comply with the laws of dominant society by bringing their farmhouses up to code by adding septic systems and putting license plates and reflector triangles on their buggies. On the other hand, Amish enjoy the benefits of tourists who buy their crafts, foods and farm products. Dominant society has made accommodations to the Amish in one community by earmarking a parking garage for horses. Even where there are relatively strong boundaries separating ethnic groups from the dominant society, some limited networking across boundaries occurs, as the examples above indicate.[6]

But ethnic groups need more than boundary control to preserve their identities, they need to maintain kin systems that bind themselves to one another emotionally and socially to mitigate hostility and aggression and enhance community solidarity. Kin exercise social control over those in the kinship system to ensure that they obey norms and provide opportunities and material and social support when necessary. Ebaugh (2000) described three types of fictive kin (family-type) relationships, based not on blood or marriage, but rather on religious rituals or close friendship ties, that constitutes a type of social capital which many immigrants bring with them that facilitates their adjustment to the host society. Fictive kin systems expand the network of individuals who are expected to provide social and economic capital for one another and thereby constitute a resource for immigrants as they deal with a new culture. Fictive kin are shared widely in Spanish-speaking countries, Asia, Africa, and the Caribbean. Three examples of fictive kin systems are: *compadrazgo* among Hispanic immigrants; *Yoruba*, which is a form of spirituality that fosters black identity and a return to things African common among African-American and Cuban communities; and the *system of respect* for elders that exists among various Asian immigrants, especially Chinese, Vietnamese and Koreans. Another basis for fictive kin relationships in Asian communities is close friendships between one's parents and unrelated persons in the community who would be accorded the same rights, respect, and obligations that would be extended to a blood relative. Fictive kin among Asians also arise from the immigration experience itself. It has been common for single Asian males to immigrate to the United States first and send for their families after they have found a job and are settled. Such unattached males are usually befriended by families in the immigrant community that are already reunited and often come from the same or nearby localities back home (Ebaugh, 2000).

Fictive kin relationships provide strong social networks that are part of the social capital that immigrants bring with them when they immigrate. Immigrants also bring with them strong differences in terms of political allegiances, immigration history, and socioeconomic background that impact the nature of their adaptation. Sonn (2002) pointed out, for example, that although an ethnic group shares cultural roots that are important to the community, the different social and political views of some members of the ethnic group cause them to respond differently to an issue. For example, expatriate Chileans responded very differently to the possible prosecution of former president Augusto Pinochet' even though they identified with the Chilean community. An ethnic group can be as different within itself as it is between itself and dominant society.

Ethnic Ties and Trust

For immigrants who have insufficient financial and personal resources, social capital embodied in family, kinship, and ethnic ties serves
as an important form of capital. Social capital is available to all classes of
immigrants. It is produced and reproduced within families and extended
families, and through social exchanges within the immigrant group (Nee &
Sanders, 2001). Immigrants with ethnically-based social capital are more
likely to find jobs in the immigrant economy, even though these types of
jobs are often low-skilled and low-paid. These jobs often meet immediate
practical needs, especially as they accommodate to the United States world
of work. There are some limitations that accompany ethnically-based jobs.
Immigrants often feel obligated to the trusted party who helped them and
immigrant workers employed in the ethnic economy generally have few social relationships outside their kinship and ethnic groups. The immigrant
community may provide a feeling of security and an ease of communication that helps compensate for the lower wage structure, however, for
immigrants who had hoped for more in their quest for a new life in the
United States being locked into low-skilled and low paid jobs in the ethnic
economy may foster distrust as well as trust in ethnic ties (Nee & Sanders,
2001). There is a debate among immigration scholars whether economic
opportunities offered in ethnic enclaves limit or promote social mobility.
Obviously different enclave economies provide better opportunities than
others (Waters & Eschbach, 1995).

The practice of using ethnic networks as employment networks explains why certain ethnic groups dominate certain services and industries.
Immigrant networks also provide financing to entrepreneurs in the form of
gifts from family members or loans from rotating credit associations. These
micro lending arrangements are available where formal credit institutions
are unable or unwilling to provide credit to small borrowers. A study of
Korean business owners found that about 70 percent used debt financing
to start their enterprises and that 41 percent of those who borrowed obtained their money from family and 24 percent from friends (Waldinger,
1996; Light, 1972).

Being able to trust others is crucial to being willing to take risks associated with productive social exchanges. In other words, trust is a form
of social capital. It facilitates relations between individuals and groups.
Groups function more effectively when members trust each other and
group authorities. Individuals and groups, therefore, have an interest in
creating and maintaining social conditions under which trust can occur
(Tyler, 2001). Researchers have found that interpersonal trust is lower in
racially heterogeneous communities, in those with high income inequality,

and in transient communities. The negative effect of heterogeneity on trust is due largely to the fact that people trust those more similar to themselves (Alesina & La Ferrara, 2002).

While ethnic and racial homogeneity may be advantageous for generating trust within a group, the separation or segregation of an ethnic or racial group has significant negative outcomes for its members. For example, in the average American city, 60 percent of blacks would have to change residences to create an even distribution of the races across neighborhoods, and the average black lives in a neighborhood that is 57 percent black (Cutler & Glaeser; 1997). This spatial separation of many blacks from jobs, positive role models, and high quality public goods has led some to speculate that segregation is a cause of the problems of the black underclass. But the segregation of a group has, according to some economists, benefits as well as costs, especially if it allows for mixing across income classes to generate positive effects for the entire group (Cutler & Glaeser, 1997).

In a study of the communication infrastructure of seven residential areas of Los Angeles comprised of different ethnic and racial groups, African-Americans in Greater Crenshaw showed the highest level of belonging to their residential area. This fact was attributed to the vigor of the neighborhood's highly integrated storytelling system (Ball-Rokeach, Yong-Chan & Matei, 2001). The neighborhood is largely lower-to-upper middle social class and moderately well educated. It became identified as an African-American area with an influx of new residents after the end of World War II. Since the 1980s there has been a steady in-migration of Latino residents. The neighborhood is often described by outsiders as a danger zone. The neighborhood has had chronic difficulties developing its economic base; grocery and department stores in the area are inferior and more highly priced than in white areas. Nonetheless, there is a high sense of belonging in the community. There is a high percentage of homeowners, long-term residents, many community-building organizations, local media that storytell the neighborhood, and people talk to each other over the backyard fence about their neighborhood. In other words, residents seem to overcome their constraints with strong collectivist values that promote interpersonal engagement and storytelling. Residents of Greater Crenshaw consider it as "our" place, one that "we" care about and therefore talk about. Residents' communicative activities account for its high level of belonging.

It is not surprising that residents of some black neighborhoods feel connected to each other as studies have shown that blacks are more alienated and less trusting of others, especially whites (Demaris & Yang, 1994). Black neighborhoods, which may appear to be disorganized and pathological to outsiders, have been found to have functional networks of kin and friends. A study of networks in three Los Angeles metropolitan neighborhoods pointed out that not all black communities are the same; blacks respond differently to economic and political forces depending on their different resources and backgrounds (Oliver, 1988). Some behaviors of blacks may not be understood in larger society but may be functional within a black neighborhood or community. For example, two black social workers overheard several white public school teachers in a city in the southwest comment, "Isn't it terrible how black boys talk about their mothers." The white teachers were not aware of "playing the dozens," a verbal game commonly played among black adolescent boys from the inner city. Learning to defend oneself verbally or to gain control of a situation through insults or put-downs of others is found in many cultures. In the United States we tend to ascribe leadership characteristics to individuals who are able to think on their feet, to hold other's attention, to be verbally persuasive, or to exhibit a quick wit. Joking relationships are part of the process of learning to cope or adapt in interpersonal relationships, especially among adolescents. While the dozens appears to have African origins, it is also played among Mexican-Americans and Anglo-Americans (Bruhn & Murray, 1985).

The dozens is usually played by two young black males, often surrounded by an interested and encouraging audience of peers in which the players insult and provoke each other with put-downs of each other's mother or other female family members. This process teaches one to take insults in stride while encouraging verbal retorts. The dozens can be clean or dirty. In the "dirty dozens," the slur usually takes the form of jingles about the illicit sexual activity of the other person's mother. Gaming is a part of black tradition. Verbal games are a way of controlling chaos and having fun. The dozens is played more often and more intensely in urban ghettos where frustrations are greater and the strategies of the ghetto are appropriate to a zero-sum game; neither player really wins. The dozens works when the players share a common ethnicity, a degree of connectedness, and acceptance of the activity for what it is—a game (Bruhn & Murray, 1985). There has to be an element of trust between the players of the dozens, and shared ethnicity is a prerequisite; it is unlikely that black and white adolescent boys would engage in the dozens. The dozens is a culturally meaningful way for black youth in inner city neighborhoods to build social capital in an environment of personal and community disadvantage.

Ethnic Ties and Powerlessness

One reason that immigrants and ethnic groups choose to live together in a common neighborhood is that they trust each other. Life in

a new country promotes distrust. Individuals who live in places where resources are scarce and threat is common, and who feel powerless to avoid
or manage threat, are more likely to be distrustful. Widespread mistrust in a
neighborhood may, in turn, interfere with neighbors to form ties with each
other. Research has shown that the environment in which an individual
lives affects his/her sense of control. Individuals who live in neighborhoods where social control has broken down, and when drug use, fights,
vandalism, graffiti, loitering, public drinking, litter, and crime are common,
perceive that they are powerless and are more distrusting largely because
they have weak, if any, social ties to neighbors. Mistrust is the product of
an interaction between a person and "a place." "A place" gathers those
who are vulnerable to mistrust and intensifies their susceptibility. Disadvantaged people, therefore, tend to live in disadvantaged neighborhoods
where they see the evidence of mistrust, fear, and powerlessness (Ross,
Mirowsky & Pribosh, 2001; Geis & Ross, 1998; Ross & Jang, 2000). It is the
informal connections with neighbors that help in buffering the negative
effects of fear and mistrust. Living in a neighborhood with people from
one's own ethnic group where there are natural support networks helps to
bolster the self-sufficiency and autonomy that new immigrants feel they
have lost (Riger & Larrakas, 1981).

There is concern that most immigrants and ethnic minorities continue to be non-participants in United States democracy (Junn, 2000). Junn
pointed out that, while asking for more citizen participation is desirable it
is unlikely the situation will change until more political space for the representation of group interests are provided. Political non-participation, and
a growing concern that Latinos and Asians are becoming more residen-
tially segregated from non-Hispanic whites, would seemingly increase the
perception that immigrants and ethnic groups are powerless. Ellen (2000)
warns of a "new white flight" from communities populated by immigrants,
particularly those of Asian and Latino descent, that is driving residential
separation. Such trends raise concerns about the prospects for immigrant
assimilation more generally in the United States.

Suburban settlement is a characteristic of contemporary immigration
in the United States. This pattern contrasts with the urban model established by European immigrants to the United States in the early 20th century. Researchers have found that the ability to enter the suburban housing
market is strongly determined by socioeconomic level. Suburbanization
among Asian groups is influenced by family and the presence of children,
reflecting household needs and preferences. On the other hand, Indians
and Koreans, who often come to the United States in search of professional
employment or entrepreneurial opportunities, look for favorable neighborhood amenities in the suburbs. Those immigrants who do not speak

English well and are seeking labor opportunities are more likely to reside in central cities (Alba, Logan, Stults, Marzan & Zhang, 1999).

Suburbanization tends to select members of immigrant and second generation ethnics who speak English well or who had abandoned their native language in daily life. There is now less of a barrier to suburban residence for recent arrivals, even when they speak English with difficulty. As immigrant groups living in the suburbs increase it becomes easier for new arrivals to settle there, since the networks and infrastructure exists to meet their needs. This is the phenomenon of chain migration whereby immigrants go where kin and other co-ethnics preceded them and collectively they share some semblance of power (Alba, Logan, Stults, Marzan & Zhang, 1999.)

THE ETHNIC NEIGHBORHOOD AND ITS NETWORKS

The ethnic neighborhood has historically been considered the core of immigrant life and continues to perform this function for some new immigrants. Ethnic neighborhoods have met immigrants' needs for a low cost lifestyle, family ties, a familiar culture, and a job. Ethnic neighborhoods have usually been considered places of safety, refuge, and necessity because of the constraints of dominant society. Recent studies of various ethnic groups in the United States have found that ethnic identity is strongly shaped by the location of the settlement (Sanders, 2002). Regional and neighborhood concentrations of ethnic groups facilitate the maintenance of social boundaries and ethnic identity. However, there is evidence that ethnically distinctive neighborhoods have declined as immigrants coming the United States have more diversified social and economic resources and human capital, using the ethnic neighborhood as a point of transition into American culture. As a result, some ethnic groups are now able to establish neighborhoods in desirable locations, often in suburbia, and group members may choose these locations. Logan and his colleagues (2002) prefer to see the ethnic neighborhood as one involving choices rather than constraints.

Therefore, Alba (1990) pointed out that there is no relationship between neighborhood and ethnic identity. For example, individuals can be embedded in ethnic neighborhoods or communities without necessarily thinking of themselves as ethnic. On the other hand, strong ethnic identifiers do not need ethnic social surroundings in order to maintain a sense of themselves as ethnic.

Figure 3.1 illustrates some of the possible settlement patterns for immigrants. Choices are mainly affected by social and economic resources and

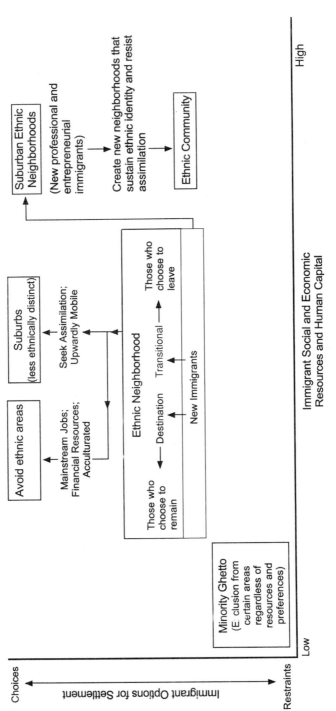

Figure 3.1. Residential Paths for Immigrants to the United States

human capital. Immigrants with few resources chose to locate in an ethnic enclave or neighborhood because their predecessors have established a network of connections that will facilitate their adjustment. Immigrants may remain in neighborhoods until they feel comfortable enough with their skills to seek jobs in mainstream society or until they have acquired the financial and social resources to become accepted in the suburbs. Some immigrants may choose to either work or live in an ethnic neighborhood so that they can benefit from networks in both their own and the dominant culture. Other immigrants who have strong resources and human capital upon entry may move directly to the suburbs where they may choose to assimilate or maintain connections with others who do not wish to assimilate and instead, form an ethnic community.

The choice of settling in ethnic places is stronger among refugees than among immigrants to the United States. The federal resettlement policy for refugees to the United States usually is one of dispersement. But some refugee groups end up undermining that policy, desiring to create distinct and recognizable communities in the United States. This is illustrated by the communities established by Vietnamese refugees in Orange County, California and Boston, Massachusetts. Orange County's "Little Saigon" contains a vibrant business district known as the capital of Vietnamese America. In Boston's Field's Corner, a small cluster of shops, restaurants, grocery stores, and social services serve as a focal point for the Vietnamese community. Place-making is a central and persistent aspect of Vietnamese American community building. Little Saigon and Field's Corner operate as territorial sites for social interaction, anchors for identity, and symbolic aggregating devices. Regional and local social structure along with population size, help to shape the prevailing opportunities for leadership. Vietnamese American community building is weakened without the presence of a main territorial place (Aguillar-San Juan, 2001).[7]

The Israeli immigration to New York City, especially since the 1980s, illustrates that, for them, social networks are more important than place. Israeli immigrants to New York City have a transient orientation to their migration. While immigrants to the United States have traditionally relied on formal ethnic organizations to help them adapt to their new surroundings, New York City Israelis have rejected this option because of: their short-term orientation to immigration (they are sojourners, intending to return to their home country); their reliance on an informal system of friendships to provide a sense of community during their stay; and, their ability to partake, at will, of already established American Jewish organizations (Levitt, 1996). This is different from the Israeli experience in other United States cities. Gold (1994) found that the Israeli community in Los Angeles was organized along traditional lines. The Israelis take part in formal community organizations, they readily hire co-ethnics, participate in joint business ventures with American Jews, and form cooperative group arrangements. In Chicago, Israeli immigrants are more divided in their orientation to the United States. Vriely (1994) found that Israelis in Chicago live a double life based on their social class, ethnic background, and long or short-term orientation to their immigration. He divided the community into three groups: settlers, permanent sojourners, and sojourners. Israeli Ashkenazic professionals acted more like permanent settlers than did the Sephardic businessmen, who were unsure of their status as long or short-term immigrants. They express the desire to leave the United States but are never able to bring themselves to do so, even after 20 years or more.

The Israeli community in New York City, according to Levitt (1996), falls between the middle of the Los Angeles and Chicago immigrant experiences. While New York City Israelis desire close relations with co-ethnics, and succeed in forming them, they rarely participate in the organizations offered by the American Jewish community. Business relations are strained because of their short-term orientation and there is competition among Israelis and between American Jews and Israelis in the same businesses. The New York City Israeli immigrants retained their ethnic identity by socializing with other Israelis and working in either Israeli or American Jewish owned firms. They were Israelis in America, not new Americans (Levitt, 1996).[8]

THE HEALTH EFFECTS OF IMMIGRATION

The Trauma of Breaking or Loosening Old Ties

Studies have shown that newly arriving immigrants have often experienced mental health symptoms during the early periods of their arrival in the United States, depending upon the nature of their immigration experience. For example, post-traumatic stress disorder has been reported among Salvadorans and Guatemalans who came to the United States escaping civil war conditions in their respective countries. Many Central Americans have endured traumatic experiences prior to departure. Escapees from war constitute a distinct class of immigrant from the point to view of psychological well-being. A study of Indochinese refugees in the San Diego area found significantly higher depression levels among women, people over 50 years of age, persons of rural background, the least educated and English proficient, and the unemployed. Lower depression levels were found for those who were married and who had relatives and friends nearby, underscoring the buffering effects of co-ethnic social support. However, when all factors were combined into a predictive analysis of depression, experiences prior to and during immigration emerged as the most powerful predictor (Portes & Rumbaut, 1990).

The same San Diego study, which followed Indochinese refugees over a year, found that the effects of past experiences tend to decline while those associated with their present condition become increasingly important. The first year in the United States is a relatively euphoric period and the lowest depression and demoralization levels are found during this time. By contrast, psychological symptoms hit their highest levels during the second year, a period that may be called "exile shock." After the third year a process of psychological rebounding seems to take place as indicated by a significant decrease in psychological symptoms (Portes & Rumbaut, 1990).

There is also a great deal of evidence on the relationship of social connections, social disruption, and social disorganization to the susceptibility to certain diseases and to mortality (Ornstein & Sobel, 1987). An example of the importance of social connectedness to health can be seen in a comparative study between people living in Japan and in the United States. Japanese who migrate to Hawaii or California have a much higher heart disease rate than those remaining in Japan (Reed, McGee, Yano & Feinleib, 1983). These differences could not be accounted for by differences in diet, serum cholesterol, smoking, or blood pressure level. Members of the group with very low heart disease rates lived a traditional Japanese life. As children they had lived in Japanese neighborhoods and they identified with the Japanese community; they visited Japanese doctors; they most often attended Japanese cultural events and Japanese political and social gatherings. For these people strong social ties may have prevented a disruption in their social world and their sense of social organization. Like a strong belief system, close ties to others can stabilize a person's view of oneself and one's world. We do not yet know the exact mechanisms by which social support enhances health, but we do know that different types of social structure influence the opportunities to express support (Antonucci & Jackson, 1990). Supportive behaviors occur in social contexts that have structural regularities such as ethnic communities.[9]

Rumbaut (1997) has noted that, although new immigrants to the United States, especially in the years since 1990, are some of the most skilled, better educated, and healthiest immigrants in United States history, the process of becoming Americanized can be a traumatic process. Studies have shown a link between becoming acculturated and adopting health risk behaviors such as cigarette, drug and alcohol use. It has been found that the more acculturated Mexican immigrants become, the higher were their rates of various types of psychiatric disorders. There is also evidence from a study conducted by a Vietnamese physician showing that the blood cholesterol levels of children of Vietnamese émigrés to the United States increased for each year they have lived in the United States. Further evidence that immigrants become similar to the native population to which they have immigrated is found in studies of breast cancer incidence and mortality rates. Immigrant women originating from countries with lower breast cancer risk than the United States have been found to increase their risk for breast cancer with their length of residence in the United States (Rumbaut, 1997). A 25 year study of the acculturation of a small Italian-American community in Pennsylvania found that the deaths from heart attacks increased as successive generations of Italians adopted a typical middle class American lifestyle, diet, married non-Italians, moved away from the community to work and live, resulting in the loosening of family and community ties. (Bruhn & Wolf, 1979; Wolf & Bruhn, 1993).

Immigration scholars point out that many of today's immigrants take different pathways and have different goals than immigrants in previous years. For example, some immigrants come to the United States temporarily for specific reasons and intend to return to their native country. Many immigrants know a great deal about American culture prior to their arrival because of mass media, computers, and the spread of popular culture. Many immigrants have personal connections to people in the United States before they immigrate. National surveys in Mexico have found that about one-half of adult Mexicans were related to someone living in the United States, and one-third of all Mexicans have been to the United States at some point in their lives (Massey & Espinosa, 1997). Extensive linkages and social networks of family and friends can soften the impact of the immigration experience. Rumbaut (1997) estimated that one-third of Cuba's population of eleven million have relatives in the United States and Puerto Rico. Many recent immigrants, for example from Caribbean countries, already have competency in English. These pre-immigration advantages facilitate the degree and speed of acculturation and assimilation. Social ties with one's own kind in the country one intends to immigrate to helps to minimize the trauma of immigration.

SUMMARY

The phenomena of immigration and ethnic communities are about seeking and maintaining social ties with others who share a common culture. Cities in the United States have been the focal point for the formation of ethnic communities, where immigrants can usually gain the assistance of predecessors in beginning their process of adaptation to a new environment. The success or failure of this process will be greatly influenced by the connections the newcomers are able, or not able, to make. Immigrants have different purposes for their immigration which offer different options and lead to different outcomes including, becoming American through acculturation and eventual assimilation, retaining one's ethnic commitment by living in an ethnic community, or remaining a sojourner. Whichever goal is chosen immigrants to the United States will interact with or encounter people from numerous other cultures of the world who either are native to North America or have immigrated. Today's cities in the United States display highly visible racial and ethnic diversity that is increasing. The challenge for the United States today is how to facilitate the development of new and broader connections and social networks so that immigrants will be able to adapt successfully and experience the American ideals that attracted them to immigrate.

The majority of ethnic groups to the United States have cultural ties with people from their countries who have preceded them. This provides a source of social capital that facilitates the development of further social connections. Connected relatives and friends can help enhance opportunities for new immigrants to obtain education, training, skill, knowledge, and language credentials. However, not all immigrants are able to use connections in their new environment to continue the progress of their predecessors.

Immigration involves challenges to social identities and a sense of community. The ethnic community provides physical and social boundaries that help immigrants cope with threats to their identity or sense of belonging. Ethnic communities will be a destination for some immigrants and a way station enroute to acculturation and assimilation for others. Some ethnic communities such as the Hasidic Jews and Amish prefer to greatly limit their contact with larger society, while other ethnic communities like the Somali's want to be included in United States culture but retain their ethnic identity and customs. Many new immigrants from Asia who arrive with substantial human capital are settling in suburbs with fellow ethnics who have been successfully upwardly mobile where they form an ethnic neighborhood.

Ethnic neighborhoods have historically been considered the core of immigrant life in cities, especially for new immigrants. Ethnic identity is strongly shaped and reinforced by the location where immigrants settle. With the growth and expansion of cities it is now common that regional and neighborhood concentrations of ethnic groups are being formed to facilitate the maintenance of social boundaries and ethnic identity. However, there is evidence that ethnically distinctive neighborhoods have declined as immigrants coming to the United States have more diversified social and economic resources and human capital, using the ethnic neighborhood as a point of transition into American society.

The choice of settling in ethnic places is stronger among refugees than among immigrants to the United States. The federal resettlement policy for refugees to the United States is usually one of dispersement, but the ties among most refugee groups is stronger than the policy. Many groups, such as the Somali's, move to areas of the United States they find more attractive. This can strain local resources if the area chosen does not have the appropriate infrastructure or attitudes of tolerance toward people who might be different from themselves.

The trauma of breaking ties and establishing new ones can have health effects. Many immigrants and refugees may have health problems that existed before they entered the United States, but early in the adaptation experience newly arrived immigrants often experience mental health problems such as depression, anxiety and post traumatic stress syndrome. The highest level of symptoms today is usually during the second year, a period often referred to as "exile shock." There is a great deal of evidence that social connections can help to ameliorate the shock of immigration. Like a strong belief system, close ties to others can stabilize a person's view of himself and the world around him. Different types of social structure influence the opportunities to express social support. Supportive behaviors occur in social contexts that have structural regularities such as ethnic communities.

The world is becoming a smaller place. More immigrants to the United States, especially those from Mexico, Cuba, and Caribbean countries have relatives living in the United States, have been to the United States, or have knowledge of United States culture through the mass media and technology. Many are competent in English. Thus, many immigrants come to the United States with a pre-immigration experience that is more realistic, making their transition less traumatic.

QUESTIONS FOR DISCUSSION

1. Discuss the dilemma of how it is important to new immigrants to the United States to retain their cultural identity and traditions on the one hand, and on the other hand be accepted as an American citizen and share in the American common good.
2. Is assimilation a realistic goal for ethnic Americans? Should Americans expect immigrants to assimilate? What are the ethical limits to pressure exerted on people of different ethnicities to conform to the dominant culture?

3. What are the issues raised when people of a given ethnicity chose to live in ethnic neighborhoods and support ethnic economies when affirmative action and equal opportunity are the laws and practices of larger society?

4. What are some of the issues surrounding the establishment of inter-personal trust between yourself and someone from a culture different from your own?

5. To what extent do ethnic neighborhoods and communities embody Tönnies idea of Gemeinschaft?

6. Discuss some of the long-term negative effects of immigration on a person's or family's health.

7. In your view, what should be the future policy of the United States toward immigration?

8. As the United States becomes increasingly diverse how do you think the manifestations of prejudice will change? Will the country become more tolerant and more accepting or less tolerant and less accepting of different ethnic groups?

9. Do you agree that the federal resettlement policy for refugees to the United States should be one of dispersement?

10. What is your opinion about President George Bush's plan to allow foreigners, including undocumented immigrants already here, to work in the United States with temporary three-year visas?

Chapter 4

Fragmented Ties
The Poor and the Homeless

INTRODUCTION

Poverty and homelessness are a part of the history of mankind. Attitudes toward the poor have deep philosophical and religious roots. Aristotle argued that the good of the community should set the direction for the lives of individuals, for it is a higher or more divine good than the particular goods of private persons. St. Thomas Aquinas argued that a right relationship to God requires commitment to the common good of our neighbors and of all creation (Hollenbach, 1999). In the early 16th century before the Reformation, Martin Luther described the customs surrounding the giving of alms.[1] Poverty has also been a political issue, periodically rediscovered by politicians (Wilson, 1987). President Bill Clinton toured Appalachia, the Mississippi Delta, the Black Hills and the Los Angeles ghetto covering similar steps made by President Lyndon B. Johnson, who declared war on poverty 30 years earlier. It was Johnson's predecessor, John F. Kennedy, in 1963, who first initiated government programs to deal with this growing problem. Despite some progress, President Ronald Reagan declared, "We fought a war against poverty and poverty won" (Hamson, 1999).

Poverty lingers in the United States as it does to an even greater degree in low income countries. The usual reasons for the persistence of poverty are the lack of education and skills, lack of opportunity to change one's social class, lack of social, human and economic capital, discrimination, and imperialism. But the major reason why poverty lingers is that it has deep cultural roots, attitudes and values that impede change. Lionel Sosa (1998) pointed to fatalism, the resignation of the poor and the low priority of education as major obstacles to upward social mobility. Many scholars have pointed to the destructive consequences of slavery on the values and attitudes of African Americans toward work, education, and social responsibility (Patterson, 1999). Isolation from mainstream society is a factor in the high poverty rate among American Indians, particularly the two million who live on or near reservations. Their traditional culture, based on man's partnership with nature, inculcates a sense of fatalism and egalitarianism that discourages initiative and upward social mobility (Harrison, 1999).

There are connections between poverty and homelessness. Not all poor are homeless, but all homeless are poor. The homeless are drawn from a pool of the extremely poor. The persistently poor who are long-term unemployed, and who engage in drug abuse and crime are often referred to as the "underclass" (Rossi, 1989; Auletta, 1999). The homeless are estimated to comprise from one-half to two and one-half percent of the poverty population.[2] The United States poverty threshold has been defined the same way since 1965. The World Almanac (2003) defines the poverty rate as the proportion of the population whose income falls below the government's official poverty level which is adjusted each year for inflation. In 2001, the poverty threshold was about $18,000 a year for a family of four. In 2001 there were an estimated 32.9 million people of all races in the United States or 11.7% of the total population who met the definition of poverty. (See Figure 4.1.) The proportion of African Americans below the poverty line is about 27 percent and black unemployment is about nine percent, but more than 30 percent of Hispanics are below the poverty line and on some Indian reservations the unemployment rate exceeds 70 percent. Nonetheless, most poor persons in the United States are white (68%) and the majority of the poor (59%) live outside central cities (Cotter, 2002). Poverty in rural areas is severe, enduring, growing, and complex. The rural poor are more likely to live in a family where the head is working at poverty-level wages (Cotter, 2002).

Homelessness, a more abstract and overwhelming concept of poverty, is defined as not having a fixed address, no private space, shelter, or home, (Jencks, 1994), and who possess limited familial support services and limited amounts of personal and public regard from which to draw support (Baker, 1994). Estimates on the number of homeless vary widely as some estimates are based on the number of homeless people in shelters on a particular night, other estimates are based on the number of persons who have been homeless in their lifetime, and still other estimates are based on the number of persons who are known to use agency resources.[3] There are "old" and "new" homeless. A study of 269 homeless males and females from six sites in Los Angeles County, and a random sample of 174 skid row single room occupants (SRO), found that these persons were not newcomers to Los Angeles or newcomers to poverty and

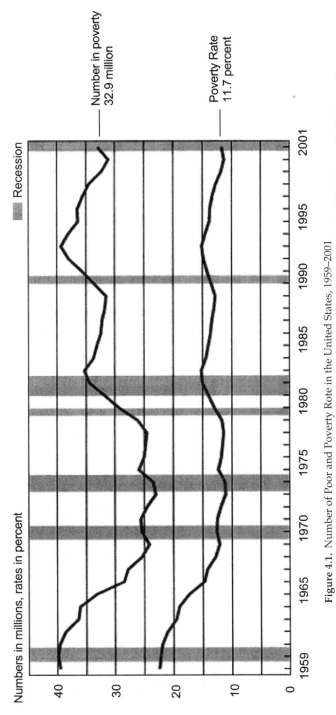

Figure 4.1. Number of Poor and Poverty Rate in the United States, 1959–2001

Note: The data points represent the midpoints of the respective years. The latest recession begins March, 2001. (*Source:* U. S. Census Bureau, *Current Population Survey, 1960–2002.* Annual Demographic Supplements) homelessness. They were part of the labor force but were socially isolated. A large number were veterans (Ropers, 1988). The "new" homeless are those who have fallen through the cracks of a social structure shaken by long-term economic, social, and political policies and changes. The causes for poverty and homelessness of newcomers is not found only in individual pathology but intertwined with local and national factors. The homeless in the United States began expanding in the 1960s but surged in the 1980s. Therefore, it is not surprising that estimates on the number of homeless in the United States increased from 350,000–400,000 in 1987 to 3.5 million children and adults in 2000 (The Urban Institute, 2000). During the 1990s estimates of the homeless population reached as high as 12 million people (Miringhoff & Miringhoff, 1999). Families with children are thought to comprise 40 percent of the homeless. The largest group of poor is the working poor who numbered 7.4 million in 1996 (Newman, 1999). Many of the newcomers to poverty and homelessness are immigrants who migrated to states with weak safety nets and that had little experience assisting immigrants in acculturation.

A survey commissioned by the Los Angeles Times concluded that there were 42,000 car garages sheltering 200,000 individuals and families in Los Angeles County. An unknown number lived in other parts of Southern California. The majority of these invisible people were immigrants from Central America and Mexico (Chavez & Quinn, 1987). Profiting from the situation were landlords who violated laws governing sanitation, zoning, safety, and adding as much as $450 to their monthly incomes. Some of these black market garage homes were remodeled. Others were simply garages. Most had no plumbing, heating, or windows. While extra housing inspectors were hired to evict the garage dwellers, Los Angeles mainly responded to individual complaints (Chavez & Quinn, 1987). Poverty is, indeed, a public health issue (Harris & Curtis, 1998).

POVERTY AND HOMELESSNESS AS INDICATORS OF NATIONAL HEALTH

Poverty and homelessness have been identified as two of several indicators of the social health of our nation.[4] The Fordham Institute for Innovation in Social Policy has studied indicators of the social health of America and published trends in these indicators each year since 1987, to increase public awareness of social conditions (Miringhoff & Miringhoff, 1999). Like economic indexes, the Index of Social Health uses key social indicators that assess the quality of life, such as child abuse, suicide, drug use, and health care, and core socioeconomic indicators that measure well-being, including average earnings, poverty, and inequality. The Institute has combined these indicators into a single number for each year since 1970, enabling trend analyses to be undertaken (Miringhoff & Miringhoff, 1999). The overall trend of the Index of Social Health for the United States from 1970 to 1996 is one of decline. This decline corresponds to a downward trend in another national index composed by the National Commission on Civic Renewal.[5] The Index of National Civic Health has declined steadily from 1965 to 1995. While the two indexes had different purposes and are therefore comprised of different indicators, they both agree on the downward trend in the quality of life in America over the past 30 years.

The Index of Social Health is comprised of 16 indicators two of which are poverty and (the lack of) affordable housing (homelessness). Poverty is broken down into child poverty and poverty among persons aged 65 and older. While poverty among the elderly has decreased from a high of 24.6 percent in 1970 to 10.8 percent in 1996, there are 3.4 million poor elderly in the United States. Among the elderly, black and Hispanic poverty rates are more than two and one-half times those of whites. Females have twice the poverty rate as males. Measured by the international poverty standard of less than one half the median income, the United States has the third worst poverty rate for the elderly among 17 industrialized countries (Miringhoff & Miringhoff, 1999).

Child poverty in the United States increased by 33 percent between 1970 and 1996. Currently there are 13.8 million children living in poverty in the United States. Child poverty is most prevalent among those under age six, and among ethnic minorities, especially African American and Hispanic youth. According to the Children's Defense Fund, the child poverty rate in the United States is now at least double that of other developed countries. One in three children will be poor for at least a year before turning age 16 (Nunez, 1996). The Children's Defense Fund, which documents the links between child poverty and pathology, reports that children are more likely to suffer malnourishment, family stress, inferior child care, frequent moves, adolescent pregnancy, overcrowding and death. They attend inferior schools, are more likely to drop-out, to become delinquent, and to feel hopeless (Myers, 2000).

Home ownership has deep symbolic meaning in the United States. Home ownership is more difficult today for young families than it was in the 1970s (Appelbaum, 1989). Rental costs remain high and the availability of low cost housing is declining. Low income households spend 50 percent or more of their income on rental housing or live in substandard housing. The high cost and shortage of low income housing along with low veteran's incomes, low paying jobs, and the deinstitutionalization of the mentally ill have all contributed to the rise in the number of homeless in the United States. What is most striking is the growing number of families with children that have no home (Miringhoff & Miringhoff, 1999).

According to sociologist Christopher Jencks (1994) the spread of homelessness among single adults was a by-product of five related changes: the elimination of involuntary commitment, the eviction of mental hospital patients who had nowhere to go, the advent of crack cocaine, increases in long-term joblessness, and political restrictions on the creation of flop houses. Among families, three factors appear to have been important: the spread of single motherhood, the erosion of welfare recipient's purchasing power, and perhaps crack cocaine (p. 103). Jencks suggests that as more shelters and soup kitchens were created in the late 1980s these resources provided an option for those homeless who did not want to return home or who were living alone. In Jencks's words, "the more people learn about coping with homelessness, the easier the boundary is to cross" (p. 106).

Poverty and homelessness are not one problem, but many; they are not a condition, but the result of a process (see Figure 4.2); the societal

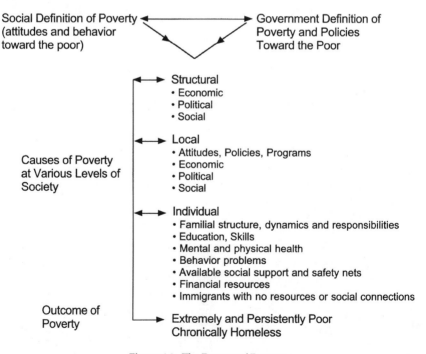

Figure 4.2. The Process of Poverty

resources needed to assist them are chronically inadequate because we only deal with those who are visible; the increased immigration of people with little education and few skills who accept low salaries and few benefits will make it difficult for them to escape poverty and perhaps homelessness; they are attributed a negative stereotype that puts the blame for their situation on personal failing, bad attitudes, or victims of bad luck (Cozzarelli, Wilkinson & Tagler, 2001); and they are often mistakenly described as persons who are disconnected, lacking social ties and networks. One of the limitations in increasing our understanding of the process of becoming poor and homeless is our tendency to stereotype them and generalize this stereotype so that they are considered a homogeneous category. Contrary to widespread public belief that the homeless are "unsocialized retreatists," peer relationships are a combination of isolation and sociability (Anderson, Snow & Cress, 1994). There is a community of the streets which includes social isolates, the pathologically disconnected, and newcomers who cannot financially afford to survive.

SOCIAL CONNECTIONS AND NETWORKS: THE URBAN POOR AND HOMELESS

The stranger in Nathaniel Hawthorne's *The Ambitious Guest* (McIntosh, 1987) asked, "Is not the kindred of a common fate a closer tie than that of birth?" (p. 84). Fate brings people together even for short periods of time. In their studies on the streets of St. Louis, Michael Stein and George McCall (1994) found that persons without homes must approach their environment in different ways, giving rise to a "community of the streets" which is different from a residential community. Daily life rounds are not home-based. Domestic life has become decentralized. The street homeless have to carry out domestic functions in public places. Their notion of a home is that of a home range comprised of "spots" and connecting routes. Community life is not communal because privacy, security and safety have changed for the homeless. Distrust creates wariness. Yet, by sharing and overlapping of home ranges and daily rounds they create a geographic community among the disaffiliated. Their "community" becomes a mutual awareness of shared and overlapping home ranges and daily rounds (Stein & McCall, 1994).

Some homeless become habituated to street life; they become anchored, and it is difficult to rescue them. They need transitional resocialization programs more than programs that thrust them back into the conventional world. They need to learn how to make new types of connections (Snow, Anderson, Quist & Cress, 1996).

Nonkin Networks among the Male Homeless

Whether housed or homeless, people are inherently social in nature. Through our social encounters we acquire a web of interpersonal social relationships. These relationships form the basis of our personal social networks. It is through social networks that we negotiate our social worlds. Even in dire circumstances, people usually manage to connect with others to maximize their survival. Life on the streets involves frequent involvement in social networks.

An estimated 80 to 90 percent of America's homeless population is male (Baker, 1994; Snow & Anderson, 1993). Studies indicate that these men: are single and without families and either have never been married or have experienced a break in personal relationships; have tenuous ties with family members; have physical and/or mental disabilities, are members of an ethnic or racial minority group; and suffer from extreme poverty (Rossi, 1989). There are a growing number of single women, women with children, and young families becoming homeless. Women comprise about 20 percent of the homeless population. Compared to men, homeless women are more likely to be accompanied by family members, usually their own children. Both Latinas and African American women are over-represented among the homeless (Baker, 1994; Burt, 1992).

Molina (2000) studied the social networks in the daily survival of homeless Latino and African men in Los Angeles's skid row. She observed that homeless men make choices about social encounters, to develop, evade, or dissolve social ties. To evaluate the extent to which social networking takes place she conducted in-depth interviews with three groups of homeless men, English-speaking Latinos, Spanish-speaking Latinos, and African Americans. Molina found that the homeless have only a handful of people they can count on for help, and it is these people who form the basis for their social networks. The lives of these homeless men were hardly one of social isolation or of passive submission to homelessness. She found a high frequency of contact, in spite of the limitations of poverty, and men who were actively involved in their own survival.

The social networks of English-speaking Latinos were comprised of associates who provided recreational companionship coupled with a high incidence of alcohol use. English-speaking Latinos became easily acclimated to a skid row way of life through conviviality and sharing of resources. The social networks of Spanish-speaking Latinos were less oriented to a skid row lifestyle. They had close connections to housed individuals and a strong orientation toward working for pay. Their networks served primarily as channels of communication geared toward job hunting. African American men suffered the effects of a harsh and entrenched form of poverty and homelessness. Molina found that most homeless African American men were driven by the hustle of skid row shelters, meal facilities, pan handling, and recreational activities with peers. Fewer than one-third of the African American men were able to secure employment for one month and their self-reported drug use was higher than the Latino groups. Molina concluded that many homeless develop a communal sense of solidarity and rely on extensive social networks of casual friends.

Snow and Anderson (1993) studied peer relationships among the homeless in Austin, Texas in the mid-1980s. They observed that friendships are compensatory in street life. They are one of the few sources of social validation. Friends are a nonstigmatizing reference group, a nexus for sharing scarce resources, and a means of self-validation. To be homeless in America is not only to have fallen to the bottom of the status system, it is also being confronted with doubts of self-worth and the meaning of existence. "Friendships" among the homeless vacillate between feelings of closeness and discounting other homeless individuals as untrustworthy and exploitive. The exchange of personal names is discouraged as anonymity is an adaptive strategy that promotes mutual survival. Snow and Anderson found four general types of peer affiliations among the homeless. The *recently dislocated* who are fearful and distrustful and shy away from friendships. The *regular straddlers* who are consumed by the present. They are oriented to the conventional world and the schedules of caretaker agencies. Straddlers develop acquaintances and friends and state that they plan to get off the street, yet their relationships are exclusively street-based. Relationships disintegrate over time and they move on to new relationships. The *institutionally adapted straddlers* are usually employed in caretaker agencies. They resist fraternizing and live in a world of marginal and ambivalent social relationships. The *outsiders* are street-based. This group is comprised of the traditional tramps who live a solitary lifestyle; the hippie tramps who are highly mobile, self-sufficient and tend to avoid street people, being gregarious among themselves; traditional bums lack mobility, are alcohol dependent, and fit the image of the skid row alcoholic; redneck bums are younger than traditional bums, use alcohol heavily, maintain a tight social network, protect their territory aggressively, and are avoided by most homeless; the mentally ill are consistently isolated and don't initiate interactions with others. They are socially disconnected lacking the ability to establish social ties.

Even bowery men have been found to have an intermediate level of intimacy (Cohen & Sokolovsky, 1989). In a study of long-term residents of skid row (averaging more than 16 years), researchers found that the bowery is a highly social world—the few who were complete loners were the psychotic, severely depressed and/or alcoholic, and the physically impaired

(Cohen & Sokolovsky, 1989). Several characteristics emerged that also typ-ify other homeless: 1) life has a cyclical quality. Schedules are determined by agencies and institutions that the homeless depend upon for meals, daily room tickets or monthly checks; some homeless are regulated by when they must be in and out of their flops. Weekends do not exist, holi-days mean very little; 2) reciprocity is the hallmark of all relationships. For example, among drinkers it is counting on a person to watch out for you when you are drunk. The moral code regarding interpersonal relationships on the streets is "what goes around comes around." 3) group formations are common in the bowery. There are bottle gangs, food programs, hotel lobbies, and small informal groups to exchange sustenance items.

Cohen and Sokolovsky pointed out that the skid rower had fewer social ties and intimates than their age counterparts in the general pop-ulation, but they are not complete isolates or incapable of intimacy. They concluded:

> [A]lthough skid row social life is radically different from middle class exis-tence, it is not without its intricacies. There are missions, social agencies, flops, bread lines, taverns, and parks that form the nucleus for the skid rower's so-cial world of bottle gangs, associates, social workers, priests, loan sharks, and hotel managers. These supports may not only fill his stomach today or cheer him up tomorrow, but they also teach him how to survive the next winter or the next drink. They teach him to be a skid row man. (p. 137)

Shapiro (1971) found that single room occupants (SROs) functioned as a village community. He stated, "in these walled-off villages of society's rejects, we found a complex, and profoundly social community" (p. 23). The lives of all but a few of the tenants were intertwined contrary to the stereotype. The nearly closed SRO system provides housing for single in-dividuals who can neither function autonomously as productive citizens nor maintain their existing meager level of functioning. The SRO way of life provides a network of social supports from within the SRO system itself. Some recurrent patterns of relationships are the matriarchal quasi-family, the all-male drinking clique, the long-term lesbian pair, the addicted prostitute and one or two male prostitutes she supports—these networks produce an informal system of mutual help. Friendship groups give mu-tual support to each other's behavior as well as provide human association. Shapiro found that the SRO social structure can be described as a series of interlocking "near-groups," with a flexible, floating membership. The SRO is a survival culture where alcohol is a paramount shared activity from which other collective activities radiate. The SRO style of living forms a recognizable pattern in which a high degree of interconnection and mutual dependency is the rule (Shapiro, 1971).

Networks among Homeless Women

Homelessness is much more likely to affect men than women, and when it occurs among women it is less isolating (Baker, 1994). Women found on the streets and in shelters are more likely than men to be homeless in the company of at least one other family member, usually their own children. Burt (1992) conducted a nationwide survey and found that 89 percent of the men sampled were alone or in a shelter, compared to 45 percent of the women. A few men with children were found among the homeless, but the majority of homeless families were one-parent families with female heads. Rossi (1989) found that homeless women, while more connected to a family of procreation than homeless men, were less likely to express interest in maintaining connections to their families of origin, i.e. parents or siblings.

The age of homeless women varies across the country, but, in general, homeless women tend to be younger (many under age 25) than homeless men. Older homeless women tend to be single and have a greater prevalence of personal disabilities (Liebow, 1993; Wright, 1989). Homeless women are also more likely to be members of a racial or ethnic minority. Homeless women with children are more likely to be African-American. Three quarters of the Aid to Families with Dependent Children (AFDC) caseload in Chicago, for example, is African-American compared to 35 percent of the city population (Rossi, 1989).

In the nationwide survey previously mentioned, Burt (1992) found that single homeless women shared a 50 percent higher rate of previous hospitalization for mental illness than did single homeless men, while homeless women with children had a prevalence rate less than one-half that of men. Homeless women in general had lower rates of inpatient chemical dependency treatment than was true for men. But all three groups—single men, single women, and women with children—all had high depression scores as measured by standardized psychiatric tests. In general, the literature shows that homelessness presents a less severe personal disability for women, particularly women with children, than it is for men (Baker, 1994).

Not only are the precursors of street life different for men and women, but the duration of the homeless experience differs as well. The average length of homelessness for single women was 33 months and 16 months for women with children compared to four years for single men. However, women with children had longer spells of joblessness than either single men or single women. Studies suggest that homelessness may be a more episodic experience for racial and ethnic minorities than it is for whites. Both African-Americans and Hispanics seem to have more frequent periods of homelessness for shorter durations than do whites. Baker

(1994) speculates that ethnic and racial minorities might avoid homelessness longer on inadequate incomes than whites, but once homeless, minority groups are more likely than whites to experience frequent episodes of homelessness.

Social networks help determine the different paths taken by the poor and homeless. Homeless families from ethnic minority groups tend to have more family-based networks while whites tend to have friend-based networks. The social networks of ethnic minorities tend to be smaller, dense and kin-based compared to those of whites. This may explain why shelters appeal to homeless families from ethnic minority groups than they do to whites. Social networks provide social support and emotional aid, but in addition they are useful in providing information, guidance, personal and material assistance. Small, strongly embedded networks cannot provide all of these resources, rather broader, wide-ranging networks are more likely to satisfy a variety of needs. Therefore, homeless white families with less dense, larger and non-kin networks often have more options than ethnic minorities. In contrast, homeless ethnic minority families are more likely to share housing, seek the services of family agencies, or seek the assistance of shelters when network resources are scarce. Smaller families, the weakening of family ties and family breakdown has left many of the very poor without relatives to help them. According to Jencks (1994), families have traditionally been more willing to provide permanent support for poor female relatives, but, today, most Americans expect a single woman to get a job. A woman who cannot get, or hold, a job may be more vulnerable to homelessness than she was in an earlier era, especially if she is mentally ill or an addict. The decline of marriage has played a significant role in the increase of homelessness among women and children. Marriage provides an economic, if not a social safety net. Married couples hardly ever become homeless as long as they stick together (Jencks, 1994). Single, unskilled women, who continue to have children, are the ones usually forced into homelessness. The shelter may be their only safety net.

The Fragile Family

The traditional family is obsolete for the poor and homeless. The poor family is a loose-knit transitory group headed by a single parent with little education, non-competitive job skills, no regular sources of health care, and lacking in basic social support systems (da Costa Nunez, 1996). Half of current homeless mothers were born into two parent households that were self-sufficient, but now comprise the "notched down" generation. Single motherhood, crack cocaine, and the erosion of the purchasing power of welfare benefits are mentioned as reasons for being notched-down. But there are other more basic reasons. In a 20-year longitudinal study of teenage mothers and their children in Baltimore, Furstenberg (1993) pursued answers to the question "what conditions enable parents living in poverty to help children escape disadvantage later in life?" One conspicuous difference between early winners and losers was the significant role that family members played in their children's lives. Parents (especially mothers) and sometimes other relatives represented the margin of difference between their children's success or failure. The connectedness or embeddedness of the family in its immediate context shapes the strategies of parenting. Furstenberg found that to succeed parents must be super motivated, that is, adept at working the system and diligent in monitoring their children. Even in the most distressed neighborhoods parents found ways to protect their children from the dangers of everyday life. Most important was whether parents were supported or undermined by their immediate community. Parents were more successful in communities where child rearing was a collective responsibility, where strong institutions supported the parent's efforts, and where there were nurturing informal social networks within the neighborhoods.

Furstenberg also noted that social isolation is often practiced as an adaptive strategy by many parents living in dangerous neighborhoods. Safety concerns affect the degree to which families become involved with or interact with neighbors. Social integration was not always beneficial to adolescents living in a neighborhood characterized by aberrant behavior. Parents and their children, therefore, often resisted contact with neighbors, established few friendships, and did not get involved with neighborhood problems.[6] Just as neighborhoods can affect families, so families can affect neighborhoods. Darling and Steinberg (1997) found that the presence of stable families in a neighborhood is associated with lower levels of youthful lawbreaking because the adults rear well-adjusted and well-behaved children. Thus, "good families" have a ripple effect by increasing the pool of "good peers" that other families' children can befriend. Although researchers have frequently found a low level of trust among the urban poor, networks of reciprocity exist that are not always evident to outsiders. Members of these networks might provide child care, cash assistance, temporary shelter, or other forms of assistance. Inner city social networks may be more fragmented and less effective than they were several decades ago, but reciprocity is an important asset to poor people as it builds social capital within and between families and establishes some degree of trust and cohesion among neighbors (Putnam, 2000). But what is important to remember is that the causes of poverty and homelessness do no lie primarily within the social fabric of poor communities rather the causes lie in the economic, political, and racial structures of society. The social capital of the poor was never considered an important asset to maintain. If social capital is not regarded as an important asset for the poor to maintain, it will be difficult to build social capital among poor neighborhoods and poor families (Warren, Thompson, & Saegert, 2001).

Many poor families in urban areas do not have contact with social institutions that represent mainstream society. The most impoverished inner city neighborhoods have experienced a decrease in the proportion of working and middle class families, thereby increasing the social isolation of the remaining residents from more advantaged members of society. The nonworking poor experience even greater social isolation that the working poor (Wilson, 1996). Wilson posited that the flight of jobs from the city destroys businesses, social institutions and the youth socialization process, leading to social isolation. Minority youth lose ties to job networks as well as to a stable community where good work habits are the norm. Social isolation deprives inner city residents of role models, whose strong presence buffers the effects of neighborhood joblessness, but also of the contacts provided by mainstream social networks that facilitate social and economic advancement. This form of social isolation contributes to the formation and crystallization of ghetto-related cultural traits and behaviors (Wilson, 1987; 1996).[7]

The effects of poverty on the social connections of children are profound. Poor children's cognitive ability and school achievement is lower than among non-poor children. Poor children are more likely to experience developmental delays and learning disabilities and twice as likely to repeat a grade in school, be expelled, or drop out before graduating from high school (Bianchi, 1999). More parents of poor children report that their child has an emotional or behavioral problem. Reported cases of neglect and child abuse are almost seven times higher among poor than non-poor children, and poor children are twice as likely to be in families victimized by violent crimes. Poor parents provide less stimulating home environments and poor parenting styles. Parental verbal interactions with their children in poor families are less frequent and discipline is usually more harsh than among non-poor families. Studies also point to poor parental mental health as a factor in child-parent conflict. Finally, poverty constrains parents' choice of residence: poor families live in less safe neighborhoods and send their children to lower-quality schools. Children associate with peers in the neighborhood who are less likely to be positive models.

While money matters in the rearing and socialization of children, there is debate about how much money matters. Deep, long-term poverty has obvious effects on children's outcomes; some theorists state that under such circumstances parents are less able to "invest" in their children. On the other hand, some theorists argue that good parents and parenting can override the lack of income, that merely increasing income would not change the model to which children are exposed.

What is one of the most important effects of poverty, especially on children, is the degree to which individuals living in poverty feel that they are able to take control over their lives and make things better for themselves, that is, the degree to which hopelessness has established itself (Bolland, 2003). Bolland studied 2,468 youth, between the ages of 9 and 19 living in high-poverty neighborhoods in Mobile and Prichard, Alabama to determine the association between risk behaviors and various levels of helplessness. He found that roughly 50 percent of young males and 75 percent of young females growing up the Mobile-Prichard inner city experienced high levels of hopelessness about their future. For males, the interaction between age and hopelessness predicted 2 of 21 risk behaviors (sexual intercourse and gang membership). Among females, the interaction between age and hopelessness predicted 5 of the 21 risk behaviors (physical fights, attempts to get others to fight, cut or shot by someone else, sexual intercourse, having a child, attempting to get pregnant.) Bolland pointed out that the predictions for three violence behaviors were consistent for males and females. When youth see their future as hopeless there may be little or no concern about the consequences of one's current behavior, indeed, hopelessness about the future could encourage one to be more aggressive in getting what one wants now; societal boundaries and sanctions don't matter.

The length of time families spend in poverty undoubtedly affects their attitude towards the future. In a National Longitudinal Survey of Youth involving children aged four to eight, McLeod and Shanahan (1993), found that the length of time spent in poverty predicted children's mental health. As the length of time in poverty increased, so did stress and feelings of unhappiness, anxiety, and dependence. The stress of poverty erodes parenting skills, poor mothers use more physical punishment, parental abuse increases with poverty, and poor nutrition, hazardous environments, violence and crime all contribute to the total effects of poverty (Coleman & Rebach, 2001).

Youth Poverty and Homelessness

The number of youth living apart from their families is unknown. The episodic nature of teen homelessness has resulted in over-estimates of duration and under-estimates of prevalence and incidence. In 1998, Ringwalt and his colleagues reported, in a national survey of domiciled youth aged 12 to 17 years old, that 7.5 percent (equivalent to 1.5 million nationally) had experienced an episode of homelessness in the prior year

(Ringwalt, Greene, Robertson & McPheeters, 1998). The National Symposium on Homelessness Research provided a comprehensive, current assessment of our knowledge of youth homelessness (Fosburg & Dennis,
1999). At that symposium Robertson & Toro (1999) presented an excellent
overview of the distribution and patterns of youth homelessness and the
characteristics of homeless youth.

The estimated annual prevalence of homeless youth in the United
States is five percent for those ages 12 to 17. This estimate suggests that adolescents under age 18 may be at higher risk for homelessness than adults.
Homeless youth are more likely to be visible in major cities, but they exist
across urban, suburban, and rural areas. Studies have found slightly more
females in shelters while street youth or older youth tend to be males.
National surveys have found no differences in rates of youth homelessness by racial or ethnic group. Homeless youth are no more likely than
non-homeless youth to report a gay or bisexual orientation. Interestingly,
youth who experience homelessness seem to come from *less* impoverished
backgrounds than homeless adults.

Youth consistently report family conflict as the primary reason for their
homelessness. Sources of the conflict include disagreements with parents
over relationships with stepparents, sexual activity or sexual orientation,
pregnancy, school problems, alcohol or other drug use, neglect, and physical, psychological and/or sexual abuse. About 20 percent of homeless
youth were removed from their homes by authorities because of neglect or
abuse. Many homeless youth report disrupted family relationships such
as single-parent families, blended families, parents were unknown or were
divorced or separated. Many lived with relatives or were placed outside
the home by officials. Homelessness appeared to be a pattern of long term
residential instability during early life including runaways, psychiatric or
correctional placement, foster care, and shelters. A consistent theme among
the youth is a history of interrupted or difficult school histories resulting in
dropping out, being placed in special or remedial classes, suspensions or
being expelled. School problems merely reflect family problems and vice
versa. It is not surprising then that homeless youth have high rates of emotional and mental problems resulting in a high number of repeated suicide
attempts.

With such a pervasive history of fractured, unsatisfying social connections in the developing years of life it is not surprising that homeless youth
seek out, or are pulled toward, others of similar age and circumstance for
association. Most homeless youth hang out with peers like themselves, especially in gangs, to share substance abuse, and/or sex. Many homeless
youth have used illicit drugs before they became homeless. Parents of these
youth are often alcohol and drug abusers themselves who have received

treatment for the abuse of drugs or psychological problems. The literature reports high rates of sexual activity among homeless youth and usually low protection against pregnancy or sexually transmitted diseases. Homeless youth present a high profile for human immunodeficiency virus (HIV) infection. Specific high risk sexual and drug abuse behaviors include multiple sex partners, high-risk sexual partners, survival sex, minimal condom use, injection drug use, sharing needles, and having sex while high. HIV is a widespread health problem among homeless youth with the rate of HIV positives ranging from two to seven percent among youth ages 15 to 24. Many homeless youth report illegal behavior, some of which may be to provide basic needs directly, to generate income, and/or to sustain addictions (Robertson & Toro, 1999).

HIV risk behaviors and seroprevalence are particularly high among street youth. Though many programs have been designed to serve them, street youth have low rates of service utilization. Auerswald and Eyre (2002) interviewed and observed street youth in San Francisco to gain insights into the lifecycle of homelessness in this population. Street youth described themselves as not having a choice. They recounted their life prior to living on the street as one of catastrophic family dynamics. Once on the street they experienced loneliness, disorientation and an intense desire to feel included along with the need to satisfy basic needs. Their initiation to the street was facilitated by street mentors who provided the youth with survival skills and helped them acculturate to street resources. Once youth are integrated into the street economy, living on the street is a way of life. The youth described a supportive community and street partnerships as a coping strategy to help them in their daily struggle to survive. While these relationships were helpful, youth had low expectations of them. Youth had a low level of trust for each other and especially of mainstream institutions such as the police, clinics and shelters. Sometimes events on the street threaten a youth's ability to survive in the streets and some return to mainstream society. Other youth overcome being robbed, assaulted, or ill, and continue viewing mainstream society as the greater of two evils. Auerswald and Eyre pointed out that street youth who are most open to intervention are those in transitional states, such as those who have just arrived on the street or those who are in crises.

The additive effects of maltreatment, poverty, parental pathology, negative parenting, difficulties with authorities, and unsatisfying experiences in school and with the law, all contribute to poor outcomes. In addition, homelessness puts the youth in an environment that is conducive to further negative experiences. Many scholars and service providers have expressed concern that homeless youth will become the next generation of homeless adults. There is some evidence that between 9 and 26 percent of homeless adults were first homeless as youth (Susser, Streuning & Conover, 1987; Zlotnick & Robertson, 1999).

Homeless Veterans

Homelessness among veterans has a long history. More attention was given to homeless veterans following the Vietnam War, some writers suggesting that this was another effect of this war. Yet, 40 percent of homeless men report past military service compared with 34 percent of the adult male population. Veterans, in general, are 1.4 times more likely than non-veterans to be homeless.

What are the military risk factors for homelessness? The three major risk factors are wartime military service, war-zone exposure, and post-traumatic stress syndrome (PTSD). Studies have shown that these three factors taken independently are not more common among homeless veterans than among non-homeless veterans in the general population. Premilitary experiences such as antisocial or delinquent behavior and childhood physical and sexual abuse have been found to be the strongest predictor of homeless among veterans. Social isolation for example, being unmarried or not having people to talk to following discharge, had a stronger relationship with homelessness than did a psychiatric diagnosis, PTSD, and substance abuse (Rosenheck, Leda, Frisman, Lam & Chung, 1996). The risk for homelessness among African-Americans is 7.3 times that for whites. Among veterans in general, mental illness and substance abuse are stronger predictors of homelessness than either combat exposure or economic disadvantage. It appears that many of the services, specialized programs and benefits offered for veterans and homeless veterans specifically, have promoted significant improvement in housing, psychiatric status, substance abuse, employment, social support, and access to health services. The fact that treatment and service programs in the Veterans Administration system are all-veteran can be of special value in maintaining a support network among veterans. However, it is also important that homeless veterans be assisted in building new social relationships outside the comfort zone of sharing time and experiences with peers. The greatest risk of homelessness among veterans is between ages 30 and 39, a time in the lifecycle where most people are settling in with families and jobs. Strong social support systems are needed for returning veterans whose lives have been disrupted by military service, but critical for homeless veterans who did not have a social support network before they left for military service, or indeed, may never have experienced strong support.

THE SHELTER: TEMPORARY CONNECTIONS

The sociologist, Erving Goffman (1961), studied the culture of what he termed "total institutions." These are places of residence where a large number of individuals are isolated from society for a period of time and lead a highly structured and controlled way of life overseen by administrators. Examples of total institutions include mental hospitals, orphanages, prisons, detention centers, sanitaria, and shelters. Public attitudes toward the homeless as a group are that they are deviants, misfits, lazy, addicts, mentally ill and have been in jail or prison. Americans tend to link homelessness with disabilities, character flaws, and undesirable qualities. Some even see the homeless as dangerous, incompetent, and unpredictable. (Link, Phelan, Stueve, Bresnahan & Struening, 1996). Therefore, emergency shelters carry a stigma even among the homeless. They are usually highly structured and paternalistic, with an emphasis on control. For homeless people to use a shelter is a further infringement on their autonomy and empowerment (Stark, 1994). Most homeless do not use shelters, therefore, shelter utilization is not a valid count of homelessness. Few homeless may use shelters in some areas of the country because of the lack of beds. For example, the United States Census Bureau conducted a one-night enumeration of emergency and transitional shelters on March 27, 2000. Only 170,706 homeless of both sexes used a shelter that night; 61 percent were male and 29 percent were female, barely the tip of the iceberg (Smith & Smith, 2001). But shelters also provide meals, a place to clean up, clothing, and sources of medical care. Shelters help with the physical needs of life, but they are not able to repair the sense of despair and hopelessness that accompanies homelessness (Liebow, 1993). Shelters provide temporary connections. They put a premium on little things. The struggle of homelessness begins at the level of human needs, then moves on to companionship.

Anthropologist Elliot Liebow (1993) was a participant observer in a shelter for single, homeless women outside of Washington, D.C. He worked as a volunteer in the soup kitchen, observed the dynamics of shelter life, and interviewed and developed life histories on many of the women over a period of nearly five years. One of the major characteristics Liebow found among the women were broken family relationships. The homeless women had not always been homeless and familyless. They were born into families and had varying kinds of relationships with family members until the family let go. For many women living with relatives and receiving support from them was the last stage in their decent into homelessness.

Many women in the shelter talked about being familyless rather than homeless. Often, relationships with children were the only family contacts.

Some adult children lived with their mothers in the shelter. Young women had children living with their mothers or other relatives. Most of these women were never married, divorced, or separated. Some women saw their children regularly and assumed some responsibility for them. Ties to children were the sole concern for married women whose families were in the process of breaking up. Liebow learned that some grown children gave emotional support to their homeless mothers, but not financial or material support. The "ghosts" of former family relationships were active in women's minds, especially their relationships with their parents. In some cases the women had been rejected by their parents; many of the women showed little affect about their parents.

Most marital relationships were in the past. Many of the homeless women had nothing to do with their former husbands. Some women came to the shelter to escape abuse from their husbands; others were abandoned by them; still others were ambivalent or didn't know how they would change their unpleasant situation. Liebow concluded that in fracturing or fractured family relationships the weakest person gets pushed out. It is the young mothers with children who fought the fiercest to maintain their family connections, and many functioned as mothers-at-a-distance. In contrast, when relationships with parents were unsatisfying or destructive, young women fought to break away. Relationships with husbands were generally no longer significant. Some women savored the memories of the few good times in their families and these memories provided them some degree of emotional support.

In general, the homeless women expected little from life; that way it minimized their disappointments. Building a relationship among each other in the shelter was what a person could do for another emotionally or psychologically. No one person could offer continued support so there was a tendency to reach out cautiously at times of need so that best-friend relationships remained a zero-sum game. With their individual resources used up, the women turned to the remaining source of social support— themselves as a group. However temporary their connections they would make it together.

RURAL HOMELESSNESS

Much of what we know about poverty and homelessness is based on observations and studies of urban areas where the poor and homeless are more visible and where the institutions to serve them are found. Rural poverty, on the other hand, is largely invisible and off the beaten path (Aron and Fitchen, 1996). Therefore, the rural poor and homeless have few social services and shelter programs and must rely on relatives, friends and self-help strategies.

The rate of poverty in rural areas is increasing more rapidly than in urban areas, and unemployment rates are as high as 20 percent (First & Rife, 1994). Social and economic changes have severely affected rural people. From 1981 to 1987, there were 650,000 farm foreclosures and 500,000 jobs were lost in rural manufacturing industries. By the middle 1990s agriculturally dependent counties experienced substantial losses in local earnings and tax revenues. For every six to seven farms lost to foreclosure, one business fails. These changes have jeopardized the well-being of people living in rural areas. Rural areas also have unique populations susceptible to homelessness. The largest Native American populations are in rural areas, as are most migrant farm workers. Veterans also make up a significant number of rural residents.

One of the first statewide studies of rural homelessness was conducted in Ohio in 1990 (First & Rife, 1994). A major finding from this study was that there are wide differences in the demographic characteristics of the rural poor and homeless compared to urban populations. Homeless people in rural areas are younger, are more likely to be single women or mothers with children, are more highly educated, and less likely to be disabled because of mental illness or drug and alcohol abuse. Five major groups of homeless persons were found in the rural areas of Ohio:

- Young families who were no longer able to close the gap between housing costs and total household income
- Individuals who were currently employed full or part-time, but who had too little income to afford housing
- Women who were unable to work because of child care responsibilities or who had limited skills to meet the demands of a changing labor market
- Older men who were homeless longer and disabled with few social supports
- Disabled people who were without the social support and social programs needed to live independently in the community

Many individuals and families were unable to secure affordable housing despite receiving income from employment or public assistance. The survey respondents were asked the main reason for their current homelessness. Almost one-half of the individuals cited economic reasons (eviction, problems paying rent, and unemployment), 30 percent mentioned family problems as the reason, only five percent indicated they were homeless because of drug or alcohol problems, and only two percent were homeless because of deinstitutionalization.

In contrast to the urban poor and homeless, half of the rural poor and homeless had connections with family and relatives that they could count on for help. The rural poor and homeless had fewer mental health problems than their urban counterparts. Yet, those rural and homeless who do need shelter, food, and safe homes find that services are largely on an emergency basis with insufficient planning for long-term solutions to meet a growing problem.

POVERTY AND HOMELESSNESS: PROCESSES OF DISCONNECTEDNESS

We usually hear that people "fall" into poverty and once fallen, they cannot "climb" out of it. The "fall" is usually attributed to either faults of the social structure or to individual shortcomings or failures. As Cotter (2002) pointed out "structuralist" and "individualist" are often seen as irreconcilable, incompatible, and competing perspectives. Cotter suggests that poverty is a multilevel problem and to understand it we need to consider the interrelationships between "person poverty" and "place poverty."

Poverty is a process of disconnectedness that involves individuals and families facing an accumulation of broken and breaking social connections to social institutions, their work, church, school, and neighborhood. Disconnectedness takes many forms, including joblessness; inability to meet financial obligations and making severe and sudden changes in one's lifestyle, i.e. the sale of a home and cars, dropping out of groups and activities that might require obligations or reciprocity; postponement of medical and dental care; dependency on public agencies for basic necessities; and drifting away from friends because of embarrassment about the progression into poverty and avoiding explanations for it. The rapidity of the progression into poverty is variable depending on individual and familial circumstances and the alternatives available. Nonetheless, disconnecting from an acceptable lifestyle to a stigmatized one is an experience of profound loss and grief. The "way out" of poverty requires social connections and social networks with the non-poor.

Similarly homelessness is a process of disconnectedness. The homeless are not only poor but they have no place to live—they carry their identity with them. Martha Burt and her colleagues (2001) have said that homelessness is a "revolving-door" crisis. Some people are homeless only once, others make multiple entries and exits, still others never exit. Homelessness is the loss of social connections and social networks with the non-poor. One's connections when homeless are temporary, superficial, and with

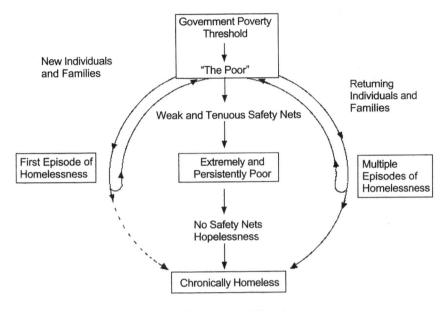

Figure 4.3. The Process of Homelessness

other homeless peers. Like the poor in general, the homeless need social connections in order to "escape" permanent homelessness and hopelessness (Figure 4.3).

There are community efforts to help the poor and homeless to re-connect with non-poor society. A nationwide community telecommunications system shared by a variety of social agencies link to a single community voice mail program to help the poor and homeless find jobs, health care, housing and other resources. Clients can personalize their own voice mail greeting, use a number that looks like any other local telephone number, and access their voice mail from any phone (See Box 4.1). This is the kind of national effort that needs to be expanded to include other services to help the poor and homeless to re-connect with mainstream society.

Burt and her colleagues (2001) outline what it will take to stop the re-volving door of homelessness. It will take making poverty and homelessness long-term high priorities for funding, policy changes, and a campaign to unstigmatize these lifestyles. This is easier said than done, as politics is both a friend and an enemy to poverty and homelessness. It is difficult to sustain programs and interventions over a long enough period of time to have an effect when politicians and funding priorities change with them.

Box 4.1

Community Voice Mail for the Homeless

Community Voice Mail (CVM) started in Seattle in 1991 as the first community based use of telecommunications technology for homeless and phoneless people in the United States. It is a basic telecommunications system shared by an entire community of social services agencies to keep their phoneless and homeless clients connected to opportunity and support. Nationally, nearly 2,000 welfare to work agencies, domestic violence shelters, veterans administration services, and others, link to one of the numerous community voice mail programs to find jobs, housing, health care, and safety. Each client receives his or her own voice mail box into which a personalized greeting is recorded in the client's own voice. A CVM number looks like any other local telephone number and therefore does not signal the client's status as a homeless or phoneless person. www.cvm.org

Yet, poverty and homelessness are favorite political topics to mobilize public emotions about how we should help the unfortunate. The interventions necessary to abate poverty and homelessness must go far beyond short-term projects, lump-sum efforts, and charity. One of the key predictors of being poor and homeless is a family history of poverty and homelessness; these problems are generational and cyclical. The revolving door must be prevented from revolving.

SUMMARY

Poverty and homelessness are co-dependents; poverty creates homelessness and homelessness is evidence of the profoundness of poverty. Despite the difficulties in obtaining accurate counts of the poor and homeless, observation tells us that both phenomena have been increasing especially over the past three decades. Poverty and homelessness are two of several indicators of the social health and well-being of America, but are among the most intransigent. The causes of poverty and homelessness are well-known. They involve a mix of inadequate social structural resources, unexpected economic tragedies and individual failures. The greatest concern is that significant increases have occurred in the last decade of the 20th century in young families with children and single women with children. As a result, nearly 14 million children are living in poverty in the United

States. Child poverty is most prevalent among children under age six and among ethnic minorities.

Many poor and homeless have no other option than to become anchored to a non-conventional community. They live their lives in a world disconnected from mainstream society. While public expectations are that, with some help, they will become mainstream citizens, there are few exits and the long-term resources to rescue them are inadequate.

The poor and homeless are not alike except that, like all humans, they have a need for social contact with others. A break in their relationships with others, especially family members, is usually a contributing factor to their homelessness. Yet, it is almost impossible to survive on one's own efforts, hence, the homeless establish new social networks to help them survive. Social connections on the street are one of the few sources of social validation. Even bowery men are not complete isolates. Most social connections among the homeless are temporary, tenuous, and temperamental, but they do produce an informal system of mutual help.

Social connections among homeless women are different from those of the men. Homeless women are, in general, less socially isolated because they are more likely than men to be homeless in the company of at least one other family member, usually their own children. Homeless women tend to be younger, single, a member of an ethnic or racial minority group, have a personal disability, lower rates of chemical dependency, and a shorter homelessness experience, compared to men. Women are more likely to use shelters than men, perhaps due to the need to meet the basic needs of the children. The shelter may be the only safety net for some women, especially those who have been the victims of abuse and violence.

Most youth who are homeless have experienced broken, rejecting and hateful, and often times violent relationships in their families. Their escape is the inner city where they find communication and associations with peers of similar age and circumstance. In this environment they find camaraderie in gangs, peace in "highs," and a fast-moving, high-risk environment for experimentation with sex, drugs, and violence. Homeless youth find the connections they need to survive from day to day, but their models are others who have failed in making healthy connections.

Most veterans who are homeless also have a pre-military history of antisocial or delinquent behavior, and childhood physical and sexual abuse. Many are unmarried and lack a social support system to return to following their tour of service. Mental illness, substance abuse and being an ethnic minority are strong predictors of homelessness among veterans. Veterans aged 30 to 39 are at greatest risk for homelessness. This is the period in our lifecycle when most young people are marrying, establishing their families, and settling into a career. The returning veterans who had not begun these early milestones before they left for the service, will undoubtedly feel behind their peers. If, the veterans, in addition, lack a support system that can help them, and if their wartime experience was traumatic, it is reasonable that "opting out" is one way to cope.

The rural homeless differ from the homeless of the inner cities. Rural poverty is largely invisible and the rural poor have few resources such as social services and shelters to assist them. Rural poverty is also likely to be the result of a family farm or a job that is dependent on the agricultural industry. Many of the rural homeless are Native Americans and veterans. Unlike the urban poor, the rural poor are likely to be employed part-time or full-time. Rural poor just do not have the income to afford housing. Most rural poor have connections with family and relatives that they can count on. The rural poor and homeless have a much lower rate of mental illness and alcohol and drug abuse than their city counterparts.

Poverty and homelessness are processes of disconnectedness. They are closely related problems that have complex causes and solutions. While programs and services are critical for survival, most critical to their return to full citizenship is the re-establishment of social connections with the non-poor. It is through social connections that opportunities are leveraged. Poverty is often viewed as a state into which one falls; homelessness is seen as a revolving door for the underclass. Both poverty and homelessness are socially isolating and degrading; the end result of the termination of positive connections. The challenge for our society is preventing the door from revolving by making poverty and homelessness long-term, high priorities for funding, make appropriate policy changes that extend beyond national elections, and remove the stigma of poverty and homelessness through innovative programs such as community voice mail. Then, in the words of Robert Putnam, the poor and homeless will not be bowling alone.

QUESTIONS FOR DISCUSSION

1. Discuss the idea that poverty and homelessness are the result of failed social connections. What are other consequences of failed social connections?
2. In what ways do the social connections, or lack thereof, among the poor differ from those among the homeless?
3. Do shelters help individuals and families to establish social ties? Why or why not?
4. If you were to construct an Index of National Health, what other indices, in addition to the number of poor and homeless, would you include?

5. What are the norms, values, and beliefs of residents of "communities of the street"?
6. Describe and contrast the socialization processes of homeless men and homeless women.
7. Discuss possible ways to intervene to stop the spread of HIV and AIDS among homeless youth considering that they do not usually use shelters or social services.
8. If the risk factors for homelessness among veterans are known, what can be done to prevent them from becoming homeless when they leave the military?
9. Discuss the short and long-term effects of homelessness on a person.
10. Why would many people feel uncomfortable talking to a homeless person?
11. Do you think the average American believes that homelessness is a choice and that poverty is the result of bad luck or poor planning? Discuss how you think your family and friends would view the differences between being poor and being homeless.

Chapter 5

Communities in Crisis
Reconnecting Frayed Social Ties

INTRODUCTION

Disaster disrupts and destroys lifestyles and lives. Hewitt and Sheehan (1969) and later, Dworkin (1974), compiled a list of all reported natural disasters occurring worldwide in the 27 years from 1947 to 1973 in which 100 or more people were killed or injured and in which at least one million dollars in damages occurred. There were 836 such reported incidents, an average of 31 per year. These reports did not include several countries where such information was not recorded, nor did it include man-made disasters. If a comprehensive list of worldwide disasters would be assembled for the period 1973 to 2000, it would no doubt contain more natural disasters than in the previous 27 years. Although the number of man-made disasters was not obtained from 1947 to 1973, the trend toward terrorism had begun. If inventoried today the number of man-made disasters would undoubtedly surpass the number of natural disasters.

There is considerable scientific evidence that human activities are contributing to climate change, which, in turn, affects natural climate variability and the occurrence of natural disasters. While it is difficult to determine the exact size of human-induced climate change, the most recent assessment of the science suggests that human activities will have an increasing influence on concentrations of both greenhouse gases and sulfate particles called aerosols. How human and natural factors interact to affect the climate system to create natural disasters is not fully known. We do know, however, that man-made disasters are becoming more common as evidenced in the epidemic of terrorism in the world which has accelerated in the last decade. Some scholars of catastrophes discuss natural and man-made disasters as separate phenomenon. Yet, both kinds of disasters, irrespective of their causes, have common effects—they produce trauma that changes the social and emotional lives of individuals, the resiliency of families, and the cultural fabric of communities.[1]

The focus of this chapter will be to examine the effects of disasters and community crises on the connectedness of people and the ways victims and survivors attempt to re-connect frayed or broken social ties following severe trauma.

What Is a Disaster?

Disasters are non-routine events that do considerable harm to the physical and social environment (Erikson, 1976a). They occur at a definite place and time. They create an urgent need to act against threats to life and/or property, and to restore a sense of routine and normality. They happen suddenly with little or no warning and their impact results in the collapse of individual and communal bases of identity. A disaster is not an isolated event, state, or condition, it is a process that sets off a chain of events that triggers further events and responses for years, and even for lifetimes (Carr, 1932). Erikson (1994) has portrayed a disaster as follows:

> We generally use the word "disaster" in everyday conversation to refer to a distinct event that disrupts the accustomed flow of everyday life. They have a beginning, and a middle, and an end. They do not begin and end at random. They have a certain magnitude, yet are easily taken in by the eye. (p. 147)

Others have viewed disasters as a discontinuous form of social change (Taylor, Zurcher & Key, 1970). Still others see disasters as "place disruptions" that interrupt the processes that bind people to their sociophysical environments. A disruption means that individuals must define who they are and where they are going without the benefits of former tangible supports (Brown & Perkins, 1992).

Disasters are unique because of the peculiarities of the event and differences in the populations affected. Therefore, they can have different short and long-term consequences at different levels of society, nonetheless all community crises share several common features (Quarantelli, 1993). *First*, most experts agree that disasters break or fracture social networks instantly. This is vividly stated by Giel (1990): "Just try to imagine the social disaster of the removal of more than 100,000 people from around Chernobyl and the resulting uncertainty about their future and that of their children and, even more so, the future of some of the unborn" (p. 8). A *second* common feature of disasters is that grieving occurs. When networks of places and people are destroyed they must be grieved in ways similar to mourning a death. Losing access to places of cultural and social significance, and the resulting loss of connections to people, undermines a community's ability to act. *Third,* people exposed to disasters develop a sense of being out of control. They experience helplessness and vulnerability. Trauma causes people to see the world differently so some will be drawn together in groups to help re-establish boundaries and structure, while others will feel estranged and want to be alone. A *fourth* feature of all types of disaster is pre-disaster behavior predicts post-disaster behavior (Logue, Melick & Struening, 1981). How well the individual, family, or community was able to deal with crises prior to the disaster, that is, how effective their coping skills were, will foreshadow how they will deal with the disaster. There are different levels of survivorship, ranging from helplessness to limited functioning to aggressively assuming new challenges. Survivorship is influenced by how connected the individual or how cohesive the family or community was before the disaster. The degree of connectedness usually determines the degree of intervention and social support needed. Traumatic events can mobilize and strengthen or it can fracture a family, group, or community. *Fifth,* the Utopian mood immediately following a disaster is short-lived and often replaced by individual and group strains and conflict. Disasters bring out both the best and the worst in people. *Sixth,* ethnic and racial minorities experience different consequences from disasters than non-minority citizens both in death and injury rates. This is related to differences in the type and location of housing, socioeconomic status, and degree of integration and participation in the community prior to the disaster. The *seventh* feature shared by all disasters is that disasters are not one-way processes back to normalcy. There may be set-backs in the recovery process especially on the anniversaries of the disaster where the event is likely to be emotionally re-experienced. Sometimes it is impossible to recover the sense of community that existed prior to the disaster creating frustration, schisms, and conflict which prevent a community from recovering its identity and cohesiveness. A disaster may be the final straw that brings to the forefront social conflicts that may have been waiting for a catalyst. Recovery therefore, is not a linear process irrespective of the type of disaster experienced. An *eighth* feature of all disasters is that, irrespective of known risks and preparation for "the" disaster, when it arrives it is always a shock. Even though there is preparation for and expectation of disaster, especially in geographic areas of the country that are known to be vulnerable based on past experience, denial is a common response to the threat. Too little worry or fear may reduce vigilance, while too much worry or fear can create panic and irrationality. Preparation for a disaster is never completely logical. It is difficult to believe the unbelievable (Giel, 1990).

A *ninth* feature of all disasters is that they create widespread tension, fear and rumor. People distort facts out of fear and the lack of knowledge. A *tenth* feature is that the focus is usually on the victims, but a community is a total system, a disruption of a part can affect the whole. The non-victims are key players in helping the entire community recover.

Disasters may differ from each other on several dimensions: the geographic scope of the impact; the length of forewarning; the speed of onset; the duration of impact; the social preparedness of the community; the degree of life threat to individuals; the degree of bereavement; the amount of geographic displacement required; the proportion of the community affected; the cause of the disaster; and whether the disaster is central or peripheral with respect to the core of community life (Giel, 1990; Quarantelli, 1993).

Knowing both how a particular disaster is unique as well as what characteristics it shares with other disasters helps in understanding the stages or processes of a disaster and in distinguishing between normal and pathological reactions or patterns of behavior. All disasters, impending or real, create interpersonal catastrophes because they disrupt established social networks. While disasters are commonly viewed in terms of losses of human life and the destruction of the physical environment or of the economy, they also alter, and even destroy, entire cultural systems as happened in the Chernobyl nuclear accident. Individuals attach to others for survival; disasters cause disequilibrium by severing those attachments. That is why individuals, families, and communities are never the same following a disaster.

HOW DISASTERS CHANGE SOCIAL TIES

Social ties provide the basis for individual and communal identity. The extent, depth and meaning of social ties are often not appreciated until they are altered by sudden trauma. There are several ways in which disasters disrupt or destroy the social attachments we often take for granted.

Place Disruptions and the Loss of the Familiar

Place disruptions interfere with the everyday way that we connect with people. Disasters disrupt routines and postpone hopes. Disruptions are difficult to deal with because the ties that bind people include multifaceted connections, occurring at multiple levels that provide a take-for-granted view of the world. A disruption means that individuals' ability to integrate their past and present life is impaired without the help of tangible social and environmental cues and symbols (Brown & Perkins, 1992). Places and the people connected to them become images and memories.

Our identification with "place" is more than comfort with a familiar home, neighborhood, church or school, it is also a location where we keep personal belongings and keepsakes, memory books, diaries, and photographs of our past life, and a central gathering place for family and friends. The degree of identification we develop with "our place" can be so powerful that after a disaster one of the first things victims feel impelled to do is to return to "their place." Indeed, half of 100,000 relocated survivors of the Chernobyl nuclear accident said that they wanted to return to their old places of residence even though these were radioactively contaminated (Sayenko, 1996).[2] It is reported that 1,000 people did return to their old residences in contaminated zones without the permission of authorities.

Erikson (1976a, b) pointed out that many of the traumatic symptoms experienced by the people of Buffalo Creek were as much a reaction to the shock of being separated from meaningful places and people as it was to the flood itself. Buffalo Creek was a tightly knit mining community until a slag dam constructed by a mining company gave way and 132 million gallons of black slag flowed into the valley below on February 26, 1972 (Gleser, Green & Winget, 1981). The loss of the entire community left the survivors without any "place" to locate themselves meaningfully in time and space. Places and objects disappeared. They had trouble finding stable points of reference to help fix their position and orient their behavior. The loss of a personal landscape is an indication of our degree of self-control. One survivor said, "We feel like we're living in a strange and different place, even though it is just a few miles up Buffalo Creek from where we were" (Erikson, 1976b, p. 304). This stunned, bewildered, robot-like behavior has been called "the disaster syndrome" (Taylor, Zurcher & Key, 1970).

People also learn who they are and where they are from other people in their environment. But when those people are gone, or equally disoriented, there is a sense of separation and loss, a loss of connectedness. Disaster creates a sudden dependence on oneself, and for those who lack resources, they may feel a loss of connection with themselves. One survivor of Buffalo Creek said, "It's like being all alone in the middle of a desert." Even husbands and wives found difficulty in relating to each other. This was reflected in a sharp increase in the divorce rate.

Disasters create place disruptions through the actual physical destruction of places and also through stimulus overload. There are numerous stimuli requiring different degrees of attention that tax an individual's repertoire of coping skills. How an individual, family, or community deals with the immediate bombardment of competing stimuli is what separates victims from survivors. Victims and survivors are similar in that both may experience the same traumatic event, but victims become immobilized by self-blame and may become so discouraged by the event that they become pessimistic, helpless and depressed, on the other hand, survivors can overcome the traumatic memories and become mobilized to rebuild and set new goals. The survivor draws on the experiences of coping with the catastrophe as a source of strength, while the victim becomes paralyzed by it (Figley, 1985). Therefore, it might be said that disasters that modify or destroy "places" call forth the use of coping skills that reflect our conceptions about life.

It is only natural upon hearing about the threats of a potential disaster (those we can predict) that we begin to assess the probability that "our place" is vulnerable and the degree to which we can prepare or control the damage. We define disasters in terms of the severity of place disruption, for example the Richter scale reading of an earthquake or the Fujita categories of a hurricane. However, it does not hold true that the greater the severity of disaster damage the greater the social and psychological consequences. For example, there were no lives lost and no property damage from low level ionizing radiation from the Three Mile Island nuclear plant accident near Harrisburg, Pennsylvania in 1979, nevertheless, 140,000 abandoned their homes for "safe places." Researchers reported that symptoms of posttraumatic stress syndrome persisted among residents within a five-mile radius of the plant for as long as five years after the plant was restarted (Davidson & Baum, 1986; Prince-Embury & Rooney, 1988). Consequences of the accident are not fully known yet. The study of Three Mile Island and other technological disasters, such as Chernobyl and Bhopal, India, suggest that they cause more severe, longer lasting, and widespread mental and emotional problems than do natural disasters of similar magnitude because they have no boundaries like natural disasters do (Baum, Gatchel & Schaeffer, 1983).

Disasters have long-term effects on place attachments. Victims and survivors may relocate to a different area of the country following a disaster, especially leaving areas susceptible to certain natural disasters. Others who are more tenacious stay and rebuild a new place. But the texture or feeling of a new community and new social networks is not the same. A community may rebuild but never restore the former degree of community feeling.

Primary Relationships Become Primary

Following a disaster relationships become more simple and intense. Many people constrict their social relationships and limit their boundaries following a disaster, especially individuals who have previously experienced a catastrophe. They want to exert some control in minimizing future trauma. One of the results of disaster is the increased bondedness with kin and primary groups, and less time is spent with voluntary associations. The church often becomes more central in the lives of many disaster victims and survivors (Drabek & Key, 1984).

The length of time victims and survivors may focus on primary relationships is related to their sense of isolation and loss which is unique to the grieving process of each individual and family. Studies have indicated that it was the broad social networks prior to a disaster that enabled individuals and families to receive help and social support and hasten their recovery from the disaster. Community resiliency is dependent upon participation from members of the community. A cohesive community affords a greater chance that the individuals and families in it will rebound sooner. Kleinman (1995) said, "The experience of suffering is interpersonal, involving lost relationships, the brutal breaking of intimate bonds, collective fear, and an assault on loyalty and respect among family and friends" (p. 181). Therefore, it is not surprising that victims and survivors would feel more comfortable in bearing their hearts and souls in the intimacy of kin groups. Primary group relationships following a disaster are simple and intense.

In primary groups, such as the family, emotions are shared so intensely that members not directly involved in the disaster can show symptoms. A study evaluated children's symptoms at periodic intervals after the 1993 bombing of the World Trade Center, and the relationship between parent and child reactions when only the children had been in the building (Koplewicz, Vogel, Solanto, et al., 2002). Parents' primary exposure during the disaster was uncertainty about their children's well being. Parents reported experiencing significant post-traumatic stress symptoms in the months immediately after the disaster. Symptoms were strongest among parents whose children had had direct exposure, but even parents of the comparison group of children who had not been in the World Trade Center that day, showed moderate symptoms. Children's distress was the best predictor of parents' distress whether or not the children were involved in the disaster. Children who were most symptomatic initially were those who showed strong distress nine months later. Trauma can create a kinship through empathy. Family members also provide physical and emotional safety during a time of fear and uncertainty.

Schuster and a team of colleagues (2001) conducted a national survey of 560 American adults about their reactions to the terrorist attacks on September 11, 2001, and their perceptions of their children. Forty-four percent of the adults reported one or more substantial symptoms of stress; ninety percent had one or more symptoms to some degree. They coped by talking with others, turning to religion, participating in group activities, and making donations. Eighty-four percent of parents said that they had talked to their children about the attacks for an hour or more; thirty-four percent restricted their children's television viewing. Thirty-five percent of the children had one or more stress symptoms.

The potential for personalizing the September 11 attacks was large even for those who lived thousands of miles away. Television was both a source of stress as it provided information, yet it also served as a method of coping. For children, television repeated terrifying images, which may have caused or worsened their stress. Although stress symptoms in parents are associated with stress symptoms in children, it is difficult to discern whether parental stress causes stress in children or whether children develop their parents' styles of reacting to a crisis. However, parents who are experiencing stress may perceive stress in their children, whether it is present or not. Therefore, while primary relationships become primary during disasters, members of primary groups may reinforce or mimic ways of coping that can be either helpful or harmful to each other.

Disasters Define Communities and Change Their Texture

Disasters put communities "on the map." They serve as the most significant event in the life history of a community. Disasters are "markers" which help a victimized community draw boundaries around the uniqueness of the disaster so that they can explain the differences in their lives before and after the disaster.[3] One Alaskan native said, reflecting on the Exxon Valdez oil spill, "I don't think we'll ever forget it. It's changed the way we talk. I know that it's going to be 'before the spill' and 'after the spill' (Picou, Gill & Cohen, p. 204).

On March 24, 1989, the supertanker Exxon Valdez ran aground on Bligh Reef about 25 miles from the city of Valdez, Alaska, spilling over eleven million gallons (260,000 barrels) of crude oil into Prince William Sound—extending along 1,900 kilometers of coastline. The social impact of the disaster touched 22 communities including 13 Alaskan Native villages and nine larger urban areas. The primary focus of public concern and subsequent mitigation efforts by Exxon and federal, state, and local agencies was initially on the direct environmental and economic impacts of the spill. However, the social and psychological impact of the spill was key in giving the city of Valdez and its environs a new identity. The spill changed traditional social relations in the community. Community conflict was created by the unequal distribution of cleanup jobs and compensation for the use of boats and equipment owned by local residents, and the influx of outsiders and the resulting strain on community services (Palinkas, Downs, Petterson & Russell, 1993).

The oil spill dominated the daily life for many in the 22 communities; most either worked on the cleanup or had contact with cleanup activities. In addition, the oil spill was a daily topic of discussion. The highly advertised wages of $17.69 per hour attracted people from all over the United States. Such high wages for unskilled workers made it difficult for local businesses to retain employees. A chain reaction affected every aspect of the culture in the region.

One consequence of the spill was the divisiveness and conflicts over participation in the cleanup.[4] While the majority of people believed it was good that people were able to make money on the cleanup, some people said the unequal distribution of income derived from cleanup activities was unfair, e.g. older people could not participate and benefit. There were disagreements among fishermen concerning the distribution of monetary compensation for lost fishing to permit holders. Instances of crew members who did not hold permits or receive any crew shares led to animosity toward those captains who declined to sign for their would-be crew members.

In some instances people who worked long hours on the spill had less time and energy to devote to their families. In other instances, cleanup created tensions related to family roles. For example, in Native communities the oldest child was often placed in charge of siblings as parents worked on the cleanup. When the parents returned home there were conflicts over the eldest child reverting to the role of a child rather than a caretaker. The spill also resulted a significant reduction in the frequency of social visits among family and friends. Cleanup workers had less time to participate in religious activities and community festivals and celebrations. Less time was spent in volunteer activities. There was also an increase in the prevalence of generalized anxiety, post-traumatic stress, depression, substance abuse, domestic violence, and a perceived decline in health status among natives and non-natives after the spill (Palinkas, Petterson, Russell & Downs, 1993).

Conflicts existed between outsiders who came to work on the spill and community members. Many of the problems involved drunkenness and obtrusive behavior on the part of outsiders. There were also conflicts among friends, some resulting in the termination of friendships, over cleanup issues such as environmental effects of the spill, issues of fault and responsibility, whether to work on the cleanup or not, and monetary issues. There were cultural differences between the Alaskans and Exxon and its contractors over how the spill cleanup should be organized and how decisions were made. Alaskans felt a loss of control and resented the bureaucratic approach of outsiders. The small native communities usually made decisions by consensus.

Exposure to the Exxon Valdez oil spill had a dramatic effect on subsistence activities for both natives and non-natives (Rodin, Downs, Petterson & Russell, 1997). Many areas were closed to subsistence activities. The safety of subsistence foods was of great concern. Marine life was threatened. Hunting was curtailed. There were conflicting messages about the safety of food. As a result, there was less resource gathering, and there was less food to share with kin and elders. As one native Alaskan said, "Ninety-five percent of our cultural tradition is subsistence . . . we worry about losing our subsistence way of life . . . about losing our identity . . . it's what we have left of our tradition." (Palinkas, Downs, Petterson & Russell, 1993, p. 8). The oil spill had a beginning, but it has not ended. Many believe that the litigation, internal conflicts, and the restoration of the environment will not end in their lifetime.

Disasters Increase Preexisting Inequalities

A year after Hurricane Hugo, a category four storm that hit large areas of North and South Carolina on September 22, 1989, 1,000 victims and non-victims were asked about the social support they received and provided following the hurricane. Victims of the disaster received and provided very high levels of tangible, informational, and emotional support. However, post disaster help was not distributed equally; some groups received more support than others (Kaniasty & Norris, 1995). Blacks and less educated victims received less help than similarly affected victims who were white or more educated. Unmarried victims received less tangible support than those who were married.

Bolin and Bolton (1986) interviewed people eight months following four different kinds of disasters, an earthquake in Coalinga, California, a tornado in Paris, Texas, a hurricane in Kauai, Hawaii, and a flood in Salt Lake City. They found that in all four instances, residential dislocation and post disaster moves, the use of formal assistance, the amount of damage suffered, and the stress endured were related to ethnicity. Poor families and large families, which tended to be black and Hispanic, had the most trouble acquiring adequate aid and in recovering from disaster than whites. Minority families had a greater number of non-productive dependents, poorer insurance coverage, less money in savings accounts, and fewer personal resources. Their disadvantaged life conditions were intensified further by the catastrophic event. While blacks and Hispanics used multiple aid sources they tended to recover more slowly and the aid they received was insufficient. Survivors of the 1993 Midwest Floods who had the lowest incomes and who lived in rural communities were found to have a greater risk for post disaster psychological distress and depression

(Ginexi, Weihs, Simmens & Hoyt, 2000). Bolin and Bolton concluded that certain ethnic and cultural traditions keep some victims of disaster out of the formal aid network.

A study of how minority citizens prepare for disaster revealed that different ethnic groups use different social networks to relay warning information about an impending disaster (Perry & Mushkatel, 1986). Mexican Americans tend to rely on social networks to relay warning information to a greater extent than blacks or whites. Indeed, Mexican Americans are less likely to believe a flood evacuation warning, for example, than whites, no matter how specific the wording of the message. Minorities are more likely to attribute higher levels of creditability to some ethnic contacts from kin and friendship networks than whites. Even in the face of previous experience with a disaster Mexican Americans and blacks are more likely than whites to rely on, and believe, their own social networks. Furthermore, minority citizens are more likely to comply with emergency measures they have helped to develop.

Victims' age has also been associated with the receipt of less help following the Topeka, Kansas tornado in 1966. Drabek and Key (1984) found that families headed by persons over 60 years of age received less aid than younger families. They concluded that elderly families did not participate as fully in post disaster recovery as young families. This neglect of older persons has been observed across a variety of disaster sites and cultures. It my also be that older people have smaller social networks. People who participate in reciprocal helping tend to be married, young, educated and have large social networks. These people are more connected and have more relatives, friends, and neighbors who can offer assistance. Elderly peoples' social networks have shrunk in size, influence, and the type and amount of resources they might be able to offer.

There are several groups of people who are high risk in a disaster because they are high risk before the disaster. These groups include: the elderly; youth; people living in rural areas; the economically disadvantaged and poorly educated; people who lack kin and live alone; and people who have been victims of disasters before, but received little or no assistance (Milgram, Sarason, Schönpflug, Jackson & Schwarzer, 1995).

Disasters do not erase social distinctions. Erikson (1976) tells about how the Buffalo Creek Flood forced the residents into a number of refugee camps with people they did not know. An increase in alcohol and drug use and in the theft and delinquency rates among some people in the camps led others to feel that they were coming into contact with persons of lower moral stature. Yet all of the people in the refugee camps were residents of Buffalo Creek. Erikson observed that it may be that relative strangers are almost by definition less moral than familiar neighbors. To live in a tightly knit community is to make allowances for behavior that might otherwise look deviant. When Buffalo Creek was intact people did not observe how their neighbors coped when they were under stress. But under stress, when bonds were severed and norms were relaxed, and residents were scattered into unfamiliar groupings, their level of suspicion and scrutiny of one another increased. When the people of Buffalo Creek were clustered together in a community they tended to overlook or minimize individual differences that became magnified in the disaster. As survivors of Buffalo Creek compared and contrasted their neighbors as individuals the differences they observed became inequalities that were more important than their collective survivorship. The cruel irony of disasters is that patterns of inequality fuel further discrimination and deprivation (Gist & Lubin, 1999).

Disasters Have Epilogues

The effects of some disasters have no end. Lifton (1982) has continued to follow the survivors of the Hiroshima atomic bomb attack. Other authors have studied the transmission of Holocaust narratives to the children and grandchildren of survivors (Adelman, 1995; Bachar, E., 1994 & Danielli, 1998). Studies have found negative mental health effects as long as 14 years after a disaster. Trauma, grief, and symptoms do not go away, they remain a part of the lives of individuals and communities to be managed (de Vries, 1995).

Disasters do not have to be extensive to have long-term consequences, but those that gain worldwide attention are usually the ones we know the most about. Gallop polls found that 20 percent of all Americans knew someone or knew someone who knew someone who was missing, hurt, or killed on September 11 (Pyszczynski, Solomon & Greenberg, 2003). A follow-up to a national study of public response to the September 11th terrorist attacks in New York City and Washington conducted by the National Opinion Research Center at the University of Chicago, found that women, minorities, low-income groups and people in poor health were having much greater difficulty recovering from negative emotional and physical symptoms than the United States population in general (Rasinski & Smith, 2002). Findings on specific groups showed that:

- New Yorkers had a recovery rate on stress items about half that of others in the country.
- Hispanics reported nearly twice as many symptoms as non-Hispanics.
- African-Americans showed a slower level of recovery on stress symptoms than other ethnic groups.

- Americans with less than a high school diploma, those with a family income of $40,000, and people who reported having poor health showed little change in reported symptoms six months after September 11.

According to Rasinski and Smith (2002), these findings support the literature that those in financially vulnerable situations have more adverse reactions to disaster over the long term. The report also showed that certain groups were more likely than others to make behavioral changes in response to the September 11th attacks and the anthrax scares that followed.

- Women were more likely than men to report discarding their mail or taking precautions in handling mail, such as wearing gloves or washing their hands. Women also reported avoiding crowds more often than men.
- Hispanics and African-Americans were more likely to have discarded their mail and avoided crowds than whites.
- New Yorkers were more likely to have taken extra precautions with their mail, to have cancelled an airplane trip, or to have sought medicine for anxiety, than people in other parts of the country.

A University of Michigan study that surveyed the same people to track changes over six months in a nationally representative sample of United States adults, found that the psychological, social, and political effects of September 11 and the anthrax scares have continued. Most Americans said they did not feel any safer six months after the attacks. Women were almost twice as likely as men to remain shaken. While anxiety and depression decreased since September 11 they remain high. People know that their personal safety level has permanently changed, but they have to get on with their lives and have found personal coping strategies that relieve them of depressive symptoms (Traugott, 2002).

Schools are settings where exposure to violence is high. A series of school shootings at Columbine, Colorado, Edinboro, Pennsylvania, Jonesboro, Arkansas, Springfield, Oregon, Paducah, Kentucky, and Pearl, Mississippi confirm the findings of studies that report 70–80 percent of children have witnessed violence at school. Rates of victimization depend on the setting, but range from one out of three students reporting having been hit or punched at school, to about one in ten reporting being beaten up or assaulted. Further, the fear of victimization is high: about one in five students report that they have taken a weapon to school out of fear for their safety, and one in twenty have stayed home at least one day in the current year because they did not feel safe at school. When considering the impact of school violence on child mental health and adjustment, violence is not just homicide or serious assault, but also chronic harassment or bullying of young children. Some children may be impacted if they are involved in or witness even a single physical fight, or if they are threatened by someone. Any of these experiences can induce fear and anxiety in young children, affecting their perceptions of safety and their ability to learn. Students who have repeated exposure to violence (including violence in the home) are difficult to engage in the classroom. Their attention is constantly focused on scanning the environment for potential threats (Flannery & Singer, 1999).

North and her colleagues (1999) found that one out of three people in the path of the bomb blast at the federal building in Oklahoma City in 1995 developed post-traumatic stress disorder, and another ten percent had some other psychiatric disorder most often major depression. Two years after the Oklahoma City bombing, 16 percent of children 100 miles away reported significant post-traumatic stress disorder symptoms. In his comprehensive study of the Oklahoma City bombing, Linenthal (2001) learned from local physicians that children were experiencing nightmares, sleep disturbances and tended to talk about the bombing over and over, five years after the disaster.

Dr. Theresa Garton, an Oklahoma City psychiatrist, said that after the bombing some of her patients started remembering their own unrelated past traumas from childhood, and some patients who had previously re-solved traumatic issues re-experienced these issues after the bombing. In general, however, experience with disasters is that post-traumatic stress disorder symptoms tend to diminish over time, but do not disappear completely. Studies investigating the psychiatric consequences of disasters have been conducted at various points of time after the event even up to several years later. This and the variability in research methods make it difficult to compare findings from one study to another, with the result that little is actually known about the longitudinal nature of symptoms and disorders after acute disasters (North, Smith & Spitznagel, 1997).

Disasters Increase Resourcefulness and Cohesiveness

When the massive truck bomb detonated in front of the federal of-fice building in Oklahoma City 168 people were dead (18 of them chil-dren) and an additional 400 people were injured. In the hours following the blast, families of 300 people thought to be missing gathered at the nearby First Christian Church searching for answers and information. Res-cue workers formulated lists and family members assembled photographs and medical/dental records of their missing relatives. Although chaos ini-tially permeated the church, a multi-agency effort was quickly organized to provide information, facilitate the efforts of the medical examiner's office, and provide emotional support. The Family Assistance Center became known as the Compassion Center. Until all 168 death notifications could be completed, the Compassion Center became a sanctuary (Sitterle, 1995; Sitterle & Gurwitch, 1995; Linenthal, 2001).

The Center provided a safe and protective environment, a sense of order and predictability, it empowered families to hear the truth, and it provided understanding in a stressful emotional climate. Families developed their own sense of community (Zinner & Williams, 1999). "People usually sat at the same tables each day, often adorned by photographs and flowers. Families offered support to each other. Even though family members were required to leave the church immediately after undergoing the notification process, several quietly returned later to remain with those still waiting" (Linenthal, 2001, p. 87). Numerous emergency and community organizations worked together with 350 to 400 mental health professionals providing mental health services such as support, family services, death notification, and stress management. But, perhaps most important, the Center provided new connections that were life-affirming.

This high level of mutual helping has been referred to in the literature as the "altruistic or therapeutic community," where there is a heightened degree of internal solidarity and an overall sense of altruism. Individuals who have lived in their communities for a long time and have high levels of community attachment are more likely to provide support to others (Haines, Hurlbert & Beggs, 1996). This is not to say that all victims or survivors of a disaster are equally involved, but there is a general readiness and willingness to give and receive social support among survivors and with care providers and the recovery team. People reached out to connect to fill a connection they were missing. "The bombing brought into being a new world of social relationships and groups. It gave birth to a commemorated community of the dead, a community of family members, survivors and rescuers, and their subgroups" (Linenthal, 2001, p. 82). During the three weeks following the bombing thousands of volunteers and hundreds of family members passed through the Center.

Quarantelli (1985) makes an analogy of the "social sponge" to portray a victimized community's ability to withstand trauma and destruction and still be able to generate positive consequences—such as the Oklahoma City Compassion Center. In some traumatized communities personal and group friction prohibits community resourcefulness and cohesiveness. Indeed, Erikson (1994) refers to this as a "corrosive community," where a disaster sets victims apart from the rest of the community.

Another example of community resourcefulness and cohesiveness comes from the experience of the sudden collapse of the Teton Dam in

Idaho in 1976. When the dam crumbled it released a tidal wave of 80 billion gallons of water. The flood path was about ten miles wide and fourteen miles long until it drained into the Snake River, which caused flooding for a distance of 70 miles. In some areas the topsoil was eroded 60 feet or more down to bedrock. In Madison County nearly 3,000 homes or more than 70 percent of the total housing was damaged or destroyed. Estimates of loss were over one billion dollars.

In the first hours after the impact county commissioners and stake presidents formed an emergency government and delivered a message to a public gathering of refugees, "Roll up your sleeves and get your homes and our communities cleaned up. Don't sit back and wait for the federal government to do it for you. Let's do it ourselves." (Golec, 1983, p. 258). More than 90 percent of the population was Mormon. This means that the population was well-organized, relatively autonomous, and highly integrated. The emergency government prioritized and coordinated all post-disaster operations and maintained public morale and social cohesion. They depended on the ward structure, which was self-governing, similar to Catholic parishes, and relied on voluntary participation. The combined efforts of community leaders, the Mormon Church, and the federal government were so effective that the emergency government ceased to function within eight to ten weeks of the disaster. Over the next year and a half the flooded area looked like a gigantic construction site. The vast majority of residents were resettled into their homes by the summer of 1978. While people agreed that the valley would never be the same, life and people were different, they felt that they were materially better off, that the flood had brought people closer together, and there was a sense of pride that the community had met the challenge of rebuilding (Golec, 1983).

Golec pointed out that the volume of resources per se was probably less important than the social arrangements for their distribution. Direct, face-to-face relationships accessed through a vast network of primary groupings worked together during the early post-impact days and weeks. Pre-disaster ties of intimacy and familiarity increased in intensity and frequency, and some new connections were formed under conditions of communal living.

The Teton dam failure, if placed on a continuum representing degrees of recovery, would fall near the extreme positive end. There are several factors that helped in the area's rapid recovery including: 1) a brief, but adequate warning; 2) a low death and injury rate; 3) a relatively autonomous, homogeneous and cohesive population; 4) an immediate disaster response; 5) local officials retained control over the recovery; 6) a supportive network of personal relationships after the disaster; 7) financial compensation; and 8) a large surplus of resources available for temporary assistance.

It should be noted that there are always some negative spin-offs in disaster recoveries. There was such a "secondary disaster" at Teton dam. Three years after the flood some disaster victims continued to experience loss and disruption in two ways. There were some flood victims who also became victims from the excessive profiteering of the owners of unregulated construction businesses. Some contractors had left town without paying local suppliers and sub-contractors. Another group of secondary disaster victims were people who had problems legitimizing their losses or who had to relocate because regulations regarding the replacement of non-restorable farms were omitted from the guidelines of the compensation program. There was no program of support for victims of secondary disaster at Teton dam, who experienced intense negative feelings of bitterness and victimization.

The strongly positive recovery response by Madison County residents to the Teton dam disaster illustrates the principle that people who can rapidly rebuild communities and refabricate social resources have a better long-term prognosis (Hobfoll, 1998). Erikson (1994) said that going through a disaster raises the ante. Individuals who view themselves in charge of their fate (control), who are committed to meaningful goals and activities (commitment), and who view stress as a surmountable challenge are more likely to integrate the trauma of a disaster into their lives and to enjoy a satisfactory level of adjustment (Waysman, Schwarzwald & Solomon, 2001).

Disasters Test Social Networks

Disasters cause people to take a quick inventory of their resources, especially if they are victims. Neighbors and friends who shared the car pool, who watched your house when you were away, or who were sources of information about where to get repairs done—these friends and neighbors suddenly become victims themselves, and they too are inventorying their resources. It is common for us to assume that our social connections will be there when we need them. Disasters test the strength of connections under duress.

Community networks are integrated webs of social contacts characterized by density. Individuals in low dense, heterogeneous networks fare better in coping with stress because these networks contain a variety of people who can provide a variety of services. According to Granovetter (1973) there is power in having weak (low density) ties because there is a connectedness between groups that is absent in strong (high density) groups, which tend to lack interconnectiveness except among kin. Dense social ties have been shown to promote the psychological adjustment of people in

disaster situations. Dense networks help to reinforce a sense of positive social identity and belongingness (Albrecht, 1994). On the other hand, people
with small homogeneous social networks seem to be adversely affected by
their isolation. They many not desire more relationships, but social ties
that lonely and isolated people have are likely to be with other lonely and
isolated people. These people are generally unconcerned with attending to
other people's psychological needs (Samter, 1994). Socially isolated people
tend to withdraw and seek individual ways to cope with stress and crises.

Involvement in various social networks and identifying with a culturally shared moral code is what motivates acts of heroism and acts of
compassion (Albrecht, 1994). There is no single definition of a hero, but
they tend to exemplify desirable traits, ideals and values that are considered important in our society. There are usually heroes in every disaster,
that is, people who do extraordinary things like the man employed at
the World Trade Center who refused to abandon a disabled worker, even
though it meant both would perish. Heroes are symbols from which people
can learn. We want to be like everyone else because we have a basic need
to be liked and respected as persons, yet we want to be different. Heroism has more to do with circumstances than with personality traits. Most
heroic acts tend to take place when a person is alone or in a small group,
when they feel responsible and there are not others around to defer to. It's
hard to be a hero in everyday life; it usually takes a disaster to uncover a
hero.

Erikson (1976) pointed out, in the Buffalo Creek flood, that community
gave people the power to care for one another in moments of need. When
the people of Buffalo Creek clustered together as a community they were
capable of remarkable acts of generosity, but when they tried to relate to
one another as separate individuals they found that they could no longer
mobilize the energy to care. Social networks are especially effective when
problem episodes intersect. Networks can provide a variety of supports
that individuals need but cannot supply individually, especially in times
of crises (Hoff, 2001). Surviving a disaster is the product of effective, time-
tested relationships. Being a hero is taking a risk to preserve a culture of
caring about valuing each other.

RECONNECTING THROUGH COLLECTIVE COPING

Symbols That Connect

The Oklahoma City bombing left a solitary tree in the immediate area
of the federal building. This tree became known as the Survivor Tree. It was

a symbol of resilience and endurance. People gathered individually and in groups around the tree, and continue to do so, leaving flowers, notes and flags to help them to reconnect with the past. The tree serves as a symbolic leader of a never ending self-help group. Countless studies have shown that social support is essential in coping with crises. The more friends upon which the traumatized person can rely, the better the person's prognosis in the years following the event. In addition to face-to-face support we find comfort in symbols, memorabilia, and talking. Therapists have long proposed that talking with others during or following a disaster is one of the most effective coping mechanisms available (Pennebaker & Harber, 1993).

Coping with situations does not involve only a single method or style. Coping strategies can change as an event unfolds. In addition, coping is very interpersonal so the degree to which people can talk about a trauma depends upon them having willing listeners. In Pennebaker and Harber's study of coping following the Loma Prieta earthquake in the San Francisco Bay area in 1989, they found that the levels at which people talked about the event dropped dramatically after about two weeks following the earthquake. While they could not explain why, the researchers speculated that people became tired of hearing about it. Nonetheless, Pennebaker and Harber said, on the basis of their interviews with 789 residents in the area, people continued to think about it for several weeks.

On the basis of their earthquake data these researchers proposed that collective coping took on different forms as it emerged in stages. In the emergency phase, which lasted about two weeks after the earthquake shock, people reported obsessive thoughts about the trauma. At the same time, social contacts increased and people were able to express their thoughts and feelings to others. Strangers would strike up conversations with each other about the disaster. During this time there were negligible changes in health problems, nightmares, and social conflicts. The second phase (inhibition phase), which lasted from two weeks to about six weeks, was characterized by significant drops in talking about the disaster, but continued thoughts about it. It was during this time that social conflict, disturbing dreams, and health problems began to surface. In the three to eight weeks following the earthquake, there was an increase in urban violence in San Francisco. The third phase (adaptation phase), began about six weeks after the quake, showing some accommodation to it. Pennebaker and Harber suggested that the degree of disparity between talking and thinking depends on the magnitude and quality of the trauma. They contend that the phasing of coping behavior is based on the relative disparity between talking and thinking. An important finding from the Loma Prieta earthquake study is that the greatest need for help in coping often does not appear among victims and survivors of a disaster until the emergency has dissipated, and people stop talking, but continue to think and dream about it.

The Talking Circle

On January 27–28, 1996, The Talking Circle was held in Cordova on the shores of Orca Inlet, organized by the members of the Village of Eyak in Prince William Sound, Alaska (Picou, 2000). The two-day event resulted in many testimonies about personal experiences with the Exxon Valdez oil spill. Traditionally, many Native American communities have used the talking circle as a way of bringing people of all ages together for purposes of teaching, listening, and learning (Running Wolf & Rickard, 2003). Talking circles are a traditional form of early childhood through adult education and provide a way to pass on knowledge, values, and culture. Talking circles are used as a healing intervention in tribal inpatient and outpatient clinics and centers. It is seen as an effective tool that fosters respect, models good listening skills, settles disputes, resolves conflicts, and builds self-esteem (Running Wolf & Rickard, 2003).

The focus of The Talking Circle was the Exxon Valdez oil spill, as framed by spiritual leaders of the village on the first day. All creatures destroyed by the oil spill produced pain and sorrow throughout the spirit world. It was only through restoration and healing that people could restore nature and themselves. Following an initial discourse on the ecological and human impacts of the spill, participants spoke, taking turns in a clockwise fashion. Over the two days, working through creative tension and discursive conflicts, the solidarity and cohesiveness of all participants increased. The transformation process led to increased cultural awareness and political mobilization. After The Talking Circle the village assumed management of many of its own programs. The village now has an active environmental program, has established a housing authority, and purchased a new building. Villagers established a team-based organization employing local tribal members to lead programs and support them with training and technical assistance. One villager said, "The pain of the spill will never go away, but, there are other more important things for us to do now..." (Picou, 2000, p. 94).

Walls of Grief

In several major disasters temporary "walls" have been constructed near the site of the tragedy where all people can collectively participate in sharing their individual grief regarding missing or deceased family members. The Wall of Missing Persons near the World Trade Center was a focal point for notices, photographs and artifacts. It provided a socially acceptable "place" where people could openly express their grief and talk with others. Similarly a 20-yard "wall" in Denver's Civic Center Park provided a place for drawings, flowers, messages of prayer and support and homemade cards for those who grieved the shooting death of the 17 Columbine High School students on April 20, 1999.

Walls provide a degree of structure and focus for family and others who are distraught, facing the uncertainty of missing relatives who were at risk, and who feel alone. They are a gathering place where people can give and receive sympathy, express empathy, and share experiences of previous loss.

Survivor Reunions

Survivors of disasters develop strong bonds with other survivors; many meet periodically to commemorate the disaster and reaffirm their ties, e.g., survivors of the Titanic, the Holocaust and Hiroshima still have reunions. Reunions serve many social and psychological purposes. They enable survivors to experience catharsis by reliving the event through story telling. Many survivors feel guilty that they survived and are haunted by the question "Why me?" Reunions provide a reminder that others also survived.

> John Morgan was off-duty and asleep when torpedoes sunk his cruiser in the south Pacific in 1945. The death toll of 880 made it the worst sea disaster in United States naval history. Morgan was one of 317 survivors. "A lot of guys couldn't talk about it for a long time," said Morgan. Decades later, talking about it helps. His buddy, Ralph, didn't make it. "If you're watching from someplace out there, Ralph, please forgive me." There wasn't anything else Morgan could have done. Knowing that may not help. But being with the other survivors does. (Strauss, 2003)

There is a sense of psychological intimacy among survivors; they can feel emotionally safe in expressing their feelings—they know the others will understand. Reunions provide an importance source of therapy for survivors who have not worked through their grief about the disaster and have not experienced peace of mind since it occurred. Reunions, theretore, provide consolidation and consolation for survivors and their families.

CONTINUING DISASTERS

Some Disasters Have No End

The global human immunodeficiency virus (HIV) and acquired im-munodeficiency syndrome (AIDS) epidemic is such an example. Since its beginning in 1980, HIV and AIDS has grown to the fourth leading cause of death worldwide. HIV infection has caused approximately 20 million deaths. The World Health Organization (2002) reported that the number of men, women, and children in the world living with HIV/AIDS at the end of 2002 was approximately 42 million. There are an estimated 14,000 new infections daily. Nine out of ten of the HIV infected live in the developing world. Figure 5.1 shows that the Sub-Saharan Africa (SSA) region of the world has the most cases of HIV/AIDS, with 70 percent of the population or 29.4 million people infected.

In the United States the National Institute of Allergy and Infectious Diseases (2002) estimates that 850,000 to 950,000 United States residents are living with HIV infection, one-quarter of whom are unaware of their infection. Approximately 40,000 new HIV infections occur each year in the United States. Of these newly infected people, half are younger than 25 years of age. The rate of adult/adolescent AIDS cases in 2001 was highest among blacks followed by Hispanics, American Indians/Alaska Natives, whites and Asians/Pacific Islanders.

The frustration with this universal health problem is that it can be pre-vented. In most cases, HIV can be stopped by individuals being respon-sible for their own behavior. Certain behaviors are known to increase the chances of becoming infected with HIV, particularly through the exchange of blood, blood products, semen, or vaginal fluid during unprotected sex; through the sharing of drug paraphernalia; or through breast milk. Pre-vention programs have been designed to eliminate or reduce the chances of HIV transmission from an infected person to someone else. Perhaps the greatest challenge in the prevention of HIV is the prevention of lapses of high-risk behavior. This is especially difficult because most lapses are re-lated to situational, emotional or cognitive experiences which encourage an individual to take the risk of a one-time relapse into high-risk behavior (Thomason & Campos, 1997). Risk perception is influenced by many fac-tors, but the one that is most important is an individual's connections with others and with the community in which one lives.

Every individual subscribes to a culture where the values and norms regarding sexual behavior and substance abuse are known and exhibited in the behavior of members of the culture. The degree to which an individual is connected to the culture will influence the degree of pressure he/she

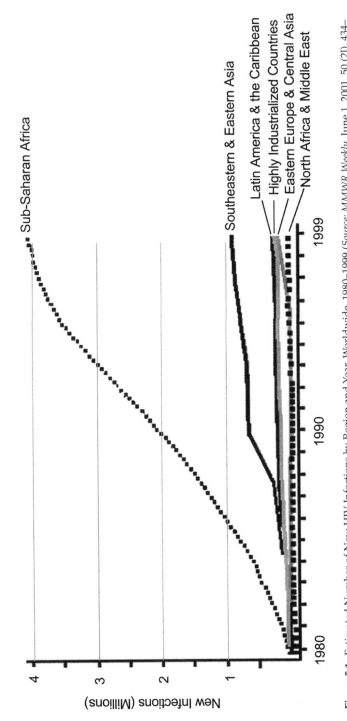

Figure 5.1. Estimated Number of New HIV Infections by Region and Year, Worldwide, 1980–1999 (*Source: MMWR Weekly,* June 1, 2001, 50 (21), 434–439)

feels to conform to its ways. If larger society regards certain behaviors in a culture as risky for the transmission of a disease, the members of that culture must be convinced in order to bring about cultural changes. How members of the culture connect with each other will need to be changed. In other words, the *triggers or antecedents* for risky behavior need to be changed. Then *current risky behaviors* will themselves need to be modified, i.e. reduced or eliminated. By changing the boundaries of risky behavior the antecedents of the behaviors can be redefined, and in turn, the *consequences* of engaging in them can be understood. If the consequences are clear and irreversible, then *relapse* into risky behavior can be *prevented*. In the case of HIV/AIDS there is no cure and there is no vaccine in sight. However, in North America and Western Europe, the availability of new more potent anti-HIV drug combinations has helped people with HIV to live longer; deaths in the United States dropped by two-thirds between 1995 and 1997. Some individuals may choose not to change their risky behaviors, or gamble on a one-time relapse, with the knowledge that death is not an immediate certainty.

There is evidence that the disaster of HIV/AIDS has not been personalized by many, especially young, disadvantaged or marginalized persons, since new HIV infections have remained constant, indicating that prevention programs have been ineffective.

Other examples of continuing disasters include famine, all types of violence and abuse, homelessness, and the abuse of drugs.

THREATS OF DISASTER

Environmental Surprises

Kates and Clark (1996) discuss three disasters occurring since 1970 that were surprises. Legionnaire's disease struck attendees at the national convention of the American Legion in Philadelphia in July 1976. The outbreak of this illness occurred because water vapor containing a bacterium *Legionella pneumophilia* was transmitted through the hotel's air conditioning ducts. It was a surprise and shock because we thought we had such organisms under control. Similar surprises include Lyme's disease and radon in homes. A second disaster occurred in Bhopal, India in December 1984 where Union Carbide had a pesticide manufacturing plant. An unexpected chemical reaction took place in a storage tank of methyl isocyanate, a toxic gas used in the production process. The heat and vaporized gas spread over 30 square miles killing thousands and injuring hundreds of thousands of people. A series of human errors and equipment failures created the chemical reaction. Much is still unknown about the causes of the accident. A third disaster is the depletion of the stratospheric ozone layer. Scientists predicted in the 1970s that chlorofluorocarbons (CFC's), synthetic chemicals to provide a safe alternative to hazardous refrigerants, were drifting into the stratosphere and breaking down, leading to the destruction of stratospheric ozone. This, in turn, would allow ultraviolet radiation to penetrate to earth, where it could cause damage including skin cancer. Kates and Clark (1996) point to four characteristics the three "environmental surprises" shared—they confounded social expectations, they were not completely unpredictable, they were harmful, and they opened windows of opportunity to better manage the problems that caused the disasters and, therefore, minimize similar threats in the future.

Terrorism: Biological, Chemical, and Nuclear

Terrorism engenders collective fear in people worldwide. Browne and Neal (2001) suggest that the collective fear we are experiencing today is similar to that following the Japanese attack on Pearl Harbor and the Cuban Missile Crisis in 1962 when we were on the brink of a nuclear holocaust. Terrorism already has a history, but, as the National Commission on Terrorism (2000) has outlined, the patterns and characteristics of terrorists today, and their methods, are continually changing. Therefore, the fear, uncertainty, and feelings of vulnerability of becoming a possible target create a daily threat, which itself is terroristic. Such a climate of distrust of others encourages people to withdraw into known, comfortable primary social networks where their degree of control is greater.

A conference on the "Psychology of Terror" was held in Jerusalem, Israel in May 2002. Terrorism was defined as "the deliberate, calculated, systematic menacing, maiming and murdering of the innocent to inspire fear for political, ideological or religious ends .... fighting terrorism means more than identifying and intercepting the person with his finger on the trigger or his hands on the controls of a hijacked plane or a bomb strapped to his body. It means a war against the entire network of people and organizations and states that trained him, supported him, financed him, harbored him, armed him and activated the fanatic hatred that caused him to pull the trigger, crash the plane, or detonate the bomb" (Foxman, 2002).

Terrorism has as its objective not only the destruction of lives but the destruction of the social fabric of a society—its infrastructure and the trusting relationships that give it vitality and meaning. Therefore, terrorists can strike anywhere, as they did in Oklahoma City, where there was a sense of astonishment that terrorists would strike at the nation's interior. On the one hand, it is impossible for a country to fully protect itself against terrorism, yet, citizens must be psychologically prepared for an unknown attack and resources must be networked to respond at an unknown time and place. The threat of terrorism requires a sustained high level of connectedness, suspicion and vigilance among people anticipating a disaster. It seems paradoxical to be supportive of each other, yet watchful of other's behavior. Such mixed emotions are part of the psychology of terrorism. In countering terrorism our country's focus has been largely on chemical and explosive weapons. After an explosion or chemical attack the worst effects are quickly over, but the effects of biological weapons such as smallpox or anthrax, on the other hand, are ongoing. Biological terrorism is more likely than ever before and more threatening than chemicals or explosives (Henderson, 1998).

The possibility that terrorists might crash an airliner into a nuclear power plant is one of the most nightmarist scenarios since the attacks on the Pentagon and the World Trade Center. There is disagreement among scientists as to whether a plant could survive such an attack as well as the consequences. According to the *Bulletin of the Atomic Scientists* in a January/February, 2002 article, the average nuclear power plant contains 1,000 times as much radioactivity than was released by the Hiroshima bomb. Nuclear power plants are designed to withstand extreme events such as hurricanes, tornadoes and earthquakes, but will not necessarily survive a large airliner. A controversial article in the September, 2002 issue of *Science* magazine authored by Douglas M. Chapin and 18 other members of the National Academy of Engineering, claims that the implications of the 1986 Chernobyl nuclear accident are not applicable to American reactors. They claim that the terrible and widespread consequences of the accident—increased suicide, alcoholism, depression, unemployment, and 100,000 unnecessary abortions—were caused by the fear of radiation and by poor planning based on that fear. Such a view contrasts with those of the United Nations, which highlights a 25-fold increase in childhood thyroid cancers in some cities in Belarus, and explicitly links this to Chernobyl (Burgess, 2003).

The aftermath of terrorism encompasses not only the victims, survivors, and physical damage but the psychological aftermath which typically manifests itself in flashbacks or nightmares that replay the traumatic event and the avoidance of reminders of the ordeal, and a hypervigilant state. These symptoms are heightened by the destroyed or fragmented social networks among people which provided social support and helped to provide the resiliency for recovery and healing to occur. The disaster of terrorism leaves more casualties than the violence of natural disasters. It appears that the threat of terrorism and a heightened state of anxiety will be a part of living in the 21st century and perhaps beyond. People will live with threats to their survival with nothing specific to fight or flee except their own feelings of vulnerability.

The Effects of Threats on Connections

Some threats of terror result in a disaster, other threats remain vacuous. In both instances terrorists have been successful. A major objective of terror is to create dysfunction among people by holding out expectations that a disaster will occur somewhere, sometime, that may take their lives. The openendedness of threats, with periodic enhanced warnings, intermingled with actual disaster, can over time create significant havoc in a society. Table 5.1 lists some of the effects of terror threats on a society.

A major effect of a terror threat is that there is no closure until either a disaster occurs or the threat stops. While people wait for an anticipated disaster they are uncertain how they will cope with it when and where it happens. This period of suspended animation, if prolonged, can have serious, disabling physical and mental consequences. In essence, people are limited in how they can cope with a threat, especially when there is little or no concrete feedback from the environment about the threat's degree of certainty (Lazarus & Folkman, 1984). This is evident in some confusion about the government's color-coded terror alert levels, the criteria used to elevate or reduce a level, and what actions each level requires of citizens. There is no question that the threat of terrorism is becoming one of the most common debilitating disasters experienced by mankind.

Table 5.1. Some Effects of Terror Threats on Society

- Fear, rumor, anxiety sufficient to disrupt useful lifestyle
- Vigilance and hypervigilance, possible panic
- Decreased spontaneity in interactions
- Increase in pessimism
- Decrease in interpersonal trust
- Decrease in cohesiveness within and between groups and organizations
- More protectiveness and less cooperation among social institutions
- Prejudice toward known or probable sources of threat
- Feelings of loss of control, sense of helplessness
- Difficulty focusing on tasks and maintaining performance
- Increased patriotism and nationalism

SUMMARY

Disasters have been a part of the history of mankind. The human, economic, and environmental impact of natural disasters has increased as populations become more concentrated in megalopolises, especially those that have a special vulnerability to certain natural disasters. In addition, the susceptibility to natural disaster has increased as a by-product of man's ingenuity and the alterations he is making to the physical environment. But it is the planned destruction from man-made interventions that is of growing concern in the world. Disasters, whatever their origin, temporarily maim a society or community, and may permanently destroy it. The effects of a disaster reach all members of a society or community and change them forever. Our concern in this chapter has been on how disasters disconnect people and how they re-connect following pervasive trauma.

What is a disaster? Disasters are unexpected surprises that disrupt, damage, or destroy the physical and social environment. On the one hand, we shouldn't be surprised by a tornado if we choose to live in the part of the United States known as "Tornado Alley," yet we are stunned when a tornado destroys our home. Even as we accept the certainty of some disasters, for example the inevitability of death, when it occurs in our family we react with shock. What is alarming in today's world is that, with the increased occurrences of man-made disaster, such as terrorism, everyone is a potential target, anywhere, at any time. Unexpected surprise is the method to achieve the objective of mass casualties and there is very little individuals can do to decrease their vulnerability. In addition, man-made disasters set off a chain of additional disasters, which have no end point. Disasters create discontinuous social change. Therefore, it is difficult to heal from man-made disasters and the frayed social ties that remain may never be reconnected.

Each disaster is unique because of the peculiarities of the event and differences in the populations affected. Disasters can have different short and long-term consequences at different levels of society, but the community level is especially important because it performs an integrative function, that links individuals and their primary groups with the larger social order. Disaster specialists often focus on individual victims forgetting that their recovery will be influenced by their connectedness in the community. Social ties provide the basis for individual and community identity. The extent, depth, and meaning of community ties are often not appreciated until they are altered by sudden trauma.

Disasters can change social ties in several ways: 1) they disrupt our connections to "place," that is, the tangible social and environmental cues and symbols that connect us with the everyday way we connect with people; 2) they increase our bond with kin and primary groups; 3) they become "markers" which help define communities and change their texture; 4) they increase preexisting inequalities; 5) they remain a part of the lives of individuals and communities to be managed; 6) they increase resourcefulness and cohesiveness; and 7) they test social networks causing people to inventory their resources. Individuals and communities that can rapidly rebuild their social ties have a better long-term prognosis. Individuals who view themselves in charge of their fate, who are committed to meaningful goals and activities, and who view stress as a surmountable challenge are more likely to integrate the trauma of a disaster in their lives and to enjoy a satisfactory level of adjustment.

Reconnecting social ties is about collective coping. Countless studies have shown that social support is essential in coping with crises. Coping with situations does not involve only a single method or style. Collective coping takes different forms as it emerges in stages. The emergency stage enables victims and survivors to express their thoughts and feelings to others. The next stage is when talking to others about the disaster decreases, but the feelings and thoughts become more internalized often being expressed through physical and mental symptoms. The final stage is the accommodation to the disaster involving a re-adjustment of lifestyle. While thinking and talking about the disaster do not cease, more effort is made toward taking action to rearrange one's life. An example of how talking can facilitate healing individually and collectively was presented in The Talking Circle initiated by Alaskan Natives following the Exxon Valdez oil spill. Other methods of collective coping are the "walls of grief" constructed at Ground Zero following September 11 or the wall in Denver's Civic Center Park after the Columbine shootings. Survivor reunions also provide a sense of psychological intimacy among survivors of a disaster for a lifetime.

There are disasters that have no end in sight, such as the HIV/AIDS pandemic that has consequences for multiple future generations. This disaster has no apparent resolution—it is not curable, only preventable. Yet, prevention efforts have not been personalized by many, especially young, disadvantaged or marginalized persons. Evidence for this is that the incidence of new HIV infections has increased, despite enormous efforts to educate persons about the behavioral risks of HIV/AIDS. There are other continuing disasters such as famine, violence, homelessness, and the abuse of drugs.

Threats of disaster are perhaps the most debilitating aspects of life in today's world. Threats of disaster hold people hostage, they manipulate entire societies with the fear of "what might happen," and they dampen the enthusiasm and hope for the future. Sources of threats of disaster come from two major directions: 1) environmental surprises that arise due to man's mismanagement of the technology he has created, or due to man's ineffectiveness in planning, anticipating, and preventing possible break-downs or loopholes in what is controllable; and 2) individuals and groups who purposefully kill and destroy for political, ideological, or religious reasons. The objective of such individuals and groups is to create an at-mosphere of terror, fear, and frustration and to periodically reinforce this terror with actual attacks. The threat of terror can be vacuous or result in a disaster. In either case its purpose is to create dysfunction, which over time can result in severe human and economic costs to a society.

The threat of terrorism over time unravels a society; it creates discon-nectedness. No society or community can socially and psychologically sus-tain a level of heightened preparedness indefinitely without lasting effects. Over time people become less innovative with coping methods, become more likely to deny that they will experience a disaster, and numb to new threats. They lower their levels of preparedness, which is when they are more vulnerable. Threats of terror is a verbal game of survival in which the perpetrators of the threats have the upper hand—they control whether or not, when, how, where, and how often. Terrorists do not negotiate so the only way to deal with terrorism is by preventing it from occurring. There are no effective ways to do away with threats except to eliminate terrorists. The real costs of man-made disasters and threats of them are the erosion of societal institutions and infrastructure and the disappearance of trust.

QUESTIONS FOR DISCUSSION

1. Has the epidemic of terrorism caused you to change how you connect with others, your lifestyle, your attitude about trust, and/or your sense of security in your community? Discuss.
2. Disasters remind us of our vulnerability and how tenuous our sense of personal control can be. In what ways does the increase in man-made disasters affect connectedness on a local level? On a national level? On an international level?
3. Discuss approaches to explaining disasters to children and the impact of different explanations on their conceptions of danger, risk, vulnerability, and trust.
4. Why do you think people experiencing a disaster pull together for the short-term, but do not sustain closer connections for the long-term? Is whether the disaster is natural or man-made a factor in sustainable relationships?

5. Why do you think it is difficult to mobilize the public to act in continuing disasters?
6. Describe how disasters can be "windows of opportunity" in cross-cultural relationships.
7. Why are we motivated as a society to deal with some disasters immediately and more completely than others?
8. In what respects is terrorism a continuing disaster?

Chapter 6

Communities of Exclusion and Excluded Communities
Barriers to Neighboring

INTRODUCTION

All animals have a need to regulate distance between themselves, and between themselves and other animals. Territoriality is a basic concept of animal behavior by which an animal lays claim to an area and defends it against members of its own species. Territoriality regulates density. It provides a framework in which things are done—places to learn, places to play, and safe places to hide (Hall, 1966). It keeps animals within communicating distance of each other. Territoriality also offers protection from predators—it provides a safe home base—and protects against the exploitation of the particular environment that a species has selected to live. Finally, territoriality is associated with status; it is, according to Hall, "...a hidden band that contains the group" (p. 13).

Man, too, has territoriality. Everything that man is and does is associated with the experience of space. But man's proxemics, unlike that of other animals, is molded and patterned by culture. And people reared in different cultures have different perceptions and values of space. The French philosopher Henri Lefebvre (1991) asserted that space is more than just a social container; it is also linked to behavior. We construct our surroundings to meet particular needs and objectives; our surroundings, in turn, affect our behavior. Therefore, people organize their daily lives and actions within the constraints or opportunities of the established culture, including the social rules about space. There is a direct relationship between the ownership of space and power. Power is expressed in the monopolization of space and the relegation of less powerful groups in a society to less desirable environments (Sibley, 1995). The owners of space exert their power by drawing boundaries which determine who will be included and excluded from their territory. Wilber (1979) pointed out that boundaries actually mark off nothing but an inside and an outside, which didn't exist before the boundaries were drawn. Boundaries create a world of opposites and a world of opposites is a world of conflict. Wilber explained that every boundary is a battle line; the firmer the boundaries, the more entrenched are the battles. Most of our problems are problems with boundaries and the opposites they create. So it is with communities of exclusion and excluded communities.

COMMUNITIES WITH WALLS AND GATES

Common interest housing first was used to create exclusivity, and later it became an instrument of exclusion. In 1898, Ebenezer Howard became impressed with Edward Bellamy's utopian model *Looking Backward* in which Bellamy proposed that a perfect society was attainable through rational planning (McKenzie, 1994). Howard conceived of a garden city, a residential area surrounded by a greenbelt. This complex would be self-sufficient and governed by a constitution minimizing competing interests and politics. The English idea of the garden city was transplanted to the United States in the 1920s, but was received with only modest enthusiasm until the new town boom of the 1960s when developers promoted the idea of common interest housing, especially in the Sunbelt area of the United States. In 1962 there were fewer than 500 homeowner associations in the United States, but by 1988 30 million people or 12 percent of the population lived in 150,000 common interest developments. The concept of the garden city coupled with Americans' concern with privatism created what McKenzie termed "privatopias." By 2004, 50 million Americans lived in 260,000 association-managed communities, 40 percent of which were in Florida and California. Each year 6,000 to 8,000 new community associations are formed (Community Associations Institute, 2003).

Gated communities are part of the trend toward exercising physical and social means of territorial control. It is estimated that between four and eight million Americans live in gated communities (Architectural Record, 1997). Some walls are meant to keep people in, some to keep people out. Some are meant to mark territory and identity, others to exclude (Blakely & Snyder, 1997). The major characteristic of gated communities is that they are introverted. Caldeira (1999) has called this new type of urban segregation "fortified enclaves." "Fortified enclaves are privatized, enclosed, and monitored spaces for residence, consumption, leisure, and work. The fear

---

Box 6.1

Wetherington Residents Cite Safety, Deny They're Elitist

Guardhouses and wrought iron gates will soon be in place at Wetherington, an upscale development of about 1,000 residents, who will enter and exit their golf and country club neighborhood with special key cards. That means that as many as 11,000 motorists will be turned away from a favorite daily shortcut through one of Greater Cincinnati's more affluent developments. Some neighbors and local workers grumble that the upper crust is keeping out the common folk. But residents of Wetherington say they simply have tired of an endless stream of vehicles using their neighborhood as a shortcut. "It's also a safety issue for children and other pedestrians," says Kevin Plank, a lawyer and president of the Wetherington's Homeowners' Association. "We are not trying to hurt others."

Mr. Plank says that Wetherington homeowners will pay $43 a month for street maintenance and share a one-time $300,000 cost of gate installation. "There will be no fences or walls. We don't plan to put any guards in the guardhouses . . . not even for special events," Plank said.

SOURCE: Adapted from W. Schaefer, *The Cincinnati Enquirer*, December 21, 2001, www.enquirer.com

---

of violence is one of their main justifications. Gated communities appeal to those who are abandoning the traditional public sphere of the streets to the poor, the marginal, and the homeless" (p. 83). Blakely and Snyder (1997) explain that gated communities go farther than privatizing individual space, they also privatize community space. Many of these communities privatize civic responsibilities such as police and fire protection, and schools, recreation, and entertainment. The new developments create a private world that shares little with its neighbors or the larger political system. This fragmentation undermines the concept of organized community life. While early gated communities were restricted to retirement villages and the compounds of the super rich, the majority found today are for the middle and upper middle class. Residential areas with walls and gates are a dramatic manifestation of a "fortress mentality" growing in America and worldwide. As citizens divide themselves into homogenous, independent cells, their interest in and commitment to sharing in the principles of citizenship and community is attenuated.

Low (2001) studied two gated communities, each located at the edge of a culturally diverse city with publicized incidents of urban crime. San Antonio and New York City are known for their multiculturalism, cultural inclusiveness, and interethnic conflicts. Both cities have large socioeconomic disparities and a history of residential segregation, including middle class residents moving to suburbia. They also differ in population size and density; history of gated community development; scale and design of gated communities; legal and governmental structure; and crime rates. Interviews with residents, key informants, and observations in and around the communities provided the data for ethnographic analysis. In New York, residents fled deteriorating urban neighborhoods citing changes in local stores, problems with parking, and frequent robberies. In San Antonio there was a similar pattern, but here the emphasis was on a fear of kidnapping and illegal Mexican workers. Residents of both cities had moved to gated communities because of fear. Yet, a gated community does not insure complete safety as service workers need to enter the community and residents need to leave to shop. Walls, gates, and guards help residents cope with "perceived" threats by regulating the physical distance between them and "others." The walls and gates merely make the system of exclusion visible in concrete.

Privatized Social Capital

Where fortified enclaves produce spatial segregation, social inequalities become explicit. Everyday interactions with people from other social groups diminish and are limited to an "as needed" basis to the gardener, service person, clerk, or gas station attendant. Fortified enclaves are usually close to high-end shopping centers that cater to the specialized needs of affluent residents. Therefore, public encounters occur within protected areas and with people like themselves. The physical reality of exclusion is carried over to social restrictions, for example, in dress codes at golf courses and restaurants. When social differences, safety concerns, and the value of privacy are combined it is easy to understand why residents of fortified communities look for differences between people. The greater the social distance between others and residents, the greater is the perceived threat. All of this works to limit the degree to which fortified residents are willing to help build social capital for others. Their residence, their needs, and protecting both, become primary. The community and society of which they are also a part become the "other," which they can easily ignore through withdrawal and non-participation. In a survey of community involvement in suburbs across America, Oliver (1999) found that the greater the social homogeneity of a community, the lower the level of political involvement. Some have argued that the suburb spells the end to civic life.

Types of Gated Communities

Gated communities can be classified into three broad categories based on the primary motivation of their residents.

Lifestyle (or intentional) communities provide security and separation for certain leisure activities and amenities. These include retirement communities, mobile home communities, healthy lifestyle communities, sexual orientation communities, Jewish lifestyle communities, family communities, a community to promote the safe use of guns, golf and country club developments, and suburban new towns. In these communities people are sold "community" as lifestyle, prestige or security, or some combination of all three. Putnam (2000) has said some of these developments resemble "theme parks" with unified architecture and coordinated amenities. There is an inward-looking cohesion of people with similar expectations, outlooks, levels of affluence or anxieties that exclude the world outside. Formal rules and regulations guarantee conformity. Social cohesion is purchased, not made, fabricating a neighborhood context (Blakely & Snyder, 1997; Forrest & Kearns, 2001). *Elite (or luxury) communities* symbolize distinction and prestige and both create and protect one's social position and project an image. These include executive home and estate developments, enclaves of the rich and famous, and developments that set limits on the cost of homes and combine home ownership with mandatory amenities such as country club membership. The third type, *Security Zone (or defensible space) communities*, include residents whose primary concern is to protect their property and its value, as well as themselves. This is often accomplished by residents forming alliances or buffer zones to regulate who buys in their area. The concern for community security has spread to the Internet. Its open architecture and easy access has created a space with uncertain boundaries. The absence of clear demarcation between public and private space has created a need to regulate privatization and abuse, such as pornography and "spam." Some authors have suggested, in the absence of government regulation, one answer may be through the creation of defensible cyberspace. Business would be transacted within the electronic equivalent of gated communities (Harshman, Fisher, Gilliespie, Gilsinan & Yeager, 1998). These three types of communities reflect concern with exclusion, privatization, and security. A sense of community is not a primary concern.

Blakely and Snyder (1997) pointed out that gated communities create a false sense of security. While guards may be hired for 24-hour coverage, the walls of gated communities can easily be scaled. The usual solitary guard only screens who enters the compound. Homeowners' associations create a false sense of community. Usually homeowners' meetings are so poorly attended that by-laws have to be amended to lower the requirements for a quorum. This apathy gives more power to the officers of the association who are usually people seeking opportunities for control and zealously monitor members' compliance with homeowners' association rules ranging from how the American flag should be displayed to how frequently lawns should be mowed. Blakely and Snyder noted that the reasons that encourage residents to choose a gated community are themselves barriers to neighboring. The presence of gates does not ensure a sense of community. The degree of apathy and noninvolvement has been found to be the same in gated and non-gated communities, even though people in gated communities *felt* more social, there were not any stronger social ties than in non-gated communities (Blakely & Snyder, 1997). Homeowners' associations do not generate high levels of participation, self-governance, or mutual trust.

Gated communities are a symbol of the underlying tensions in larger society. Indeed, gated communities can be thought to reinforce people's fear because they provide an illusion of control and stability. Gated communities are also a barrier to interaction among people of different races, cultures, and socioeconomic groups and add to the problem of building social networks in the larger community. People who live in fortress enclaves perceive themselves as friendly, yet feel isolated in them. The essential mutuality of community is missing. Neighbors are often unneighborly and patterns of social interaction are similar to those found in apartment and condominium complexes. Guards and association officers are substitutes for community responsibility. Most residents of gated communities want to be left alone in their homes with protected value and only responsible for paying monthly association dues.

The Minimal Moral Code of Suburbs

More than sixty years ago Lewis Mumford observed that suburbs are a collective way to lead a private life. Escape from urban problems has no doubt been a key factor in people leaving the city for the suburbs and retreating behind walls and gates. Conflict is rare in suburbia. In a study of Hampton, a suburb of New York City, ethnographer M. P. Baumgartner (1988) found homogeneity, autonomy, independence, relative indifference, and weak ties among people. There was an aversion to conflict and confrontation and a preference for weak strategies of self-control, such as avoiding the problem person or situation. Baumgartner found that the people of Hampton "got along" because they allowed people to restrict their dealings to those with whom they felt most compatible. This allowed people to avoid confrontation by fleeing (moving out) rather than by fighting when a conflict did arise. Baumgartner characterized what she found as "moral minimalism," that is, a considerable degree of indifference to the wrongdoing of others. People cannot be bothered to take action against those who offend them, neither can they be bothered to help them. She said that moral minimalism dominates the suburbs. The suburbs are a culture of weak, fluid social ties, which undermines social control and promotes moral minimalism.[1] The decrease in connections and social contacts weakens the bonds of mutual responsibility and the social contract. We no longer speak of citizens, but rather of taxpayers or members of an association who exchange money for services.

PRIVATE NEIGHBORHOODS AND TENTATIVE NEIGHBORING

Robert Frost's poem "Mending Wall," expresses Americans' ambivalence about neighboring, about feeling close and staying apart. People want the close ties of a cohesive neighborhood yet want to assert their rights of protection and privacy from their neighbors. Walls and fences make for good neighbors because they reduce the chances for conflict. When a conflict occurs neighbors turn outside their neighborhood to the police for intervention. Sally Engle Merry (1993) studied the role of law in maintaining social order in four urban neighborhoods, each with about 1,000 residents, in and around Boston, Massachusetts. Specifically she examined how often people had family and neighborhood problems and what they did about them. Two of the neighborhoods were working-class, one of which was stable, and the other undergoing transformation. A third was a middle-class suburb of single-family homes, economically homogeneous but ethnically diverse. The fourth neighborhood was similar to the third only upper-middle class.

Merry found that the law regulates social life in different ways in transitional and in private neighborhoods. Those who bring their problems to court come from the poorer neighborhoods, where there are fewer regulations and less helpful police. Consequently, when problems become severe, they erupt into a direct confrontation. In the private neighborhood, there is less confrontation because there are more options and a stable hierarchy of resources to solve problems. When a violation of the social order occurs in a private neighborhood, the complainant calls the police to intervene, but the complainant wants to remain anonymous and does not intend to pursue an arrest. They want the officer to remind their neighbor of the importance of quiet, the detraction of an improperly parked vehicle, or the inconsiderate effects of an unleashed dog. In private neighborhoods the law reduces resident's reliance on their neighbors. Residents chose to live where they are free from obligations to keep up informal contacts with neighbors so they can enjoy the luxury of autonomy.

It is important not to see the neighborhood as a territorial bounded entity but a series of overlapping networks (Forrest & Kearns, 2001). The lack of ties with neighbors does not mean that a person is devoid of friendships. Particular friendships will change with people's circumstances and interests, but the role of friendship remains key even in this era of privatization (Allan, 1998).

There is a difference between neighborhood and neighboring (Forrest & Kearns, 1999). Research has shown in disadvantaged neighborhoods it may be the *quality* of neighboring which is an important element in peoples' ability to cope with a decaying and unattractive physical environment. In more affluent areas, however, neighborhood and its physical ambience and location may be more important than neighboring. Neighbors and neighboring retain greater importance for the poor, elderly and excluded groups, while mainstream society develops new and spatially diffuse social networks apart from their neighborhoods.

Forrest and Kearns (2001) examined the concept of neighborhood from four different perspectives. They viewed the neighborhood as "*community*," a local domain of friendships and casual acquaintances. There is the neighborhood as "*context*" particularly in the negative sense of labeling behavior that is the basis of social exclusion. There is the neighborhood as "*commodity*," a domain of safety and security, of a comparable lifestyle, and purchased as an enclave. Finally, there is the idea of neighborhood as "*consumption*" or the classification of neighborhoods in terms of consumption patterns and lifestyle groups. Neighborhoods have different forms and amounts of social capital. Social groups that have limited social capital are excluded from wider social networks that could help with the negative effects of exclusion, therefore they are limited to coping with problems rather than overcoming them.

Neighborhoods and neighboring are embedded in social structure and culture which includes factors such as social class, age, gender, marital status, and region of the country, but also by race and ethnicity.[2] For example, Campbell and Lee (1990) found that women are better neighbors not because of greater leisure time or more consistent presence in the neighborhoods, but because American gender roles encourage women's extensive involvement with others, including neighbors. Lee and his colleagues

(1991) demonstrated clear racial differences in urban neighboring behavior using data from a survey of black and white residents of Nashville, Tennessee. They found that blacks interacted with their neighbors more often and in greater variety of ways than did whites. For blacks, neighbor relations were more often instrumental than casual; for whites, the opposite was true. The only noteworthy similarity between the two groups was the positive impact of neighboring on feelings of community. The results support the view that neighbor relations have helped blacks cope with constrained social opportunities and provided them with access to resources unavailable through formal institutional channels.

In general, the residents of gated communities generate little, if any, social capital for their neighborhood, or community. It is the author's experience from living in two gated communities, both managed by homeowners' associations, that there are few friendships among neighbors and most neighborly interactions are abbreviated gestures of civility. Many neighbors avoid contact with others, and some are never seen. Of course, there are exceptions, neighbors who "house watch" when another neighbor leaves town, or the rare neighbor who helps another with an emergency repair. But, working for increased social capital for the common good is not on the priority list of most residents of communities of exclusion.

EXCLUDED COMMUNITIES

Social exclusion is the process of being shut out, fully or partially from any of the systems that determine the social integration of a person in a society (Barata, 2000). Social exclusion usually arises from a combination of low income, unemployment, poor health, lack of skills, inadequate housing, stigmata associated with lifestyle, stereotyping and prejudice, and self-imposed geographic isolation. Social exclusion is an interactive process. Social exclusion involves limiting interaction with those who look, act, and believe differently from the majority and those who sense, feel, or experience their differences and withdraw from others. Frequently the result of social exclusion is the grouping together in specific geographic areas, by choice or by force, those who are different. However, members of excluded communities can also be geographically dispersed.

Social exclusion results in economic, social, political, and cultural disadvantage. There is a vicious cycle of exclusion and disadvantage; individuals or groups cannot change their position of exclusion if they do not have access to the proper resources to do so, but the appropriate resources are out of reach or limited for the socially excluded. Therefore, socially

Table 6.1. Characteristics of Communities of Exclusion and Excluded
Communities

Communities of exclusion	Excluded communities
• Moderate to high geographic mobility	• May be geographically cohesive or dispersed
• Homogeneity in lifestyle	• May have excluded groups within their community
• Low interpersonal trust	• Moderate to high level of social cohesion and trust
• Loosely configured social networks	• Tightly knit social networks
• Low neighborhood social capital	• High neighborhood social capital
• Formal social control	• Informal social control
• Very little neighboring	• High degree of neighboring
• Security and self-protection a major concern	• Equality and full participation in society important goal
• Leaders are usually volunteers who like policing/monitoring roles	• Members are stigmatized; Leaders emerge from the group
• Diversity and discrimination are not of concern	• Efforts made to be socially inclusive

excluded groups cannot fully participate as citizens in the society in which
they live.

Table 6.1 shows some of the contrasting characteristics of communities
of exclusion and excluded communities.

The Excluded American Indian

Native Americans have a legacy of exclusion dating to the 1700s and
the founding of our country. They were initially excluded from citizenship,
moved to reservations, their religions and spirituality were outlawed, their
tribal nationalism was quelled by war, they became citizens and their tribes
could acquire land and become self-governing, but the federal government then set out to disband tribes by relocating them. In 2004, only about
one-third of the 4.1 million Indians in the United States live on reservations, the remaining two-thirds live in cities (Fixico, 2000). Wherever they
live the stereotype of the Indian is similar to that of African-Americans
and Hispanic-Americans, uneducated, unskilled, poor, and "out-of-place."
Most reservations are located far from cities and even large urban Indian
concentrations appear small compared to the size of metropolitan areas.
Therefore, much of the information about American Indians is not based
on accurate information or direct contact with them; ignorance has helped
to perpetuate anti-Indian bigotry.

Many urban Indians are descendants of those who first came to cities during the federal government's relocation program between the late 1940s through the 1960s. Under the relocation programs many Indians looking for jobs and housing moved to large cities. Relocation brought Indians from various tribes together to form new communities. Urbanized Indians have not completely assimilated into the dominant society and still retain some of their traditional tribal values. The loneliness of the city has caused some Indians, especially those under age 25, to relocate back to the reservation. Anthropologists who have studied urban Indians have noted that those from traditional hunting cultures have more difficulty assimilating into the culture of the city than Indians from agricultural traditions. The sedentary lifestyle of agrarian life has made adjustment to factory work in the cities easier than for those from mobile hunting traditions (Fixico, 2000).

Community and family are strong cohesive forces in Indian culture. Relocation and urbanization have had profound effects on the traditional social structure. In some instances, urbanization has alienated the father from his family. Fathers are the primary provider for the family, but in the urban setting an inability to obtain a job have forced many families to receive welfare and undermine the traditional role of the father. Poor working conditions, low pay, seasonal or limited work, specialized skills, and discrimination keep the unemployment rate at 40 percent or higher during the winter season especially (Fixico, 2000). This, in turn, harms the father's pride and creates guilt and shame, which threatens family unity. Young Indian males in this situation often leave the city and return to the reservation leaving the wives alone to raise the children. The effects on Indian children without the presence of a father are especially traumatic. Even with all family members present Indian youth experience psychological difficulties in adjusting to urban life.

Retaining cultural identity is often an individual undertaking. Indians are more scattered within the population than other minority groups. There is no neighborhood or barrio to go to. Urban Indians are not a place-based community; they are networked people who know each other. That is the reason Indian people are so easily ignored or forgotten. Cultural ties that were once second nature on the close-knit reservation are more difficult to retain. Distance from their families creates another hardship in carrying traditions from generation to generation.

A difference in perception and outlook on life distinguishes the cultural values of Indians in the city from the urban mainstream. This difference has maintained a gap between Indian and Anglo cultures. Indian values include: respect for elders; living in harmony with all living things and supernatural forces; oriented to the present time; and regard for spirituality. While urban Indians can retain these values Indian children may have some difficulties because of them in Anglo schools. The urban environment is so strange, and conflicts with Indian values to such a degree, that it is not surprising that the Indian feels alienated and lonely. When loneliness occurs an Indian feels disenfranchised from the spiritual bond that ties him or her to family and community (Fixico, 2000).

Alcohol has become a means of coping for both urban and reservation Indians. The reasons, Fixico has said, are both external and internal. External factors include socialization, difficulties in urban life, mainstream educational and occupational standards that are difficult for Indians to meet, physical abuse by a family member, death in a family, poor housing environment, and continual racism. Internal factors include feelings of self-destruction, depression, feelings of inferiority, loss of self-esteem, and the need to escape reality. Alcohol provides a temporary solace from the struggles of living on a reservation and the unmet expectations of an inhospitable alien culture.

On the other hand, it should be pointed out that relocation and urbanization have led to various degrees of acculturation among Indians that have enabled them to create an Indian middle class of professionals and business owners. But the dilemma remains for the present day American Indian, how much of their native culture are they willing to relinquish to become more inclusive members of the dominant culture? The alternative, to remain struggling outsiders, does not bode well for the health and well being of new generations of American Indians.

Low-Income Communities

Public housing was originally intended as an economic stimulus program as a way to provide housing to families who were temporarily unemployed, or employed at low wages, during the Great Depression. Public housing has now become housing for the very lowest income families, seniors, and disabled. In 2002, the median annual income of public housing residents was about $10,000, below the national poverty level of $14,128 for a family of three. Seniors and persons with disabilities make up 52 percent of the residents. There are about one million children living in public housing. Despite the fact that most residents have very low incomes, over 40 percent of all public housing families with children report that wages are their primary source of income. Most families have lived in public housing for less than ten years.

The public housing system has concentrated very poor people in very poor neighborhoods and offered no incentives for self-sufficiency. As a result of an innovative redevelopment strategy of the United States

Department of Housing and Urban Development (HUD), many public housing projects have been replaced by attractive low rise town houses. The HOPE VI experiment was initiated in 1992 to revitalize severely distressed public housing communities by creating new opportunities for public and private partners to develop mixed income communities. Each HOPE VI revitalization strategy is unique to its location. Reknitting the fabric of neighborhoods requires not only economic activity but also schools and services. Implementation of the HOPE VI program has been slow and only about half of the $5 billion provided by the federal government has been spent. Now, instead of building more public housing, the federal government wants to create more opportunities for home ownership and it wants states to play a larger role in administering the existing public housing voucher program, which subsidizes rents so poor people can afford to live in privately owned housing. Therefore, it is unlikely the HOPE VI program will be continued, although no national studies of the social impact of HOPE VI have been made. Federal funding for HOPE VI grants has been reduced by one-half and with more public housing units demolished than have been built, many former tenants are left without housing.

Advocates for HOPE VI believe it has been useful in deconcentrating and blurring the lines of poverty. Interspersing market-rate and subsidized public housing has created a healthy environment of working families. Networking is one of the benefits of intermingling low-income residents with those who are better off, since people looking for jobs often learn about them from talking with working neighbors. Another advantage of mixed-income housing is that middle class residents provide an economic base essential to creating the sort of amenities needed in a community.

Gay, Lesbian, Bisexual, and Transgender Communities

The most visible and active focus of gay life in the United States is in urban districts or "gay ghettos" such as West Hollywood, Castro (San Francisco), Key West, or Montrose (Houston), but often small communities of gay men or lesbians are embedded in rural culture where attitudes toward homosexuality are many decades behind the times. By keeping a low profile they can avoid the limitations of social exclusion (LeVay & Nonas, 1995). While the 50 some national gay and lesbian organizations work for their social inclusion, others work around their exclusion by not challenging it, still others cross the boundaries of social exclusion and inclusion by alternating or crossing genders.

Gay and lesbian communities are a microcosm of larger society. There are also excluded communities within the gay and lesbian cultures. For example, racism, ageism, and discrimination against gender, disability, and sexuality exist in gay and lesbian culture as they do in larger society. Gays and lesbians who are African-American or Hispanic-American are often excluded by the dominant culture, their own racial or ethnic group, and by other gays and lesbians. Ageism is also strongly practiced especially among gay men who value youth and physical appearance. Older gays and lesbians are often marginalized and find acceptance in gay and lesbian retirement communities. There are also gays and lesbians with children whose lifestyles require modifications in priorities and are excluded, or exclude themselves, from peers without parental responsibilities. Finally, within the broad culture of sexual orientation and sexual preferences there are individuals who choose to associate with others who share their mode of dress, fetishes, or uniquenesses, and, in this way exclude themselves from mainstream gay and lesbian culture. One way to cope with exclusion by dominant society is to consider gay or lesbian culture as the basis for kinship. Kinship ties can help build mutual trust and compensate for the hurts of discrimination (Gardner, 1994).

Persons with HIV/AIDS

The AIDS epidemic is largely a struggle with social exclusion. The link between stigma and HIV limits the actions and effectiveness of efforts to control its spread.[3] Once a person has developed AIDS stigma restricts the kind of care he or she will receive. Some people have access to life-saving treatments, while others are excluded; some classes of a population have comprehensive care, but others have no chance of access. More than one in 100 sexually active adults across the world are infected with HIV, yet only a small fraction of these people have access to counseling, testing, or actually know they are infected. About 16,000 people are newly infected with HIV daily. More than 36 million people are infected worldwide, and most of them can be expected to die within the next decade.

HIV/AIDS thrives in the context of social and economic vulnerability. Marginalization, whether arising from ethnicity, mobility, occupational segregation, cultural practices, racism, sexuality, sexual practices, or drug use impacts on vulnerability to the disease, and poses even greater challenges in terms of interventions to curb its spread. HIV/AIDS is also enmeshed with other behaviors common among marginalized groups, such as alcohol and substance abuse, especially intravenous drug use. These behaviors can lower the threshold for engaging in high-risk sexual behavior that can lead to HIV/AIDS (Gonzalez, 2001).

The stigma associated with HIV is so powerful that it is estimated that 90 percent of all HIV infected people worldwide do not know that they have the disease. People whose behaviors are high-risk may prefer to avoid testing for HIV to confirm their fears; deny that they might be HIV positive, or be unwilling to change their behavior and leave the outcome to chance. Others find out about their positive HIV status through testing, but choose to keep it a secret, fearing the social consequences. Still others prefer to wait to see if they develop HIV symptoms. Perhaps one of the core reasons for avoiding HIV testing is that a positive result would reveal an identity they would prefer to keep hidden. It is common knowledge that HIV is associated with lifestyles and sexual behavior not generally approved by most cultures. Not all persons who are HIV positive develop AIDS and many who are HIV positive may not see the onset of AIDS symptoms for several years due to continual advancements in treatment. Indeed, it is the ambivalent status of HIV and its clinical controllability that encourages HIV positive persons to behave as if they were disease free and hide their health status from sexual partners by not practicing prevention.

Once a person develops AIDS he or she is confronted by stigma from health professionals. A study by Kelly and his colleagues (1987) showed that the strongest attitudes held by physicians were that persons with AIDS are responsible for their illness. Physicians may react negatively to an AIDS diagnosis or to the patient based on presumptions about their lifestyle. But a diagnosis of AIDS widens the opportunities of stigma to family, friends, job, housing, church, and almost all aspects of life, even funeral homes. The primary assumption by the majority of the public in many cultures is that AIDS is a homosexual disease and homosexuals are responsible for initiating the epidemic that now extends into the heterosexual community. Despite large-scale efforts to educate the public and professionals about the scientific facts of the disease, fear and anxiety lurk below the surface of many people's emotions about a disease still thought to be contagious.

The Behaviorally Ill

In his classic book, written four decades ago, psychiatrist Thomas Szasz (1964) presented a view of psychiatry that stimulated a great deal of anger and controversy. He believed that what is considered mental illness has come to be defined as whatever psychiatrists say it is and that psychiatry has increasingly called more kinds of behavior "illness." Problems that once were considered matters of individual responsibility and choice are now considered as part of the domain of medicine, such as mental illness, drug abuse, homosexuality, behavior disorders in children, and cigarette addiction. As values and norms in society have changed the boundaries separating "normal or healthy" behavior from "abnormal or unhealthy" behavior have changed. Therefore, more behaviors that violate societal norms have become labeled public health problems. Interestingly there has also been a shift in medicine and psychiatry, in particular, away from psychotherapy and community-based programs, towards treating the symptoms of many of these problems with drugs. Indeed, many of these newly excluded groups have found more comfort and cures in self-help groups or from non-traditional healers or therapies than from mainstream medicine.

There have been efforts over the past several decades to minimize the stigma of mental illness by releasing hospitalized mental patients to outpatient status and maintaining them on drugs, support groups, and various rehabilitation and work programs. Many of these previously hospitalized patients have not been able to effectively make this transition and have become homeless or victims of violence or abuse. The social exclusion of the chronically mentally ill has effectively isolated them from social networks that are essential for survival. The transitory or episodically mentally ill, on the other hand, can negotiate the struggles of daily survival with some support and assistance. Their illness may be sufficiently hidden or controlled so that they are not socially excluded.

But being mentally or behaviorally ill is relative, depending on the norms of one's culture and social circumstances. For example, a person may be a highly respected CEO at work, but a tyrant when in his automobile on the freeway en route to work. His aggression and impatience, tailgating other drivers, frequently changing lanes, shaking his fist and swearing at other drivers, would predict that he could engage in more violent forms of road rage. While his driving behavior might be considered "the norm" on many United States freeways today, when he crosses the boundary of losing control of his anger and takes violent action against another driver, perhaps shooting them, then his behavior is considered abnormal. The point here is that anger is not a bad emotion unless abused, then it leads to behavior that ultimately may cause the person to become a member of an excluded group, i.e. a prisoner.

Anger and depression are emotions commonly seen together. Depression affects more than 19 million Americans. It is estimated that as many as one-third of office visits to physicians involve depression. The World Health Organization predicts that by 2020 depression will be second only to heart disease as the leading cause of disability (National Institute of Mental Health, 2000). Depression and anger are emotions that occupy the whole body, complicating existing disorders like heart disease and cancer, and there is evidence that they might trigger these and other medical conditions. If anger and depression are increasing behavioral responses in our society, people must sense threat in much of their environment on a daily basis. Therefore, there may be a greater tolerance of angry and depressive behavior, that is, people may just be considered uncivil, until physical acts of violence are committed.

There is some effort to "normalize" behavior of some currently socially excluded groups. For example, marijuana smokers are a socially excluded group where smoking marijuana is illegal. But efforts to make small amounts of marijuana legal for medical purposes or reducing the punishment for possessing small amounts of marijuana might help to lessen the social stigma of marijuana smoking. Given certain circumstances the behavior of a socially excluded group may become socially acceptable. On the other hand, cigarette smoking, which was a decade ago considered socially acceptable, has now become socially unacceptable with cigarette smoking increasingly becoming excluded from most public places. Cigarette smoking is now regarded by the American Psychiatric Association as an addiction.

Older Americans

Perhaps the most dramatic indicator of social exclusion is suicide. Suicide rates are highest among Americans aged 65 and older. Americans are living longer, but many experience the limitations of chronic disease as they age, and therefore may be dependent upon others to get around. Members of the family may live at great distances and with the death of a spouse and friends meaningful social ties disappear, leaving many elderly socially isolated and depressed. Aging itself is a process of social disengagement, but in addition, the high value placed on youth, appearance and activity in our society devalues the consequences of growing old. Even retirement housing is a reminder of the gradual progression of social decline and isolation as people move from lifestyle retirement and independent living communities, to assisted living, and then to nursing homes.

Ageism is age prejudice. The term was introduced in 1969 by gerontologist Robert Butler. Butler was involved in a controversy over the use of a high-rise block as public housing for older people in an affluent city in Maryland. The arguments focused on the amenities of parking, swimming pool, and air conditioning, which middle-aged local residents felt were appropriate for their comfort but not needed for elderly residents. They saw elderly newcomers as an unsettling force upsetting the harmony of the community. So the concept of ageism originated in community action. Ageism was defined by Butler as a process of systematic stereotyping of and discrimination against people because they are old. Ageism allows younger generations to see older people as different from themselves. In 1979, Robert Kalish introduced the concept of "new ageism," which he suggested took the emphasis away from chronological age, and instead focused on the problems that were thought to be representative of the entire population of elderly. New ageism tends to magnify or generalize the problems associated with a category of people.

Ageism generates and reinforces a fear and denigration of the aging process and opens the door for stereotyping. Ageism legitimates the use of age to differentiate classes of people who are denied resources and opportunities that people in younger age groups enjoy. Ageism suggests that older people are less competent, dependent, and in need of protection. Evidence of ageism in health care delivery and in the attitudes of health care professionals has been well documented. The incurable chronically ill elderly represent the limitations of medicine and view their illness as unchallenging.

But the process of aging is not the same, nor does it have the same consequences, for all elderly. A poor, black, disabled elderly person living in a rural area will have experienced social exclusion in many ways before they became elderly. While the overall well-being of older Americans has never been better, some minority group elderly are not so well off. In 2000, ten percent of those 65 years or older were below the poverty line. Lifetime patterns of lower wages and lower levels of education mean that on the average, non-whites enter old age with fewer resources than whites. Older minority women who live alone are the poorest. In 2000, 43 percent of older black women who lived alone fell below the poverty line. Generally, women are less likely than men to have had jobs that qualify them to collect maximum Social Security benefits, to be eligible for pensions, or to have accumulated savings.

Senior citizens are the largest dependable and growing voting block in the country. As such they have the attention of politicians on issues of special importance to them such as the cost of prescription drugs. As baby boomers age, and the number of citizens age 65 and over continue to increase the voice of senior citizens will become stronger. Senior citizens are not voiceless or powerless. They have the important resources of time and experience to organize effective networks. One example of such a network is The Gray Panthers.

In 1970, Maggie Kuhn convened a group of five retired friends to look at the common problems faced by retirees—loss of means and loss of contact with associates and one's job. They also discovered a new freedom to speak personally about what they believed in. The group began meeting and acting and in 1972 The Gray Panthers was organized, comprised of local networks headed by a convener. Maggie Smith's motto was "The best age is the age you are." The group has grown to a national multi-issue intergenerational organization engaged in issues of aging, war, health care, challenging the status quo from a progressive, and even radical point of view.

Despite the aging of the American population, aging and its consequences will continue to be the subject of negative stereotyping in the mass media, reflecting the strong emphasis in our culture on youth and vitality.

The Obese

Obesity is the second leading cause of preventable death in the United States. Approximately 127 million adults in the United States are overweight; 60 million of them are obese, and 9 million severely obese. The number of adults and children who are overweight has continued to increase. The rate of childhood obesity in the United States has increased more than 30 percent in the last decade. Obese children will most likely become obese adults. Obesity increases steadily with age for both genders, but is more common in men and the less educated. Obesity tends to run in families, suggesting that it might have a genetic cause. However, family members share not only genes, but also diet and lifestyle habits that may contribute to obesity. Overweight and obese individuals experience social stigmatization and discrimination in general, but especially in employment, despite many federal and state laws and policies.

Obesity is not just a cosmetic problem. It is a health hazard. The more obese a person is, the more likely he or she is to have health problems including mood disorders, diabetes, stroke, heart disease, gall bladder disease, and cancer of the breast, prostate and colon and consequently, shorter lives. Blacks have the highest rates of both obesity and diabetes among all races and ethnic groups.

The social and psychological costs of obesity are substantial. Obese job applicants are less likely to be hired, especially for face-to-face jobs. If they are hired discrimination continues. Obese employees are perceived to be lazy, sloppy, less competent, lacking in self-discipline, less conscientious, and poor role models. These negative attitudes contribute to discriminatory practices such as inequality in wages, denied promotions, and wrongful termination. Obese men are underrepresented in higher paying managerial and professional jobs and are more likely to hold lower paying jobs than non-obese men.

Negative attitudes have been documented among health professionals. Obese patients are seen as unintelligent, unsuccessful, weak-willed, unpleasant, overindulgent and lazy because it is assumed that obesity is the result of emotional problems and that it can be prevented by self-control. Physicians report low rates of discussion of weight issues with their patients and admit not interviewing as much as they should with obese patients. These negative attitudes may lead obese patients to avoid seeking medical treatment. Research demonstrates a delay in seeking medical care by obese women for pelvic examinations and preventive services such as breast and gynecological exams.

Obese students face multiple forms of weight discrimination. Many studies have shown the lasting negative effects of peer rejection and teasing. Peers consider obese children as least desirable friends and attribute their exclusion in social activities and lack of friends to their weight. These attitudes may be found as early as preschool. Obese students are less likely to be accepted to college than average-weight students despite having equivalent application rates and academic performance, especially overweight females. Average weight students received more financial support from parents than did overweight students, who depended more on financial aid and jobs.

Christian Crandall's (1994) social ideology perspective proposes that traditional, conservative North American values of self-determination, individualism, and self-discipline represent the core of anti-fat attitudes and these values are key in understanding why North Americans see obesity as controllable. This leads to stigmatization toward people who are perceived to be responsible for their fate.

No federal laws in the United States prohibit weight discrimination, although Title VII of the Civil Rights Act of 1964 has been used in weight discrimination cases. Victims of weight discrimination have to depend on the American Disabilities Act for protection and compensation, however, courts have been inconsistent as to whether obesity meets disability criteria.

The Anorexic, Bulimic, and Binge Eater

Anorexia and bulimia, also known as binge-purge behavior, are not about weight loss. They are about deeper intrapsychic conflicts that manifest themselves in obsessive weight loss. They are usually associated with other obsessions such as exercising, studying, or cleaning. Many authors have pointed out that anorexics have a strong self-destructive urge and some have labeled anorexia as civilized suicide. Ninety percent of anorexics and bulimics are found in adolescents and young women; it is less common among men and older women. The prevailing thought of the anorexic/bulimic is that no matter how thin they are, they consider themselves overweight. Societal norms for young women, which are strongly reinforced in all forms of media, are of the thin, attractive model. There is a societal obsession among women with physical appearance and the fear of being too fat.

Binge eating is like bulimia. It is characterized by episodes of uncontrolled eating or binging. However, binge eaters do not purge their bodies of excess food. Individuals with binge eating disorder feel that they lose control of themselves when eating. They eat large quantities of food and do not stop until they are uncomfortably full. Usually they have difficulty losing weight and keeping it off. Binge eating is found in about two percent of the general population, more often in women than men.

Most people with eating disorders share certain personality traits: low self-esteem, feelings of helplessness, and fear of becoming fat. Eating is a way of coping with stress and anxiety. By controlling their weight they can take control of their bodies and gain the approval of others. Anorexics, for example, keep their behavior to themselves until it becomes clear to others that they are dangerously thin.

Some individuals with bulimia also struggle with the abuse of alcohol, drugs, and compulsive stealing. Many of the people with eating disorders suffer from depression, anxiety, obsessive-compulsive disorder and other psychiatric disorders. These problems, combined with their impulsive tendencies make them high risk for suicide (National Institute of Mental Health, 1993).

The obese and the variety of eating disorders are strongly linked to American culture where food is plentiful and sharing it is a part of fellowship and compliments to the host. But it is also a culture that values physical appearance, attractiveness in women and fitness in men. To violate the height-weight table of expectations by becoming too fat or too thin immediately elicits warnings from gatekeepers of appearance, one's family, peers, and doctor, which if ignored, will lead to social pressure to seek help to lose or gain weight. To deny one's problem and not conform to expectations of others is certain to lead to social exclusion.

Persons with Disabilities and Impairments

Society has historically imposed barriers—*attitudinal barriers* such as fear, ignorance, prejudice, and stereotypes; *physical barriers* such as transportation, architecture, and communication; and *institutional barriers* such as policies, practices and procedures, that subject persons with disabilities to dependency, segregation, exclusion, and paternalistic treatment. Sometimes these barriers are intentional. More frequently they are the result of thoughtlessness, indifference, and lack of empathy and understanding. In addition, our country's public policy and laws regarding disability have not changed until recently. The signing of the Americans with Disabilities Act of 1990 (ADA) provided an omnibus civil rights statute, often referred to as the 20th century emancipation proclamation, for people with disabilities.

There are no completely accurate statistics on the total number of disabled children and adults in the United States. However, the National

Center for the Dissemination of Disability Research estimates that 43 million Americans are significantly limited in their capacity to participate in work, school, family or community life. Most of the available numbers are derived from handicapped persons who identify themselves as such, who seek assistance and utilize specialized services and resources, and/or receive benefits because of their disability. Some handicapped persons choose to be socially isolated to avoid the stigma, inconvenience or embarrassment of their disability, while other handicapped persons choose to participate as fully as possible as citizens, but are prevented from doing so because their needs cannot or have not been accommodated. Social exclusion is the result of the interaction between how the non-disabled perceive the disabled and how the disabled perceive themselves.

Nearly all definitions of disability identify an individual as disabled based on a physical or mental impairment that limits the person's ability to perform an important activity. The possibility that the individual is limited by a barrier in society or the environment is rarely considered. A new perspective of disability has been proposed by Saad Nagi (1991), a sociologist at Ohio State University. He has suggested that disability is a function of the interaction of the individual with social and physical environments. The "Nagi model" suggests that an individual with a disability be viewed as a person who requires an accommodation or intervention rather than as a person with a condition or impairment. Because accommodations can address person-centered factors as well as socio-environmental factors a "need for accommodation" paradigm is more appropriate.

Many handicaps remain hidden, for example communication and learning disabilities such as dyslexia, unless they are exposed by the affected person. The social and physical situation will determine whether it is important for the handicapped person to reveal their handicap. For example, it is usually important to let a teacher know one is dyslexic, but it is not necessary information for a coach. Persons who do not have obvious handicaps can protect their hidden identities and avoid possible stigmatization. The person who is addicted to alcohol, drugs, gambling, or sex, and the closeted gay, lesbian, cross-dresser, or person who is HIV positive, are all examples of hidden identities. If a person is able to engage his or her hidden identity without requiring special accommodations or without it having negative consequences for others, and has counterbalancing positive social statuses, the hidden identity is often "normalized." For example, William J. Bennett, former United States Secretary of Education, right wing Zionist, and author of numerous books on how to live morally, gambled away more than eight million dollars at casinos without negative financial consequences to his family. Friends of Bennett were reluctant to criticize him stating, "It's his own money and his own business." Bennett said, "I view it (gambling) as drinking, if you can't handle it, you don't do it." He exempted gambling from his list of contemporary weaknesses and vices of modern culture but vowed to give it up (Seelye, 2003).

Many persons with disabilities have multiple handicaps that may each carry different stigmas and have different consequences. One handicap may complicate getting accommodation for another. For example, being a poor, black, obese, 16 year old high school student and single mother with a learning disorder is a not uncommon illustration of how disabilities interact and complicate each other. This student undoubtedly has experienced social exclusion. To restore her self-esteem and pride will require the coordinated efforts of family, school officials, health professionals, and learning specialists. While disabled persons need accommodations to help meet their needs for survival and quality of life, most have more than one disability, which makes it necessary for social institutions, caretakers and helpers to coordinate their efforts to take a person-centered approach to the handicapped client. Unfortunately, the public makes judgments about the disabled based on single observations in public places, and tends to categorize people on the basis of the handicap that is most meaningful to them. This often leads to judging or comparing handicaps and forming a negative stereotype, which is then generalized to support social exclusion for those who have that characteristic.

One of the greatest challenges we face in our society is to educate the public that having a disability or impairment is not always a choice, but whether chosen or not those who are victims of a handicap cope with it more effectively if they experience empathy, understanding, and accommodation, than they do if they are excluded and isolated.

SOCIAL INCLUSION

There are several views of the concept of social inclusion and how it relates to a modern society that is fractured by many communities of exclusion and excluded communities. One view is that of the German sociologist Niklas Lukmann (1995), who believes that social inclusion and social exclusion are two sides of the same coin. The difference between inclusion and exclusion is in the way people are treated. In modern society inclusion and exclusion are regulated by different systems, e.g. family, political, religious. Society makes no attempt to ensure that people who do not belong to one system belong to another. Therefore, it no longer makes sense to ask whether or not a person or group is integrated into society. In today's society there is no longer a stable environment that shapes an individual's identity or develops a sense of belonging to society, but rather individuals participate in various independent social systems. For example, if an individual by choice never votes or participates in any local, state, or national political activity or organization they would exclude themselves from the political system. On the other hand, they may be a very involved member of a church and/or religious organization and an involved member of the religious system. Therefore, it is possible for individuals to be included in and excluded from various societal systems at the same time. However, none of the systems alone are able to provide an individual with full integration into society. Lukmann believes that there is no need for the various systems to reciprocate with each other, yet he is aware that society's existence can be threatened if individual systems become narrow, independent, and concerned with only their self-interest.

Another view is that of Anver Saloojee (2003), a political scientist, who proposed that social inclusion begins from the premise that it is democratic citizenship that is at risk when a society fails to develop the talents and capacities of all its members. For social inclusion there is no contradiction between democratic citizenship and differentiated citizenship, where people can hold dual or multiple loyalties. The value of social inclusion is that it meets the challenges posed by diversity, namely to build on traditions of equality and incorporate equality as a national value. Social inclusion is about engaging in continuous evaluations of laws, policies, and practices to ensure that they promote social inclusion. Saloojee offered five points about social inclusion:

- Social inclusion is the political response to exclusion. Social inclusion is more than the removal of barriers, it is about a comprehensive vision that includes all.
- Social inclusion is proactive. It is about the active intervention to promote rights and responsibilities.
- Social inclusion is both process and outcome. It can hold social institutions accountable for policies and it is a yardstick to measure good government.
- Social inclusion is about advocacy and transformation. The vision of social inclusion is a positive vision that binds individuals, groups, and social institutions to action.
- Social inclusion is embracing. It posits the notion of democratic citizenship as opposed to formal citizenship.

In the context of accommodating differences there is the opportunity to ensure equal treatment. This will enable all members of society with the chance to develop their talents and participate in the benefits of citizenship free from discrimination.

"Managing" Inclusion/Exclusion

Our society is becoming more culturally diverse and social institutions and organizations are socially and legally accountable for implementing programs to enhance social inclusion and minimize social exclusion. Many leaders consider diversity, like affirmative action, a phenomenon to be "managed," that is, as long as an institution or organization is within legal guidelines it is satisfying the requirements of diversity. But inclusion and exclusion relate to how people are treated when a third party is not present overseeing interactions to ensure that they are fair, respectful, and equitable. The issue is not to "manage" or minimize the differences of socially excluded groups so they are not a problem, rather the challenge is to reduce inequalities that are barriers to full citizenship for all.

SUMMARY

One way humans have to emphasize their uniqueness is to exploit the differences between themselves and others in the use of physical space. We construct our space to meet particular needs and objectives; our surroundings, in turn, affect our behavior. There is a direct relationship between the ownership of space and power. Power is expressed by the monopolization of space and the relegation of less powerful groups in society to less desirable environments. The owners of space exert their power by drawing boundaries which determine who will be included and excluded from their territory.

Gated communities are part of the trend toward exercising physical and social means of territorial control. Some walls keep people in, some are meant to keep people out. Gated communities are a symbol of the underlying tensions in larger society. They provide the illusion of control and stability and are a barrier to interaction with people who are different. Whether they are lifestyle communities, elite communities, or security zone communities, there is an inward-looking cohesion of people with similar expectations, outlooks, levels of affluence or anxieties that exclude the outside world. Social cohesion is purchased fabricating a neighborhood context.

Walls and fences reduce the chances for conflict, but also privatize social capital, free residents from obligations to keep up contacts with neighbors, and turn concerns away from issues in the larger community. Communities of exclusion are a popular escape from urban problems. Conflict is rare in the suburbs where the predominate code of ethics of "moral minimalization" is focused around homogeneity, autonomy, independence, weak social ties, and indifference to the wrongdoing of others.

Social exclusion involves limiting interaction with those who look, act, and believe differently from the majority and those who sense, feel or experience their differences and withdraw from others. Frequently the result of social exclusion is the grouping together in specific areas, by choice or by force, those who are different. Social exclusion results in economic, social, political, and cultural disadvantage. There is a cycle of exclusion and disadvantage; individuals or groups cannot change their position of exclusion if they do not have access to the proper resources to do so, but the appropriate resources are out of reach or limited for the socially excluded. Therefore, socially excluded groups cannot fully participate as citizens in the society in which they live.

There are many examples of excluded communities in our society. Several were selected for brief illustration including, the American Indian; low-income communities; gay, lesbian, bisexual and transgender communities; persons with HIV/AIDS; the behaviorally ill; older Americans; the obese; the anorexic, bulimic, and binge eater; and persons with disabilities and impairments. Members of these communities are excluded from full citizenship because they are powerless due to a combination of low income, lack of a job, poor health, lack of skills, inadequate housing, stigmata associated with lifestyle, stereotyping, prejudice and self-imposed isolation. The challenge for our society is to create greater inclusion and cohesiveness by valuing diversity. Social inclusion and exclusion are two sides of the same coin. The difference between the two is how people are treated. Because of rapid social change, immigration, and geographical mobility it is difficult to provide a stable environment which helps develop a sense of belonging to a society. In addition, it is easy to belong to some social systems and not others, making it difficult for individuals to become fully integrated into a society.

The ability of future generations to respect and honor differences among each other will depend upon the willingness of the present generation to reduce the barriers to exclusion and give people the opportunity to learn about their similarities as well as their differences. Nathaniel Hawthorne expressed this fully when he said, "every individual has a place to fill in the world, and is important in some respect whether he chooses to be so or not."

QUESTIONS FOR DISCUSSION

1. Discuss why gated communities are popular and prevalent in the West and Southwestern regions of the United States.
2. Discuss the difficulties excluded groups and communities experience in participating in the benefits of the larger society.

3. Discuss how it is possible for individuals to be included in and excluded from various communities at the same time. Give examples.
4. In your opinion, do people who are members of communities of exclusion generate social capital for the society as a whole?
5. What are some of the norms that keep communities exclusive? How are deviations from these norms controlled? Who holds the power in communities of exclusion?
6. What is meant by privatized social capital? How do social homogeneity and privatized social capital reinforce each other?

Chapter 7

Connections of Faith
Religion as Community

INTRODUCTION

Much of religion is communal. Church going produces social connections; religiously involved people know more people (Putnam, 2000). The fellowship of like-minded believers also provides a sense of community and group solidarity. Putnam (2000) observed, "connectedness, not merely faith is responsible for the beneficence of church people" (p. 67). Nearly half of all associational membership in America is church related, half of all personal philanthropy is religious, and half of all volunteering takes place in a religious context.

Religion is a source of social capital. It brings people together in networks and creates interest in each other's welfare. It serves as a social resource and meets individual needs. This was especially true of the early history of the United States when there was a recognition of religion's unifying impact on American society. However, today immigrants are more diverse and so are their religions. Moreover, established religions have changed in what Kosmin and Lachman (1993) describe as an "open and free marketplace of faiths and cultures." Religion counts in American society. It is an intrinsic part of our country's history including the First Amendment. Religion is also a part of character education. Religion means a personal affirmation of faith in God and an identification with a religious denomination, it does not necessarily mean joining or being an active member of a particular group. Religion is a personal commitment and a shared experience (Kosmin & Lachman, 1993).

There have been two major trends in religion in the United States over the past several decades. One is that, in general, churches have become less engaged in the larger community and have focused more on reinforcing within-group networks (bonding social capital) and, therefore, have neglected or discouraged ties outside of the congregation (bridging social capital). New denominations especially, seem to be directed more inward rather than outward. Second, almost 40 percent of Americans have no connections with organized religion (Fuller, 2001). In order to benefit individually and as a society from a sense of community and group identity which religion provides, it is important to be affiliated with a religious congregation. Some writers have suggested that our disconnectedness with religion is one of the causes of our current social problems. American society has been described as being in a social recession, or a spiritual vacuum, or experiencing spiritual poverty (Myers, 2000). Religion is not the only aspect of American culture that is experiencing a decrease in social capital and disconnections among individuals. Similar decreases have been found in political, civic, workplace, and informal social participation. Putnam (2000) found civic malaise and weakening community bonds to be widespread in the United States at the close of the 20th century. This view contrasts with the findings of the Hartford Institute for Religion study conducted by Carl Dudley and David Roozen at Hartford Seminary which surveyed 14,301 congregations in 41 denominations in the United States and found the great majority to be vital and alive. Half of the faith communities saw themselves as growing in numbers especially those using or blending contemporary forms of worship and those located in newer suburbs. Most of the problems in faith communities were related to the lack of infrastructure, volunteers, financial support, and a willingness to change.

In the largest ever survey on the civic engagement of 30,000 Americans, the John F. Kennedy School of Government at Harvard University looked at how connected family, friends, neighbors and civic institutions were on local and national levels. The survey also included faith-based participation and affiliation (Putnam & Feldstein, 2003). The survey found religious participation and affiliation were highest in the South and Midwest. Eighty-eight percent of the sample reported some religious affiliation; 58 percent were members of a local church, synagogue or other religious or spiritual community. Ninety-one percent of blacks and 93 percent of Hispanics reported religious affiliations versus 88 percent of whites. Sixty-four percent of blacks were members of religious communities compared to 59 percent of whites and 43 percent of Hispanics. There were also large differences in survey responses by age. Younger respondents (18–34 years of age) showed more diversity in religious affiliation compared to older respondents. This reflects the diversity associated with the rapid growth of racial and ethnic minorities in the general population.

The survey uncovered several important findings with respect to religion in the 21st century.

- Americans are more likely to trust people at their place of worship (71%) than they are to trust people they work with (52%), their neighbors (47%), or people of their own race (31%).
- Involvement in a religious community is among the strongest predictors of giving and volunteering for both religious and secular causes.
- Religious involvement is positively associated with most other forms of civic involvement. Even comparing people at similar educational and income levels, religiously engaged people are more likely to be active in community affairs, to give blood, to vote, to know the names of public officials, to socialize with friends and neighbors, and to have wider social networks.
- Poorer, less educated Americans are less likely to be involved in community life than other Americans, but they are as fully engaged in religious communities.
- Religiously engaged people have a more diverse circle of friends than those who are less engaged in religion.
- Religious involvement is sometimes associated with intolerance, for example, favoring banning unpopular books from libraries, antipathy to equal rights for immigrants, lower levels of support for racial intermarriage and lower levels of friendships with gays.
- Greater religious participation is associated with less support for reform groups and less participation in marches and boycotts.

Many social scientists consider statistics related to religious membership to be unreliable, because membership means different things to different denominations, and since we tend to think of religion almost exclusively in terms of organizations, there is some social pressure for individuals to admit to membership in, or affiliation with, some religious organization, albeit unimportant to them. Fuller (2001) has pointed out that it is possible to be religious or spiritual on a personal level without having a religious affiliation. Therefore, survey data on religion should be interpreted with the cautions applied to other types of data obtained by survey methods. What is important in this chapter is that there is a great deal of consensus among many authors and observers of social change in America that the form and practice of religion is changing.

THE RELIGIOUS COMMUNITY IN TRANSITION

Current Patterns of Change

Almost four decades ago Martin Marty (1967) described the search for a new spiritual style in secular America. He detected a powerful "new language of the spirit" which began in the 1960s. The quest for spiritual style ranged from the rise of cults, communes, and mystical faiths to experimentation with drugs in attempts to create a new meaning by combining inner and outer life. Those people growing up reacting against the bland religious establishment of their youth continue in their explorations. The search for spiritual style goes on (Roof, 1993).

Roof (1993) described four patterns of change to show how religion is being transformed. First, there is a deepening of the meaning of spirituality. Spirituality is more focused, specialized, and tailored to meet individual needs. For example, there are Eastern spiritualities, Native American spiritualities, feminist spirituality, men's spirituality, new age spirituality, and so on. The diversity of spirituality reflects our consumer culture, the increasing diversification of traditions and religions in our society, and the need for spirituality to be personally relevant.

Along with the trend toward specialized and personalized spirituality is a broader ecological spirituality. Terrorism has made people aware of the interconnectedness of all things. This is perhaps best illustrated by Americans' unity and collective empathy for victims and survivors of the events of September 11, 2001, in New York, Washington, DC and Pennsylvania. Spirituality can be shared as well as privatized, and this can be accomplished without affiliation with organized religion. A second change in religion over the past several decades is religious pluralism. This is evident in the increase in nondenominational churches. The structure, dogma, and formalism of denominations is being rejected by baby boomers and their children in favor of seeing religion as an affirmation of basic human values which should have generic applicability. It is not uncommon to see spouses from different religious backgrounds alternate attendance between churches of different denominations to meet their different spiritual needs. A third change in religion is what Roof called "multilayered belief and practice." The old spiritual style emphasized homogeneity, which is still evident in churches that hold traditional services. Many churches have attempted to retain members by offering both traditional and contemporary worship services. There are now many more options by which individuals and families can satisfy their spiritual quest. Some have termed this "mix and match" religion. There are in-home Bible studies, seminars for singles, youth, families and seniors, sports, retreats, hikes, social ministries and self-help groups, along with traditional Sunday school, choirs, fundraising, volunteering, and fellowship dinners so that members can layer activities according to their needs and time. Churches with parochial schools often have a large number of students from families that are not church members, but who actively participate in financially supporting the school. A fourth pattern of change in religion is more self-exploration. There is more searching for a personal philosophy and for ways of sharing one's talents that are personally meaningful. The boomer style of self-searching is different from previous generations in that earlier generations were more likely to accept truisms, whereas boomers are more likely to question them, and boomers' spiritual views are more dynamic and changeable. Changeability is often why boomers are thought to lack commitment.

Roof's view is that the boomer generation (born between 1946 to 1964) is so deeply divided spiritually that only segments will ever return to conventional religious denominations. Many post-boomers (born between 1965 and 1976) have little, if any, direct experience with a church or the Bible. Roof said that boomers are looking for sharing, caring, accepting, and belonging—qualities that are more important than the places where they find them. New patterns of religious community are emerging and mainline denominations such as Roman Catholic, Methodist, Presbyterian, and Lutheran, have internalized the pluralism of lifestyles and contemporary culture with a wide array of groups, activities, and programs, to attract and retain boomers and their children. While nondenominational mega churches (so called Bible-based churches) are growing in number, large numbers of denominations and faiths are turning to small groups to connect with their members.[1] These small groups, or "faith communities," blend the search for self-actualization with group spirituality ("seeker spirituality"). Individuals come together to share spiritual experiences thereby building a sense of community. Roof suggested that where these group activities will eventually lead is unknown, but he predicts that religious communities in the future will look like loose federations made up of many smaller communities. This is similar to Wuthnow's (1998) idea that our social institutions have become porous. As a result people feel loosely connected to, or even alienated from them, seeking other ways to meet their needs. One person expressed it, "We all access God differently" (Roof, 1993, p. 258). About eight percent of Americans say that they do not access God at all (Kosmin & Lachman, 1993).

The Congregation as a Community

The boundaries of American religion are being redrawn. Fuller (2001) pointed out that the "unchurched" who are not members of congregations are now viewed differently. In previous decades the unchurched were usually viewed as lost souls. They are now viewed as people who have made a choice not to join or become actively involved with a religious organization. But many unchurched are people who, for various reasons, are in limbo about church membership. Many people who at some point in their lives are unchurched, later become church members. Pastors of nondenominational churches report that most of their members come from unchurched traditions and people who are "burned out" with denominational traditions. Twenty percent of the United States population aspires to be spiritual, but not religious, piecing together those beliefs that meet their personal needs or interests. Even members of liturgical and mainline denominations incorporate this new religious eclecticism. There is now more freedom about whether a person wants to join a church or not (Fuller, 2001). Not everyone, however, feels comfortable with establishing their own religious agenda and some remain stalwart members of denominations that have characterized their families for several generations.

While the pendulum has swung away from mainline denominations, the congregation remains an enduring voluntary religious community. For many the collective expression of traditions is essential to the religious experience (Warner, 1994). Members sing hymns, pass the peace, pray, commune, and fellowship together. Worship is a sensual and communal experience. All religions serve to socialize individuals to the norms of their group. This is achieved through congregating. Through this gathering together the skills, resources, and "spiritual gifts" of individuals are discovered so that they can assist in carrying out stewardship activities. Members volunteer or are "called" by reason of skill and inclination to teach, visit the sick, usher, witness, head committees related to fellowship, outreach, new member orientation, or serve as a trustee, elder, or member of the parish council. The congregation has also served as a place for many activities that are not religious, ranging in scope from English language instruction for immigrants to providing entertainment for teenagers. Congregations can function as protected enclaves in a hostile world. They can offer temporary assistance with basic necessities, locate possible jobs through members, and support and comfort the socially isolated. The congregation has the capacity to nurture members and non-members through life transitions from birth to death.[2]

Gilkey (1994) suggested that mainline congregations have remained too religious for a changing secular world and have been too accommodating to meet the evolving new needs of modern society. The growth of conservative fundamentalist congregations and decrease in the size of liberal congregations seems to affirm Gilkey's suggestion. Putnam (2000) noted that growth has occurred at both ends of the religious spectrum, the most orthodox or evangelical and the most secular, while the middle has collapsed. However, the fact that evangelical Christianity is rising in popularity and mainline Christianity is falling means that religion is less effective now as a foundation for civic engagement and bridging social capital (Putnam, 2000). The trends we see in religious life reinforce the measurable decrease in social connectedness in society at large.[3]

Moral Values and the Socialization of Youth in the Changing Church

The church is the only social institution that teaches, advocates for, and models moral values across the lifespan. Changes in societal norms and laws, and changes in the meaning of family, have had significant impacts on the type and extent of involvement of the church in character education. As in society in general, individuals and families are busy and have limited time. Time commitments to the church are usually not at the top of family's priority lists. Yet, parents expect the church to be the teacher of moral values.

A director of youth services at a mainline Protestant church said that parents sometimes complain that the church is not offering enough programs for youth. To some parents keeping their children busy is a high priority. The director said that he reminds parents that the church is not the spiritual center of their lives, the family is, and the church is there as a support system. The director speculated that many boomer parents may not know how to connect their children with a church since many of them didn't become engaged in a church when they were children.

As many parents, especially the more affluent, become unhappy with the social climate of public schools and place their children in parochial or charter schools, their expectations of the church as "spiritual guru" for their children have increased. The link between church and school has become more critical as these parents feel that they have insufficient time to provide continuity and reinforcement for their children's character education. Just as parents expect the church to teach their children moral decision-making, such as sex and drug education, parents want retreats and workshops on parenting, conflict-resolution, and rejuvenating their own marriages.

Churches have become specialists in offering a variety of age and gender appropriate programs for all members. However, one director of family ministries stated that rather than narrowing and specializing moral education there is a need to broaden it by involving generations within the family. Without cross-generational communication and sharing in teaching moral values in families, there will be large gaps left untaught. The church just doesn't have the same amount of time with children that parents do. As the director said, "We see the children for a few hours once or twice a week; the parents are with the children for the majority of every day." Indeed, character education takes more than a one-time video course or discussion group at church. To learn to be a "good" parent and a "good" child is a process. It takes commitment and time. The socialization of children in moral education also requires an active partnership involving parents with the school and church.

The bottom line issues in teaching moral values are commitment and prioritization. One director of family ministries told this author, "Years ago the marketing of youth and family programs were unheard of. Now you have to promote an event. Parents and children each have their list of priorities. When the church is low on one or both parents' lists they are unlikely to interfere when their child receives a call from a friend to "hang out at the mall" and chooses to miss a church youth group activity. Children mimic their parents' priorities and when the child needs to make a choice, parents don't want to fight a battle, so they back away." Another youth director at a mainline Protestant church said that the church sees youth from preschool until they are confirmed. After confirmation about half of the seventh and eighth grade youth drop out. The director speculated that as youth gain more independence, their choice is to decrease the time they spend at church, unless they participate as a family.

Religious Individualism, Choice, and the Reactive Church

There are several consequences for greater religious individualism for mainline denominations. Individualism erodes loyalties to specific denominations and local churches. Churches are chosen because of stimulating preaching, exceptional music, their neighborhood location, a particular youth program or emphasis on community outreach. Therefore, it is common to see church shopping, especially visiting the newest local church. The lack of loyalty encourages a cafeteria approach to religion and to measured involvement in church activities, should one be found interesting enough to join. Roof (1993) quoted a practicing Catholic who disagreed very strongly with her church's stand on birth control and abortion who said, "It's hard to find a religion you can believe totally in" (p. 213). As many church shoppers discover, it is rare to find what they are looking for all in one place. Religious individualism is a convenience religion and encourages turnover among members, which in turn, disrupts the sense of community in churches.

Membership in many mainline churches has remained stable at best. Transfers in and out along with poor attendance and reluctant involvement make it difficult to retain a sustainable membership. Parents go to church where their children want to go. Often children's friends in Sunday school or parochial school are the major influence on where parents attend church. Many parents drop off their children so they can be with their friends, but pick them up after the school meeting or event without attending worship services. Youth learn that church is a necessary, but not a fixed priority.

A major effect of religious individualism on mainline churches is the general lack of enthusiasm for evangelism and witnessing. With the emphasis on religious choice many people are reluctant to take the initiative to contact others about visiting their church. This is due in part, to the fact that many members consider their church as a temporary home, or believe that recruiting members is the pastor's responsibility.

Of course, the effect of losing members and the difficulty of engaging new members in volunteer activities is of great concern to church leaders. Many churches have become introspective and even defensive, critically asking themselves what they are not doing or doing wrong. In conducting this self-analysis there is often a comparison with the program offerings and worship styles of nearby growing churches. Mainline churches are often inclined to overreact by trying to add activities they financially cannot afford. A church with a stable or declining membership may decide that it needs to offer more programs and can do so only by adding more staff. This, in turn, impacts the budget and requires pastors to make appeals for increased offerings. If members feel little loyalty or commitment to a church they are not likely to support it with their financial gifts.

Strategic planning is an important aspect of the life of mainline churches as they live with increasingly tight budgets. Like businesses and other organizations churches must decide what their future goals are and how they are going to reach them in a climate of rapid societal change, religious choice, and non-commitment. Mainline churches will continue to be challenged in how to grow and flourish in a society where instant gratification and individual achievement flout the benefits of communalism.

THE GROWTH AND CIVIC ENGAGEMENT OF NON-CHRISTIAN IMMIGRANTS

Census Bureau data indicates that the number of immigrants living in the United States has more than tripled since 1970 to over 28 million accounting for 10.4 percent of the total population, the highest percentage in 70 years. As the United States has become more ethnically diverse it has also become more religiously diverse. Since 1970 Buddhists have increased by 1.8 million, Hindus by 850,000, and Muslims by six million. Meanwhile, in the last decade about 25,000 Protestant churches have closed their doors. During the 1990s the proportion of Americans who considered themselves Christian decreased from 86 percent to 77 percent, while non-Christian religions grew by 3.7 percent. Buddhists surpassed Episcopalians in number and Islam became the fastest growing religious group in the United States.

Religious institutions have historically played a key role in assisting immigrants in acculturating to American society. On the one hand churches have been important agents of socialization for citizenship. Some congregations help immigrants develop civic skills, especially women, minorities, and the poor by involving them in church activities. On the other hand, some churches are havens from larger society in which immigrants can feel at home and reinforce ties with others from the same country of origin. However, protective bonding can impede immigrant's adaptation to American society. Congregations offer adults and youth extended social networks that provide acceptance, trust and resources that enhance steps in adaptation to American society. Congregations vary in their degree of bridging social capital that can link immigrants beyond their own group ranging from job opportunities to political participation (Foley, 2001). Foley found, in a survey of congregations in the Washington, DC area, that while immigrants in general are more likely to actively participate in congregations, they do not worship regularly in congregations with large immigrant populations. Therefore, it is not surprising that some Christian churches have established outreach ministries to attract immigrants to their congregations. However, religious and ethnic solidarity tend to be intertwined and reinforce each other among some groups such as the Chinese and Koreans, who attend congregations serving large numbers of immigrants from their own ancestry.

Foley found that congregations differ in the degree to which they provide opportunities for immigrants to socialize and develop and use civic skills relevant to civic engagement. The ideology of the congregation shapes immigrant's attitudes toward civic engagement; some churches explicitly discourage it, others encourage it, and still others never allude to it. In Foley's study he found that immigrants from groups with pressing political causes were more likely to become civically engaged and to promote civic engagement among others.

Interfaith Connections

For non-Christian immigrants the process of becoming accepted by Christians can be an ordeal, especially when divisiveness among Christian groups has been part of the history of a community, as Jaquith (1999) discovered in Topeka, Kansas. Jaquith conducted in-depth interviews with representatives of different religions in Topeka, a city of about 126,000, to obtain views on how divided or unified the city was regarding religious collaboration and tolerance. The Interfaith Council was originally the Christian-based Council of Churches until 1979 when a community member insisted it was important to include Jews and Bahai's, who had the longest continuous history of non-Christian religions in Topeka dating to 1870 and 1920 respectively. Since 1979 there has been episodic participation in the Interfaith Council by Muslims, Buddhists, and Hindus and most of the literalist and fundamentalist Christian churches withdrew from Interfaith to form their own organizations claiming intolerance to world faiths.

Jaquith points out that, although the Jews, Bahai's and Buddhists equal or outnumber the membership of smaller Christian denominations, and many non-Christians participate in community affairs, most Topekans are probably not aware of the growth of non-Christian religions in the city. She states, "Topeka is divided into white Anglo-Saxon Protestant versus other religions, but in low-key aspects." For example, although some official rules and policies of the Christian public and businesses conflict with the religious calendars and holy days of non-Christians and are seen as discriminatory by them, there has been no open conflict about this.

There are some positive community trends noted by Jaquith such as students studying comparative religions at school, an official multicultural calendar for all schools that includes recognition of religious days for all faiths, and there are few overt verbal attacks on religion in public. Religious leaders agree that all of the religious communities face the same problems including those of family and youth related to excessive work demands and materialism. They also agree that identifying common needs and tasks appears to be a way of working together rather than focusing on differences that create artificial barriers.

The ability of Christian and non-Christian religions to work together is tied to the issue of "generalized trust" and how generalized trust can be developed and maintained in a socially diverse society. Thomas Pettigrew (1971), in his research on interracial contact emphasized that increasing interaction, whether of groups or individuals, intensifies and magnifies processes already underway. Hence, more interracial contact can lead to either greater prejudice or greater respect and acceptance, depending upon the situation in which it occurs. Pettigrew found that contact had positive effects on interracial attitudes and beliefs when the groups 1) possessed equal status, 2) sought common goals, 3) were cooperatively dependent upon each other, and 4) interacted with the positive support of authorities, laws, or customs. Pettigrew's work suggests that the negative effects of the interaction of social beliefs increase as the degree of inequality between the groups increases, as the degree of conflict of interest increases, and as the level of support for positive interactions between authorities declines (Knight, 2001). As long as the benefits of working together exceed the benefits of not doing so, generalized trust can be developed between groups despite differences in beliefs. Communities that allow relative strangers to identify with each other to seek a common cause across racial, ethnic, linguistic, religious and national boundaries will create generalized trust.

RELIGIOUS/SPRITUAL CONNECTIONS

Levin (2001) has pointed out that some New Age authors and media who are hostile to organized religion, but open to religious expression, have reserved the term "religion" to include those beliefs, behaviors, and rituals that occur in the context of organized religion. They include other forms of religious expression under the rubric of "spirituality." Spirituality is the larger phenomenon, religion is that part of spirituality that involves organized religious activity (Koenig, McCullough & Larson, 2001).[4]

There are many types of religious practices and many ways of being spiritual. Some of the more common include: prayer, worship, fellowship, altruism, renewal, observation, and controlled interaction. These connections can be highly personal and private, for example, individual prayer; others are focused around participation in groups, such as Bible study, prayer circles and worship services; still others are anonymous and observational, such as television ministries and the Internet. Most people who are religiously connected are involved in more than one way. And, these connections change in type and degree as personal needs and circumstances change. The type and degree of religious connections individuals make will depend upon whether they seek to strengthen existing ties, cultivate new and/or broader ties, or select ties on an as-needed basis (Figure 7.1).

Religious beliefs and practices have a long history of association with health and healing practices. Only in recent decades has it been considered

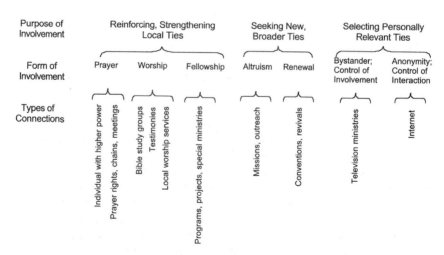

Figure 7.1. Types of Religious Connections: Their Forms and Purposes

that religion might have an impact on physical and mental health through social, psychological, and behavioral pathways (Koenig & Cohen, 2002). There is scientific evidence that religious and spiritual connections are positively associated with enhanced physical and emotional health, well-being, and longevity. While religious faith and participation in religious activities is thought to be good for health, religious coping can have negative effects such as using religion to replace traditional medical care, the overzealous use of religious activities instead of seeking timely medical care, using religious beliefs to foster, encourage, and justify child abuse, replacing mental health care with religion, and refusing types of medical intervention or care (Koenig, McCullough & Larson, 2001). Like other types of social connections religion has its healthy and unhealthy boundaries.

RELIGION, SPIRITUALITY, AND HEALTH

Longevity and Religious Attendance

There is intriguing evidence that the frequency of attendance at a church or synagogue is an important element in reducing the death risk among average people. The mortality rates of 5,286 people between the ages of 21 and 65 in Alameda County, California, were studied over a period of 28 years to determine the long-term association between religious attendance and mortality (Strawbridge, Cohen, Shema & Kaplan, 1997). Frequent attenders had lower mortality than infrequent attenders. The results were stronger for females. During follow-up, frequent attenders were more likely to stop smoking, increase exercising, increase social contacts, and stay married. The lower mortality rates for frequent religious attenders were partly explained by improved health practices, increased social connections, and more stable marriages occurring in conjunction with attendance. The lower mortality of frequent female church attenders fits with research at Duke University that found that religion is more important for women because of their traditionally more limited involvement in activities that bring them social recognition and prestige outside the home. Becoming active in a congregation often gives women a sense of purpose, self-esteem, and satisfaction that is more fulfilling than career achievement (Koenig, 1999; Helm, Hays, Flint & Koenig, 2000).

One of the most salient findings about church attendance is that its benefits may extend many years into the future. Levin (2001) reports the findings from several studies that have showed frequent church attendance can help prevent mood disorders as long as a decade in the future. Levin explains that continuous religious participation and sharing a common purpose with others provides the protection of social support, which is a buffer against the harmful effects of stress and life changes.

Several studies have also documented an association between increases in suicide rates nationwide and a corresponding decline in church attendance (Matthews, McCullough, Larson, Koenig, Swyers & Milano, 1998). It has been found that the rate of church attendance within a given population predicted suicide rates more effectively than any other factor studied, including unemployment. Koenig and his colleagues (1994) examined the associations between religious factors and alcohol abuse among 3,000 North Carolinians aged 18 years and older and found that recent and lifetime alcohol disorders were less frequent among weekly churchgoers.

In a review of published studies Levin and Vanderpool (1987) found a beneficial effect of religious attendance on health status across an array of illnesses ranging from cancer to cardiovascular disease in 81 percent of the studies. In a study of five year mortality rates among adults in Washington County, Maryland to assess whether church attendance was related to longevity it was found that the risk of dying from arteriosclerotic heart disease for men who attended church at least once a week was 60 percent less than the risk of men who attended church infrequently. For women, the risk of dying from arteriosclerotic heart disease was twice as high among infrequent church attenders than among once a week attenders (Comstock & Partridge, 1972). Other studies have shown that spirituality may be beneficial to one's health. People who attend religious services or who feel they are spiritual have lower levels of depression and anxiety, show signs of better health, such as lower blood pressure and fewer strokes, and say they feel healthier. Explanations for these findings might be that the people who attend religious services benefit from the social networks they form. It's also known that religious belief leads to less risky behavior such as less alcohol consumption and smoking. And, religious beliefs, or a strong sense of spirituality, may improve an individual's ability to cope with the stresses of everyday life.

Certain personality types ("hardy personalities") cope better with life, and these are the types of people who attend services regularly. Harry R. Moody (1997) a gerontologist and co-author of *The Five Stages of the Soul*, said the message is not "go back to church and you will live a long time," but rather "stay connected with people on your own wavelength."

Faith, Coping, and Emotions

There is substantial evidence indicating that optimistic people are better able to overcome defeat and are more likely to be successful, happier, healthier, and recover from illness faster than pessimists. And, persons from fundamentalist Christian churches have been found to be more optimistic than persons from liberal religious traditions (Sethi & Seligman, 1994). There is also a connection between faith and happiness. Persons with strong religious ties tend to be happier and more satisfied in life than those who do not have religious ties (Riekse & Holstege, 1996).

National surveys have found that 78 percent of those sampled agree that "religion provides personal comfort and support." This percentage rises to 90 percent among older adults. Half of the sample said that religion helps them in coping with physical illness. Koenig (1999) reviewed 100 published studies, 79 percent of which reported a significant positive association between religious involvement and greater well-being. Ten of these were prospective studies that found that religious beliefs or activity predicted greater well-being over time. Religion, therefore, provides a foundation or resource to use when coping with problems whatever their duration. Bergin (1991) said that, in many ways, religion is like psychotherapy. It can promote personal healing or transformation.

Koenig and his colleagues (1992) studied the level and effectiveness of religious coping among 850 men over age 65 who had medical diagnoses of cancer and gastrointestinal, neurological, respiratory, renal, and cardiac diseases. When the men were asked about how they coped with their physical illness or disability, 20 percent replied that religion was their primary method of coping. This involved trusting in God, praying, reading scripture or inspirational literature, attending church services, listening to religious programs, and visits from clergy or members of their congregation. Analysis of the data showed that the more a patient relied on religion, the lower his level of depressive symptoms. The benefit of religion appeared to be strongest among the men who were the most severely disabled. The religious patients told the researchers that their strong personal belief and faith in God and their relationships to their church congregations gave them comfort and peace. In examining the patient's responses by denomination, the researchers discovered that members of conservative, black, or fundamentalist/evangelical Protestant churches appeared to use religion the most in helping them cope with their health problems. The men who relied on religious coping also reported high levels of social contact, which suggests that they had strong social support networks. Most of the men's close friends were from their churches. What is most striking, however, is that Koenig and his colleagues could predict a 70 percent greater remission of depression and less suicide among the religious patients. In addition, they found that religious interventions were more effective in reducing anxiety among the patients than either secular treatment or no treatment at all.

Religiously involved people report greater social support than do the religiously uninvolved. Support from religious sources is more resilient and satisfying than support from secular sources, especially for older persons with declining health. Indeed, a deep inner faith characterized by a close personal relationship with God ("intrinsic religiosity") has been found to be directly related to the morale and life satisfaction of elderly people irrespective of their physical health, social support from their religious community, or their financial status (Koenig, Kvale, & Ferrel, 1988).

Prayer Connections

The possibility that prayer for others can promote health or healing has been studied. One of the most well known studies of absent prayer was conducted by Byrd (1988). He designed a randomized, double blind study of 393 adults in a coronary care unit. More of the patients who were prayed for by Christian prayer groups outside the hospital recovered uneventfully than patients who did not receive prayer. Patients were randomly assigned to treatment and control groups so that neither patients nor staff knew who was in which group, and patients and pray-ers never met.

Patients in the treatment group were assigned from three to seven intercessors who were given only their assignees' first name, diagnosis, and general condition. Treatment consisted of daily prayer until the patient was discharged from the hospital. Prayed-for patients, in comparison with the control groups, had fewer cases of congestive heart failure, cardiopulmonary arrest, and pneumonia, and less need for diuretics, antibiotics, and intubations. Byrd concluded that intercessory prayer has a beneficial therapeutic effect in patients admitted to a coronary care unit. Other researchers are attempting to replicate this study.

Researchers studying absent prayer or distant spiritual intercession state that effects on healing have little to do with the religious background or ideology of the pray-er or healer (Dossey, 1993). Psychologists Duckro and Magaletta (1994) reviewed evidence linking prayer to health and healing and concluded that, despite design limitations, studies on this question suggest a real connection. Levin (2001) is more cautious, stating that linking prayer to healing in humans is not as conclusive as the link between religion and health. It is impossible to *prove* that prayer heals as even the results of sound experiments will not be accepted by some scientists and physicians no matter the type and extensiveness of the data.[5]

RELIGIOUS GROUPS, SPIRITUAL CAPITAL, AND FORGIVENESS

Many authors attribute our social problems to people unwilling or unable to forgive others, such as revenge killings, community and domestic violence, child abuse, alcoholism, and the consequences of repressed anger. Forgiveness is a process of pardoning and making amends to aggrieved persons, overcoming feelings of anger and guilt, quelling impulses for revenge, and being able to re-establish effective relationships. Forgiveness does not just happen, but is produced by people who mobilize and expend resources to promote it. It takes social connections to create a climate for forgiveness to be practiced, not only once, but repeatedly by favorable attitudes about forgiveness.

A nationally representative survey was conducted of adult Americans who were currently involved in prayer groups, Bible studies, or other religiously oriented small groups (Wuthnow, 2000). The purpose of the study was to determine if these respondents had engaged in forgiving behavior as a result of being in their group and, if so, to ascertain which group activities were most likely to facilitate this behavior. Of the 1,379 participants, 61 percent said that their group had helped them to forgive someone, 71 percent said that they had experienced healings of relationships as a result of their group, and 43 percent said they had worked on improving a broken relationship in recent months. Further analysis suggested that forgiving behavior is especially facilitated by groups that emphasize prayer, share problems, and learn about forgiveness.

The study did not find that a single religious activity facilitated forgiveness, rather forgiveness happens when people experience a variety of social interactions and reinforcements. It is the spiritual capital that religious groups generate that affects the likelihood of forgiveness, rather than just getting together socially to eat, party, or talk. The religious content of groups appears to give people a language in which to think about forgiveness, and sharing personal problems generates an emotional climate in which relationships needing forgiveness can be explored. Since forgiveness is not an objective form of behavior that can be easily identified by an observer, the evidence that forgiveness has taken place involves the perceptions of group members, attitudes toward another person or toward oneself, and an actual change in the behavioral aspects of the relationship (Wuthnow, 2000).

RELIGIOUS COMMUNITIES AND HEALTH

Snowdon (2001) had a unique opportunity to study aging and Alzheimer's disease in a community of Catholic nuns between 75 and 106 years of age. The stable and consistent environment and the similar lifestyles of the nuns made it possible to reduce confounding variables. The availability of personal historical records, participation in regular mental and physical evaluations, and the donations of their brains for autopsy made this a powerful longitudinal study. Researchers know that the longer a person lives, the more likely he or she will develop the symptoms of Alzheimer's disease. But we also know that about 55 percent of people who live to be 85 or older do not develop symptomatic Alzheimer's disease. The autopsied brains of nine centenarians in the nun's study showed that the progression of Alzheimer's pathology increases with age, then hits a plateau, and declines. The study's most striking finding is that Alzheimer's disease is not an inevitable consequence of aging.

Snowdon obtained the early life autobiographies of 74 sisters who had brain autopsies by 2001 and found that the power of "idea density" in predicting Alzheimer's disease was about 80 percent (Snowdon, Kemper, Martinez, Greiner & Wekstein, 1996). Idea density reflects language processing ability, which in turn is associated with a person's level of education, general knowledge, vocabulary, and reading comprehension. Idea density was assessed among the nuns by a psycholinguist who read the nun's autobiographies, which they wrote on entry to the convent decades earlier. Autobiographies that were more grammatically complex were judged to have higher idea density. High idea density seemed to be a protective factor against Alzheimer's disease. Snowdon speculated that low idea density early in life may indicate that the brain was already compromised in some way. The level of idea density was strongly related to scores on cognitive tests, but not related to verbal and analytic intelligence. Idea density may be related to other properties of the brain, such as those of perception, encoding, and memory retrieval. Other investigators have found the incidence of Alzheimer's disease to be thirty times less among the well educated than it is among the poorly educated (Mark & Mark, 1999).

Snowdon also observed two factors which could not be quantitatively tested by the data, but he regarded these as important to longevity. The first factor is the profound faith and positive outlook that these women shared. The power of community is the second factor. The sisters benefited from a constant network of support and love. Snowdon (2001) commented "the community not only stimulated their minds, celebrated their accomplishments, shared their aspirations, but also encouraged silence, understood defeat, and nurtured each other when their bodies failed." The risk of death in any given year after age 65 is about 25 percent lower for the sisters than it is for the general population of women in the United States. It appears that the people who make it through their nineties without developing Alzheimer's disease are at a lower risk than people in their eighties. What is unique in this study, and potentially enormously important, is the ability to link findings at autopsy with autobiographical data collected numerous decades before. As more nuns die and their brains are autopsied, the strength of these links will become more firmly established.

Certainly, one could argue that nuns live relatively healthy and stress-free lives, so physical factors could be responsible for prolonging life and maintaining mental sharpness. Snowdon thinks the effect of social support is a life force in the nun's longevity. When he first visited the order he noticed a friendship, understanding and tolerance that could only come from years of shared history. Snowdon quotes one nun, aged 95, as she recounted her 53-year teaching career. She said, "The older sisters took care of the younger ones. They lived together and spent time studying, preparing for classes, talking about their families, playing games and having fun. We were always together in community."

Kark and his associates (1996a) carried out a survey in five secular and five religious kibbutz (communes) in Israel. They found that residents of the religious kibbutz had a higher sense of coherence than residents of secular kibbutz, although there was no difference in social support or frequency of social contacts in the two settings. They concluded that membership in a cohesive religious kibbutz community may increase host resistance to stressors and thereby promote overall well-being and positive health status. In a larger, 16 year longitudinal cohort study of mortality, Kark and his colleagues (1996b) matched eleven secular kibbutz with eleven religious kibbutz. Even after eliminating social support as a possible confounding variable they found that people residing in religious kibbutz lived longer than those in secular kibbutz. There were only ten divorces over 15 years in 17 of the kibbutz, reflecting the stability of family life in both secular and religious kibbutz.

The socially isolated Old Order Amish of Pennsylvania have persisted despite predictions in the 1920s that they would disappear. The Amish use sacrifice as one of the mechanisms by which each member becomes invested in the community. Amish are required to give up most worldly luxuries and adopt uniform styles of grooming, uncut hair, and the banning of electricity, telephones, and cars. Their equipment for farming also excludes tractors and electric machines. They discourage relationships with non-group members and renounce relationships that are potentially disruptive to the community. Common life experiences, communal sharing of property, regular group contact and rituals help bind the group together and increase loyalties. The Amish meet weekly for church services, but religion is inseparable from other aspects of life. Religion permeates the classroom by reading the scriptures, singing hymns and praying. However, religion is personal; the Amish have no churches but instead hold religious services in a family's home. These three hour services are followed by lunch and socializing (Kraybill, 1997; Hostetler, 1997).

The longevity of the Amish is a challenge to medical researchers who are looking for a longevity gene and clues to age-related diseases such as diabetes. The Amish are ideal for these studies because they are a genet- ically homogeneous population. It is easier to find genetic mutations in populations that are genetically similar. And, the Amish have a homoge- neous lifestyle including diet and physical exercise. The high degree of social support and spirituality is an equally important factor contribut- ing to longevity and good health, but has not received the same level of investigative attention as medical factors.

While Seventh-day Adventists are not unique because of the social or- ganization of their community as are convents or kibbutz, they are unique because of their philosophy of health and spirituality. The emphasis of the church is on a strong concern for the prevention of disease and the maintenance of good health. Personal health habits are an observable as- pect of the life of Seventh-day Adventists: most abstain from the use of alcohol, tobacco and drugs. The Old Testament prohibition against the use of unclean meats is strictly followed, and many Adventists are vegetari- ans. Studies of Adventists show that the risk of death from lung cancer, bronchitis, emphysema, coronary heart disease, cancer, diabetes, and traf- fic accidents is lower than for persons of corresponding age and gender in the general population of the United States. Life expectancy at age 35 for Adventists has been found to be six to seven years greater than for the general population. The longevity of Adventists is strongly related to the differences in personal health habits. The church supports community pro- grams concerned with smoking, diet, weight control, physical fitness, and other health-related services. These are linked with the evangelic mission of the church.

RELIGION AND DISEASE PREVENTION

One of the key reasons why religion and longevity are related is that religious people are more inclined to promote their health, seek health care early, and therefore, prevent the onset or progression of disease. Re- ligious persons are less likely to smoke, abuse alcohol, use illicit drugs, engage in risky sexual activities, drink while driving, and forget to wear seat belts. Some religious groups eat healthier diets and exercise more than the general population. When religious people seek health care they are more compliant with medical advice (Koenig, McCullough & Larson, 2001). There are several reasons why religion might influence medical com- pliance. Religion influences beliefs about the illness. Religious beliefs and practices help people to cope better with physical disease and disability. Religious persons have larger and more satisfying support networks than non-religious people. Religious people may be more likely to follow advice because of their general attitude toward compliance. Religious people tend to be low risk takers and are less likely to disagree with what is prescribed. They tend to follow rules, especially those from experts.

Religion should increase medical compliance as religiousness is associated with lower rates of depression, greater hope, more stable families, and large non-family support groups. High levels of religiousness or spirituality, regardless of religious affiliation, appear to be related to better compliance.

FAITH-BASED COMMUNITIES AND ORGANIZATIONS

During the 2000 presidential campaign, George W. Bush proposed a faith-based approach to government's role in helping those in need. Faith-based initiatives are not new in the United States, dating back to the early days of this country's founding, nor are faith-based interventions unique to the United States. The President's plan allows faith-based groups to bid for federal dollars on an equal footing with other organizations. Bush noted that faith is often essential to spark a personal transformation and to keep people from falling back to addiction, delinquency, or dependence. Religious congregations stand out as the most viable institution to create the social capital necessary to improve many of our current social problems. The 350,000 congregations in the United States are the largest source of financial and human resources for faith-based social service programs (Bane, Coffin & Thiemann, 2000). Religious participation accounts for roughly half of America's stock of social capital. Despite a significant decline in church attendance since the 1960s, about 40 percent of Americans still attend weekly worship services and almost 70 percent claim church membership. In many poor communities, churches are often the only social institution left with any degree of vitality. Inner-city churches, like their suburban counterparts, play the largest role in structuring community life. Religious institutions embody strong traditions through which people can learn and express the value of community, as well as the obligations members have towards each other.[7] Religion can also offer a moral vision for political action. What faith-based initiatives need is a broad basis for political participation, not approaches that are rooted in the narrow politics of religious teachings on controversial social issues (Warren, 2001).

According to Sherman (2003) the best data we have concerning the community outreach activities of religious congregations comes from the Hartford Seminary Faith Communities Today survey (http://www.fact.hartsem.edu). This survey examined 14,000 congregations of diverse faiths. The survey found that 85 percent of these congregations provided at least one community service. Most common were relief/benevolence activities, providing food, money, clothing or emergency shelter. But over half of the congregations were involved in more extensive services including providing health care services, one-third were involved in tutoring children, ministering in prisons, offering substance abuse programs, or providing housing for the elderly.

Faith-based organizations offer several distinctive contributions for social welfare programs. First, they appeal to common community bonds. People are more inclined to support programs "for their own kind" and programs that address local problems. People want to see visible pay offs for their dollars and time. Second, faith-based organizations have the ability to address problems of poverty of body and soul (Wuthnow & Evans, 2002). Too often churches focus on either of two extremes, they provide basic necessities of life without providing appropriate intervention and support for spiritual needs, or they become so concerned with fixing the blame for the poverty of soul that they postpone helping people with their immediate physical needs. Third, faith-based organizations provide a basic framework of meaning. As Bane, Coffin & Thiemann (2000) have expressed it, feeding the poor is not only a simple act of charity, rather this, and other acts, help define a community's identity. Acts of compassion, justice, and sharing are religious obligations, but they are also commitments of service to others, irrespective of the source of funding.

Three of the concerns raised about the long-term viability of faith-based organizations are: 1) they must retain the responsibility to be communities of dissent should they become at odds with larger society or government policies. If faith-based organizations become little more than an extension of government policies, then their authority will be compromised; 2) they must have clear and realistic limits to which they can meet the needs of the poor and disenfranchised. While faith-based organizations are likely to grow, their resources are limited. It has been suggested that faith-based organizations can best serve communities by providing special services not available from other sources; and 3) they must develop strong leaders who are embedded in the community and who have the ability to develop cooperative initiatives that bring people together across the lines of class and race, that often separate communities (Warren, 2001; Glenn, 2000).

Are Faith-Based Organizations Effective and Cost Efficient?

There is anecdotal evidence (Wallis, 2001) and some empirical evidence that faith-based programs are effective. Sherman (2003) described the positive results of Teen Challenge, a drug rehabilitation program, recidivism among prisoners who participated in prison fellowship Bible studies, and a program to reduce deviance among black inner-city youth as examples of effective programs.

Sherman pointed out that anecdotal and descriptive evidence of the effectiveness of intervention programs usually make social scientists skeptical because of the absence of "hard, objective data." Nonetheless, client interviews and the observations of outside observers have indicated that faith-based programs are effective because: 1) they rely on volunteers; 2) they are holistic and meet wide-ranging needs; 3) clients who participate in these programs come to look at themselves in a new way; 4) faith-based programs "are there"—they have a presence in the community; and 5) participants in religiously affiliated initiatives are often introduced to a faith that changed their lives for the better.

There are criticisms of the government's lack of accountability for faith-based funds. Barr (2001) pointed out that, according to an Office of Management and Budget survey, despite the billions of dollars that have been distributed in discretionary and formula grants over the past five years, fewer than one in five of the programs have received a General Accounting Office or Agency Inspector General's review to analyze actual performance and results. Virtually none of the programs has ever been subjected to a systematic evaluation of their performance that meets rigorous evaluation research standards. Barr stated that these federal programs may be doing significant good; and the grantees that win renewed support may be the best available. However, in the absence of meaningful performance reviews, agencies have no concrete evidence for concluding so. Some critics of the expanded federal collaboration with faith-based and community-based organizations complain that there is little proof that these organizations are effective or have the capacity to manage large-scale social service programs.

SUMMARY

Religion is an important source of social capital. People of like-minded faith come together to form social networks that create interest in each other's welfare and provide an ongoing resource for social support and trusting relationships. Religion in the United States has been undergoing substantial change. Most of the boomer generation grew up not connected with a religious denomination so they have no experience with the earlier strong denominational tradition in the United States. Almost 40 percent of Americans have no connection with organized religion. New nondenominational churches are growing in number and size, while membership in mainline Protestant churches is declining. Pastors of growing churches say that most of their new members are from unchurched backgrounds or are former members of mainline denominations burned out from dogma and traditionalism. Religion is not the only social institution experiencing a decrease in social capital and disconnectedness. Civic malaise and weakening community bonds has been increasing in the United States since the 1960s.

Religion is being transformed by a spirituality that is more focused, specialized, and tailored to meet individual needs. There is also a trend toward a broader spirituality that can be experienced without organized religion. Terrorism, for example, has shown the world that we are all interconnected and dependent upon each other as inhabitants of the same planet. Another facet of religious transformation is the heterogeneity of programs and services that churches provide, or what has been called "multilayered belief and practice." Family members may come from different religious experiences and become involved in activities in several different churches to meet the different needs of family members. As the traditional boundaries of religion are being redrawn people feel only loosely connected to, or even alienated from, social institutions and are seeking other ways to meet their needs.

Churches have become specialists in offering a variety of age and gender appropriate programs. There is still the expectation by parents that the church should be responsible for teaching moral values to their children, but youth directors are often challenged in marketing programs exciting enough to counteract peer invitations to engage in nonchurch activities. Youth directors lament that after completing the ritual of confirmation almost half of the seventh and eighth graders disappear from church functions. As youth become more independent from parents, their choices more often exclude religious activities.

Religious beliefs and practices have a long tradition of association with health and healing practices. There is evidence that the frequency of church attendance is an important element in longevity and the risk for cancer and cardiovascular diseases. Frequent church attenders have lower mortality than infrequent attenders. One of the most salient findings about church attendance is that its benefits may extend years into the future. Religious participation and sharing a common purpose with others provides the protection of social support, which is a buffer against the harmful effects of stress and life changes. Studies have shown that spirituality is associated with lower levels of depression and anxiety and signs of better health. There is also evidence that people of faith are more optimistic and better able to cope with defeat and recover from illness faster than pessimists. Religion offers hope, support, encouragement, and through faith, characterized by a personal relationship with God, it improves morale and life satisfaction.

Researchers have studied the power of prayer and its correlation with healing. It is impossible to *prove* that prayer heals, as even the results of sound experiments are unacceptable to some scientists. There is evidence, however, that intercessory and absent prayer have beneficial effects on hospitalized patients.

Interesting studies of religious communities such as Catholic nuns, kibbutz, Seventh-day Adventists, Mormons, and Amish have shown low rates of chronic illness and greater longevity when compared to persons of corresponding age and gender in the general population. These communities are characterized by their high degree of social cohesion, common values, low risk-taking, and usually a strong orientation to positive personal health habits. Their philosophy of health and spirituality are linked and provide a concern for the prevention of disease and promotion of health and well-being.

Faith-based communities are a way of intervention to spark personal transformation and keep people from returning to addiction, delinquency or dependency. Faith-based communities are not new or unique to the United States, but they have been given the opportunity to obtain government funds under the George W. Bush administration to expand their work. Faith-based organizations offer several contributions for social welfare programs. They appeal to common community bonds to address local problems. They have the ability to address problems of both body and soul. And, they help define a community's identity through acts of compassion, justice, and sharing. The recent renewal of faith-based organizations has not enabled their programs to be rigorously evaluated to know of their long-term impact. However, short-term anecdotal evidence and some empirical evidence have shown that faith-based interventions are effective in changing lives for the better.

QUESTIONS FOR DISCUSSION

1. What are some of the criteria you would use in evaluating the effectiveness of faith-based community programs?
2. What are some of the alternatives that are being used by the Internet generation to take the place of church membership and organized religion?
3. What are the responsibilities of organized religion to individuals and families in the 21st century?

4. Discuss how you might design a study to test the hypothesis "there is a direct positive relationship between prayer and a person's health status."
5. What do you see as the possible effects of the continuing growth of non-Christian faith communities on the future of influential organizations such as the National and World Councils of Churches?
6. In your opinion, is there a "tipping point" at which ethnic and religious diversity can become a liability to a community?

Chapter 8

Vital Bonds

Social Support, Social Networks, and Health

INTRODUCTION

For some people it is so enmeshed in their daily lives that they take it for granted, others experience it when people rally around them in a crisis, and still others may never experience it at all. This tangible and intangible aspect of human behavior is called social support. The term "social support" is generally not used in everyday conversation, rather it is referred to as "she is always there when I need her," or "she is the only person I can trust and confide in," or "I get lots of help from my neighbors," or "he is someone I can always count on." Socially supportive behavior indicates that people have a reciprocal helping relationship, that they genuinely care about one another and that the needs of others equals or surpasses one's own needs.

We are born into social environments with different degrees of social support. We first encounter different experiences with social support in our early years in our family, and later in school with teachers and peers.[1] Events throughout our lifecycle challenge and change our personal attitudes and feelings about social support, and in turn, influence how supportive we are of others. Social support is not only an individual behavior, its attributes apply to groups, communities, and even nations. The characteristics of social support, that is, how important it is, the ways it is expressed, and the appropriate contexts for sharing it vary culturally. The main feature of social support is the acknowledgement that humans are social animals; people need other people throughout their lives to provide nourishment for their spirits, feedback and guidance to shape their behavior, safety to express their emotions and feelings, and hope and encouragement to overcome barriers and to excel. Social support is the fulcrum

187

that makes us secure in our interdependence and keeps us from moving toward greater dependence or isolation. Social contacts with others promote social integration by reducing tendencies toward self-centeredness, egoism, or isolation (Durkheim, 1897/1951).

Social support is what we experience when we form bonds, ties, or attachments to people and places. We form ties of different types and complexity (or density) for different reasons, at different points in our lives (Granovetter, 1973). It is through these networks of social support that we obtain resources to use in our daily lives. Not all of the networks we connect with are supportive, and not all provide the same kind of support. For example, the social ties that lonely people have are likely to be with other lonely people who do not expect social support from others nor provide social support for them (Samter, 1994). We connect more strongly with "personal networks" that meet our needs (Wellman & Wortley, 1990). By expressing and embedding our social identities in personal networks, we establish "personal communities" (Hirsch, 1981).

The kind of social networks we connect, or do not connect with, have been shown to be related to our health. Specifically, numerous studies have shown that socially isolated persons are less healthy and more likely to die prematurely.[2] Social ties have also been found to play a role in the maintenance of psychological well-being (Kawachi & Berkman, 2001). Furthermore, social connections provide a cushion when crises appear and contribute to individual's survival from various diseases. In this chapter, we examine the ways in which social support, through the medium of social networks, works to enhance the health and well-being of individuals, families and communities.

UNDERSTANDING SOCIAL SUPPORT

To many people showing social support to someone means giving them a pat on the back, a kind word, a note, card or e-mail, or a hug. A recipient might view these as gestures of kindness, but not as social support. A student told me how his dad responded in a family crisis:

> My stepmother was diagnosed with cancer a few years ago, and two weeks before she died my dad bought her an expensive sports car. I think he thought that buying the car would fill a void in her life before she died. The thing is she was never able to set foot in the car and he sold it right after she died. I think my dad wanted her to feel that he cared.

While some people might regard the gift of the car as an inappropriate way of expressing social support to a dying person, it may have been the only way the father knew to express his feelings. His machismo or denial of his wife's impending death may have inhibited him from giving her a hug or two and saying, "I love you," or asking her about any special wishes she had before she died. What is considered supportive and what is not is hidden in the expectations and perceptions of the giver and receiver. And these expectations and perceptions vary with our changing situations throughout the lifecycle. Perhaps the most useful definition of social support is that provided by Cohen & Syme (1985). They suggest that social support is defined as the resources provided by other persons. Pilisuk and Parks (1986) expand this definition by stating that the resources provided can be material and physical assistance, social contact, and emotional sharing along with the sense that the person is a continuing focus of concern by others.

Unraveling the meanings and origins of social support is not as important to us here as understanding the *effects* of social support. Social support usually has positive effects, however, it is possible that too much social support in closely-knit families and communities could be stifling or social support we receive from some people may be considered gratuitous, or social support may be more demanding and draining than nurturant. Most studies have found social support to be more salubrious than deleterious.

Social support is not a substitute for stress. We need stress *and* social support. Social support and stress become meaningful in their relationship to each other. The same stress is not assessed in the same way, nor does it have the same effects, on all individuals. When stress is negative (threatening, incapacitating) social support has been shown to buffer its effects. Social support is also not assessed in the same way, nor does it have the same effects, on all individuals. Social support has generally been considered unimportant until it is absent, while stress has been viewed as significant when it is present. Stress and social support each have the potential for generating positive or negative effects when they lose their homeostasis and their imbalance impedes individual functioning.

There is debate among some researchers in the behavioral sciences about whether: social support is a personal experience based on perceptions, social support is a set of objective circumstances, or a set of interactional processes (Turner, Frankel, & Levin, 1983). I believe that how circumstances or events are *perceived* activate different interpersonal processes that lead to different outcomes regarding social support. For example, a student was frequently absent or late for class. When her professor asked for an explanation, she said that she had an infant and that she depended upon her boyfriend to stay home with the infant so that she could attend the evening class. Her boyfriend, who was the father of the child, assisted minimally in childcare and homemaking chores, and was not supportive of his girlfriend completing a college education. The student and her boyfriend perceived the circumstances differently; the student needed social support, the boyfriend gave minimal support reluctantly and sporadically. When the student stayed home her boyfriend was pleased and she was angry. When the student attended class their emotions were reversed.

Another student who was also frequently absent or late for class related that she was a single mother. She had to take her infant son from a day care facility to her mother's house after she left work in order for her to attend class. This required that the student drive an extra 15 miles after work to the day care center to retrieve the child and then take him to her mother's house. The student's mother did not understand why the student wanted to continue to take courses under these stressful conditions, yet the grandmother was delighted to care for her grandson anytime. During times when the infant was tired and irritable the grandmother scolded her daughter about continuing to create unnecessary stress, which angered the daughter and created feelings of guilt. No one in the family had attended college so the student had no support from others to encourage her to continue. So she dropped her courses.

It would seem relatively simple to offer alternative solutions to these two scenarios by focusing on the objective circumstances and/or the interpersonal transactions that occurred between the people involved. Social support is about relationships, but relationships occur within larger contexts of culture. Expectations and perceptions about social support are shaped by culture. In these two scenarios both students were Hispanic females. In Hispanic culture it is not widely accepted that females attend college, especially if they have to subjugate their role as a mother to that of being a student. Alternative care providers outside the family were not an option for the two student mothers because of their financial circumstances. They perceived that delaying taking courses toward completing their baccalaureate degrees to when their children would be older and less dependent on them was unacceptable. Furthermore, while some social support was helpful in coping with the immediate circumstances of childcare, much more support was needed to help them deal with their total life situation. For example, the student in the first scenario had a history of bulimia and experienced continuous ridicule from family members and her boyfriend about being overweight. Her response to stress was to eat. Her attempts at therapy failed repeatedly. Her dissatisfaction with her boyfriend's lack of interest in fathering and his continuing challenges to her educational dreams, kept her poor self-image, feelings of guilt, and anger alive. She recognized that her need for support required more time and finances than she could afford, therefore she stopped asking for help and continued her bulimia.

In the second scenario the student's decision to drop out of school could be considered a good solution to her situation. However, at work she witnessed the promotion of her friends after they completed their baccalaureate degrees and their advancement was a daily reminder of her unfulfilled goal. As a single mother the increased costs of living exceeded her income, and receiving no child support, she was forced to move in with her parents. Her other brothers and sisters were married, had families, were self-sufficient, and while being verbally supportive, could offer no financial help for her situation. She considered her situation embarrassing and, to avoid explaining it, she withdrew from most of her friends.

These examples illustrate the importance of building and maintaining networks of social support. Some resources in a support network may be used more than others, but without a variety of available supportive resources, a person can find themselves in the dilemma of the two students. They attempted to overcome a barrier to satisfy a need and called upon resources they thought would be supportive, but instead the resources became a source of stress themselves, and they had few, if any, options other than to suspend their plans for completing a baccalaureate degree.

SOCIAL SUPPORT AND SOCIAL NETWORKS

People affect their society through personal influences on those around them. We construct our own personal networks and join others as opportunities arise. We tend to build networks composed of others like ourselves and associate with people like ourselves (Fischer, 1982). Jeremy Boissevain (1974), an anthropologist, who has studied social networks, said that people have both intimate and extended types of relationships. He conceptualized relationships as a series of six concentric circles or zones extending outward from a core that he called "the individual." The circle closest to the individual he called a "personal zone," which was the family. The next two circles were "intimate zones" comprised of close relatives and friends. The fifth circle was the "nominal zone" made up of people who are acquaintances. Finally, the circle the farthest from the individual was the "extended zone" composed of people who were only recognizable faces. The circles each have connections to different networks of people who can be accessed for different purposes. These networks continually change as people drop-out, divorce, die, relocate, or choose to become disconnected. New people are continually added to broaden our zones of relationships that we acquire through family, relatives, close friends, acquaintances at work, through marriage, neighbors, church, clubs and organizations, leisure activities, hobby groups, and volunteering.

The major point related to social networks is that we can choose to make connections of different intensities ranging from intimacy and intense involvement to aloofness and detachment. Our social networks provide the mechanism by which we obtain social support from others when we need it. Sometimes just knowing that support is available is sufficient. Other times we need to ask for help. Social networks are like cushions of different sizes and composition. We have networks we use for general purposes and networks that are specialized. Research has shown that people who have extensive networks (both general and specialized) also have extensive sources of social support. Another way of expressing this is that people who are well integrated or networked into their communities have a ready reserve of sources of social support. Networks create and mediate social support and social support can, in turn, strengthen and expand social networks.

SOCIAL SUPPORT, SOCIAL NETWORKS, AND HEALTH

Almost 30 years ago, epidemiologists who were interested in how social conditions might influence health status developed the idea that one of the most fundamental conditions that protect people from becoming overwhelmed or immobilized by crises is their close, personal relationships with others. Hammer (1983) has referred to close relationships as "core" relationships. Core relationships are, in turn, sustained by additional "extended" relationships that help individuals to become socially integrated into their communities, and thereby have access to numerous resources when they need them (Berkman, 2000). Social support and social networks work to affect individual health in two ways: 1) they can enhance health and reduce mortality, and 2) when illness strikes, they can ameliorate its effects.

Enhancing Health and Reducing Mortality

A closely-knit family is one of the most significant influences on health behavior. A wide variety of behaviors are a part of health maintenance and enhancement. Studies have shown that everyday health behaviors such as physical exercise are easier to sustain when other household members support the behaviors through encouragement or mutual participation (Geertsen, 1997). Husband-wife households tend to engage in healthier behaviors. For example, married persons are less likely to be smokers and heavy drinkers. Marital status also predicts mortality. A marital partner has a positive influence on mortality for young people, while friends and relatives have a greater positive impact on mortality for those over age 60. Widowed, separated, and divorced women have been found to be greater users of health services regardless of the severity of symptoms compared to married women. And, the unmarried who use health services attribute their symptoms to psychological factors more often than married users.

Phyllis Moen and her associates (1989) found that social integration, defined by the number of roles occupied, promotes longevity, and one form of integration, membership in voluntary associations, is especially salutary for women. The authors point out that being involved in multiple roles accomplishes more than just preventing social isolation. They speculate that the effect of multiple roles could reflect the value of a diverse social network in promoting health-related behavior. Wives and mothers with few roles beyond the family may be more vulnerable to risk factors or more exposed to unhealthy lifestyles than those who are more socially integrated.

Indeed, the degree to which individuals are involved in associations can influence how they perceive their own health. Mossey & Shapiro (1982) found that people who volunteered once a week were ten times more likely to rate themselves as healthy than people their age who volunteered only once a year.[3] The authors suggested that raising a person's perceived health status leads to positive emotions that can reduce stress and create real improvements in one's health.

There is evidence that household members engage in similar health behaviors, for example, the influence of mothers on their children's health behaviors. There is some indication that more cohesive families make less use of maternity and pediatric services. Children from families experiencing conflict have been found to have a higher volume of health care. The household influence on health behavior is shaped by daily interaction and social support. Social ties through relatives and friends connect families to sources of influence outside the home. Studies show correlations between the use of health services and social involvement with relatives and friends. Social contacts seem to be more important for the young, while social support has greater importance for the elderly. Belonging to organizations has been linked to lower mortality risks for women, less frequent smoking and drinking, and greater seat belt use. Religious participation also is linked to the use of health services. Highly religious elderly make more visits to doctors and highly religious mothers have higher utilization rates for pediatric care. The most consistent findings are for Jews, who have more physician visits than any other religious group. They are more likely to participate in screening exams and to travel long distances for care. These findings indicate that religious group culture can influence health behavior.

There have been three key studies that indicate that social support and social networks are associated with mortality risk (Berkman & Syme, 1979; Berkman, 1985). One of these is an analysis of nine-year mortality data from 6,928 adult residents of Alameda County, California. Information on several aspects of an individual's personal network was collected. A Social Network Index was developed based on four types of social connections: 1) marriage; 2) contacts with extended family and close friends; 3) church group membership, and 4) other group affiliations. Contacts with friends and relatives were measured by the number of close friends and relatives an individual reported and the frequency with which he/she saw them. Correlation of mortality rates from all causes in relation to the Index showed a consistent pattern of increased mortality associated with each decrease in social connection. When the Index was examined in relation to separate causes of death, people with few connections were found to be at increased risk of dying from heart disease, cancer, cerebrovascular and circulatory disease, and all other causes of death. The relationship of the Index to increased mortality held independent of physical health status, socioeconomic status, level of physical activity, smoking, alcohol consumption, obesity, race, life satisfaction, and the use of preventive health services.

A second community study of mortality risk was conducted in Tecumseh, Michigan of 2,754 men and women who were medically examined and interviewed and then followed for 10 years. This study used four general measures of social relationships and activities, 1) intimate social relationships (marital status, visits with family and relatives, and going on pleasure drives and picnics); 2) formal organizational involvements outside of work (going to church, meetings, and voluntary associations); 3) active and relatively social leisure activities (going to classes, museums, movies); and 4) passive and relatively solitary leisure activities (watching TV, reading, listening to the radio). Of the components of social relationships those that were significantly related to mortality among men were: marital status, attendance at voluntary associations, spectator events, and classes and lectures. For women, only church attendance was significant. Frequency of visits with friends and relatives and going out on pleasure drives and picnics were not significant for men or women (House, Robbins & Metzner, 1982).

A third study of mortality risk was carried out in Durham County, North Carolina in 331 men and women 65 years of age and older. Eleven items of social support were included in this survey. The items were divided into three dimensions: 1) roles and attachments available; 2) frequency of interaction (phone calls and visits with friends and relatives); and 3) perception of social support (lonely even with people, someone cares what happens to you, difficulty speaking to new people). The item with the highest predictive value was *perceived* social support.

Each of the three studies used different methods of assessing social support and social networks. As a consequence each study found that different aspects or dimensions of social support predicted mortality. In Alameda County it was contacts with friends and relatives. In Tecumseh it was marital status and involvement in associations and/or church. In Durham the item that was the strongest predictor of mortality was the subjective appraisal or perception of the adequacy of support. Ideally, if all three studies had used the same measures of social support we could make a stronger and more accurate statement about which or what kind of indicators of social support are the most consistent and valid predictors of mortality. We can conclude, however, that deficiencies in social support predict increased risk of mortality.

Ameliorating the Effects of Illness

Cohen and his colleagues (1985) found that social networks have a direct effect on reducing physical symptoms. The greatest symptom-reducing effects were found to occur among individuals experiencing high degrees of stress. The authors concluded that intervention to reinforce a network can be as clinically significant as implementing a medical procedure.

Supportive social relationships are thought to help people cope with their illness. A major explanation for why close relationships are beneficial is that: 1) other people are sensitive to the situation of the ill person and respond by providing support; and 2) the support that others provide meets the needs of the ill person and is therefore effective in reducing problems and stress associated with the illness. In a prospective study of men and women over age 65 who were hospitalized for a heart attack it was found that the degree of emotional support available was a predictor of death in the hospital and following discharge. By the end of the first year following discharge the percentage of patients with a cardiac cause of death was 45 percent among those persons with no sources of social support, 27 percent among those who had one source of support, and 19 percent among those with two or more sources of support (Berkman, Leo-Summers & Horowitz, 1992).

People with major psychiatric illness such as schizophrenia or serious depression have social networks that differ from the general population, and even from those individuals with less severe neurotic problems (Pilisuk & Parks, 1986). The psychotic person typically has a small primary network of four or five family members with nonexistent friendship ties. The ties among family members are often non-supportive and negative.

Psychotic individuals have few opportunities for reciprocal relationships. People with less severe mental disorders often have large social networks, but they tend to be negative, unconnected, and non-reciprocal (Gottlieb, 1981). Additionally, social marginality frequently characterizes the victims of suicide, alcoholism, and multiple accidents (Pilisuk & Parks, 1986).

Studies of social networks among clients from different mental health service units (outpatient, day treatment, and full-time residential treatment) and of residents of a single-room occupancy hotel, reached the same conclusion. An individual's degree of psychiatric disability was related to network size and the specific characteristics of the network. More disturbed individuals had fewer complex relationships with others and fewer reciprocal relationships. Indeed, some mentally ill persons establish a pseudo-community in which delusions and hallucinations provide a self-perpetuating and verifiable network. These studies do not tell us whether deficiencies in social networks came before or after the symptoms of mental illness. However, the major goal of mental health services is to connect the mentally ill to healthy supportive social relationships as part of their rehabilitation.

While the mentally ill tend not to have close and intense networks, potential drug users seek out networks of individuals who share their values about drugs and their use. Adolescents who are disenfranchised from their families and feel socially isolated are more likely to gravitate toward friends in a similar situation. The more these teenagers are removed from the influence of conventional norms, the greater the likelihood they are to engage in activities to gain status and acceptance. These include alcohol consumption, marijuana use, use of hard drugs, and some delinquent activity such as shoplifting. As Johnson (1973) explains, if one has marijuana-using friends, one tends to use marijuana; if one does not have marijuana-using friends, one tends not to use marijuana. Marijuana use is an index or measure of involvement in the social network; the more involved in the network the more a person will become influenced by its values and engaged in its activities. This selective interaction pattern of drug use continues with the use of cocaine and ecstasy in the late teens and college years with what Kandel (1992) has referred to as "drug sequencing." The challenge in the rehabilitation of drug abusers is quite ominous—to change individuals' values and assist them in the selection of personal networks to match these values.

Social Support and Recovery from Illness

Social support appears to be a salient factor for patients with heart disease in maintaining compliance with their rehabilitation programs.

Patients who receive support from family and friends are more likely than others to comply with risk factor modification and post-coronary rehabilitation programs. Lack of social support increases the risk of death once heart disease has become manifest. The relationship between mortality from heart disease and social isolation (or low social support) has been documented in men and women after ten and twenty years of follow-up. Men and women with few social networks have been found to have significantly increased mortality rates from all causes including heart disease. An especially increased mortality was found for men living alone and for men reporting low social participation and inadequate emotional support (Orth-Gomer, Rosengren & Wilhelmson, 1993; Brummett et al., 2001; Frasure-Smith et al., 2000).

Helgeson (1991) interviewed patients who had suffered a heart attack before their hospital discharge and at three, six, and twelve months following discharge. He found that the amount of disclosure to one's spouse was the greatest single predictor of recovery. Married patients who were less able to disclose to their spouse were more likely to have a difficult recovery compared to married patients who were more able to disclose to their spouse. Furthermore, chest pain was also predicted by less spouse disclosure.

It is not completely clear how social support influences recovery from illness. There are speculations that it may enhance a patient's motivation to adhere to difficult treatment regimens. Patients who receive support may develop greater self-confidence and feelings of autonomy. Social support might protect recovering patients by protecting them from the negative effects of stress by altering their mood. Although these and other mechanisms have been discussed in the literature, few studies have been designed to discriminate among the different effects of social support (Wortman & Conway, 1985).

Social Support for Caregivers

We know very little about how close relationships respond to stress. We do know, especially through the experience of hospice, that a strong network of social support is important in maintaining the physical and mental health of caregivers. Caregivers usually are intensely and single-mindedly focused on providing continuous care to their dying spouse or family member, sometimes neglecting or denying their own need for support. Events found most strongly related to caregivers' distress are not the tasks involved in providing daily care but witnessing the decline in functioning of a loved one and low levels of support they receive from others. Providing caregivers with a team of hospice professionals and volunteers to assist them in coping with an inescapable and usually chronically stress-ful situation enables caregivers to make their losses more psychologically tolerable (Hobfoll & Stephens, 1990).

Lyanne McGuire and her colleagues (2002) studied how social sup-port can blunt the effects of stress of caring for a spouse with Alzheimer's disease. She found that caregivers who had good social support had mea-surably stronger immune responses over time than those caregivers who had no such support.

SELF-HELP AND SUPPORT GROUPS

The self-help clearinghouse database lists 1,100 national and interna-tional model and online self-help support groups and networks for addic-tions, bereavement, health, mental health, disabilities, abuse, parenting, caregivers, and a host of stressful life situations. In addition, there are an unknown number of "self-help" connections through e-mail and in person throughout the world. There are also self-help groups for persons suffering from dual illnesses. Dual Recovery Anonymous offers groups for individu-als who have chemical dependencies and comorbid psychiatric disorders. Through networking a person can find someone with whom they can share their most specialized needs and hopefully elicit their understanding and support. There are guidelines for establishing self-help groups but their form can vary depending on the changing needs of members. Self-help groups attract people who wish to remain anonymous while exploring an issue or problem they share with others, who can leave and return as their needs dictate, who can seek help without the constraints of financial cost, and who have no obligations or responsibilities except to follow the rules of the group. These factors influence the degree of trust and disclosure experi-enced by group members individually and collectively. In addition groups can specialize by focusing on gender, age, ethnic, and religious related is-sues, by meeting in places that ensure more socioeconomic homogeneity, and by how they determine group leadership.

Heller and his associates (1990) stated that there is evidence that self-help groups are more attractive to middle-class persons because their mode of operation is more congruent with middle-class lifestyles. The same is true for professionally run support groups, as they attract motivated indi-viduals who are comfortable reaching out and sharing emotional experi-ences with similar others. On the other hand, investigators have reported that those same findings are attributes of support group failures. The great-est number of dropouts and the least infrequent group attendees came from those in the lower social classes and those with the greatest number of preexisting problems. These findings support reports of difficulty in involving low-income clients in either prevention or treatment activities (Heller, Price & Hogg, 1990). Wituk and his colleagues studied factors that contribute to the survival of self-help groups and found that low attendance was the major reason groups disbanded.

Marty Tousley (2003), an experienced grief counselor, believes that the appeal of self-help and support groups makes differences in social class unimportant. Using bereavement groups as an example, she explains that mourning is an interpersonal process in all social classes. When death occurs we feel a need to be with others who understand because their experiences are similar to our own, and we feel a need to tell our stories of loss. But most of us don't know how to grieve and we look to others to help us. Most of our exposure to death and dying takes place somewhere other than home, such as hospitals and nursing homes. We don't live near extended family and our neighbors and acquaintances don't know us well enough to know what we need or how to respond to us. The appeal of self-help and support groups is their availability and accessibility; they are even available on the Internet in the form of Web sites, chat rooms, discussion groups, grief forums, and message boards. Grieving individuals or individuals with other needs can compare experiences with others and get needed validation without having to leave home to go to a group.

The benefits of self-help groups include offering people a place to tell their stories, discuss their reactions and frustrations, discover new coping skills, be with and supported by other people, learn skills they may have forgotten, share information, resources, and learn about problem-solving techniques that work for others, be encouraged and inspired by seeing others cope, and perhaps acquire new friends and connections.

Support groups can be either led by members (self-help) or facilitated by a professional mental health counselor who themselves have experienced the topic of the group, understands group dynamics, and can address complicated issues that may arise, for example, intense anger or thoughts of suicide.

It is possible to evaluate the benefits of self-help and support groups by administering a questionnaire at time one and comparing the results with time two. Even simple post-group evaluations indicate the degree to which a group meeting has had an effect on them. In the case of on-line groups members can be explicit about how they are progressing and benefits they derive from a virtual support group.[4]

Partnerships between health professionals and some mutual aid groups have led to innovative service delivery arrangements that ensure comprehensive treatment for a variety of target populations. For example, the introduction of self-help groups in the health field has meant that patients recovering from heart ailments, mastectomies, and serious burns are not left on their own to deal with the psychosocial aftermath of their medical conditions. Persons diagnosed with chronic diseases such as multiple sclerosis, diabetes, and Hodgkin's disease are routinely referred by physicians to local chapters of self-help groups serving these patients; their relatives and caregivers are also given access to family support groups. Support groups help to fill gaps in the continuum of care that patients require (Gottlieb, 1985).

SOCIAL SUPPORT AND COMMUNITY HEALTH

Social support cannot be easily quantified at the community level. What is valued as support can vary according to situations, groups of people, social contexts, and cultural values. Social support is also a phenomenon that is not absolute, but varies by degrees. The baseline of social support available in a community is closely linked to the nature of the relationship between the community's social institutions. A community with social institutions that work together is more cohesive than a community whose social institutions act independently and competitively. A high degree of social integration in a community has been found to be related to lower rates of psychiatric disorders. Collective ways of coping with the hazards of life (or stress) has been found to be beneficial in helping people deal with adversity (Corin, 1995). Corin has pointed out that culture frames how individuals perceive and react to real life circumstances. If a community's culture provides collective and positive ways for dealing with the disruptions of stress and change, for example, then individuals will benefit in similar ways. If a community's culture emphasizes a "go it alone" way of dealing with the hazards of life, one would expect a wide variation in individual reactions.

In Corin's research (1995) in six remote communities in Quebec she found that the underutilization of mental health services was associated with certain communities and for certain categories of people with the presence of a strong network of social support, and in other cases, with isolation or marginality that prevents contact with these services. On the one hand, high utilization of mental health services appeared to characterize the best socially supported people. However, the best supported people in a community may underutilize mental health services because they turn first to resources in the family, or clergy, or traditional healers, before they seek help from public sources. The traditions of a culture, therefore, define the context and appropriateness for using social support.

Wilkinson (1996) took the macro perspective when he asked, "Why are some societies healthier than others?" He speculated that factors that make some societies and communities healthier than others may be quite different from factors which distinguish healthy and unhealthy individuals within the same society. By taking a broad view of the determinants of health he proposed that we could learn about the interface between the individual and society and the effects of social structure and culture on health.

Wilkinson studied several healthy egalitarian societies in Britain, Eastern Europe, Japan, and the United States and found that they all shared social cohesion as a common characteristic. They had a strong community life. The individualism and values of the market were restrained by a social morality. People were more likely to be involved in social and voluntary activities outside the home. These societies had more social capital. There were fewer signs of anti-social aggressiveness, and these societies appeared to be caring. Wilkinson argued that the social fabric or social cohesiveness of a society is an important determinant of its quality of life, which in turn influences its health.

The Roseto Story: Culture as a Health Advantage

The discovery of the secrets of health and longevity in Roseto, Pennsylvania was largely serendipitous. In 1961 Dr. Stewart Wolf, Professor and Chair of the Department of Medicine at the University of Oklahoma Health Sciences Center, during a summer visit to his farm north of Easton, Pennsylvania, met Dr. Benjamin Falcone, a physician who had been practicing for 17 years in the nearby town of Roseto, Pennsylvania. Wolf was engaged in studies of coronary heart disease in Oklahoma City at the time so the conversation turned to that subject. Falcone said that he had observed that coronary heart disease was uncommon among Rosetans compared to the inhabitants of the adjacent town of Bangor. Roseto was exclusively Italian-American and Bangor was primarily English and Welsh with some Italian-Americans. It was the Wolf-Falcone conversation that aroused interest in Roseto and led to its study beginning in 1961–1962 for the next 30 years (Bruhn & Wolf, 1979; Wolf & Bruhn, 1993).

Wolf's first step was to obtain individual death certificates from the Pennsylvania State Department of Health for Roseto and four other neighboring communities (Bangor, Nazareth, Stroudsburgs and East Stroudsburg), covering the years 1955 to 1961. The cause of death was verified with the physicians who had cared for the deceased. He found that the death rate from heart attacks among men in Roseto was less than half that of four surrounding communities and for the United States as a whole.

This finding prompted Wolf to organize a team of researchers from the University of Oklahoma Health Sciences Center to determine the reasons for Roseto's immunity from fatal heart attacks.

In the 1960s the medical community in the United States focused on the study of individuals to find the causes of heart disease. Possible causes included high blood pressure, high serum cholesterol and blood lipids, lack of physical exercise, cigarette smoking, obesity, diabetes, and stress among others. There was little interest, on the part of physicians, in the contribution of the social environment to understanding heart disease. Therefore, there was skepticism among many physicians when Dr. Wolf organized a total community approach to studying risk factors for heart disease, which included the social environment. This unconventional approach to studying disease was antagonistic to the strong clinical tradition in epidemiology where, in order to find possible causes of disease, physicians looked at individuals and their characteristics. Furthermore, the social environment is more subtle, less quantifiable, and therefore was thought to lack the scientific rigor of quantifiable science (Syme, 1994).

Nonetheless a comprehensive medical and sociological study of Roseto and two of its neighbors, Bangor (Bruhn, Chandler, Miller & Wolf, 1966) and Nazareth (Bruhn, Wolf, Lynn, Bird & Chandler, 1966), which served as controls, was launched during five successive summers (1962–1966), with the cooperation of the mayors and town councils. The approach to studying the three communities was the same. Local coordinators from each community helped to locate a convenient place for residents to undergo a complete physical examination without cost. The clinics were well publicized in the local newspapers and radio, in speeches to local social and civic groups, and by word of mouth. The clinics were open to all community residents aged 18 and older. The clinics were staffed by physicians from the Department of Medicine at the University of Oklahoma Health Sciences Center who carried out the physical exams and obtained medical histories, laboratory personnel obtained samples of blood and urine for a variety of specialized tests (lipoproteins, uric acid, serum cholesterol and blood sugar), electrocardiograms were taken, dieticians carried out interviews and also obtained weekly food diaries and food samples for laboratory analysis, sociologists conducted extensive interviews with each participant, which included their histories of tobacco and alcohol use and exercise habits.

The clinics in Bangor and Nazareth were each conducted one time, but the clinics in Roseto extended over several more years to include former Rosetans who had moved away and returned for a visit. Following the medical clinics special studies were made of the prevalence of peptic ulcer, reported illness and smoking (Philips & Bruhn, 1981), of life events and illness patterns in three generations (Bruhn, Philips & Wolf, 1972); and incidence of treated mental illness in Roseto (Bruhn, Brandt & Shackelford, 1966). In addition, sociologists conducted a house to house survey of the community in 1966 to interview residents who did not attend one of the community clinics. When Rosetans died sociologists interviewed family members to discuss life circumstances surrounding the death, especially if it was a heart attack. The researchers were not able to follow Bangor and Nazareth in as much detail as Roseto over subsequent years because of the lack of funds.

The investigators, in 1963, after the initial period of study in Roseto, made a prediction that the loosening of family ties and community cohesion would be accompanied by loss of relative protection of Rosetans from death due to heart attacks. By the late 1960s and early 1970s the predicted change was evident, as was the predicted increase in the incidence of heart attacks. These changes were reflected in the increased number of new heart attacks among young adults (Wolf, 1992).

The earlier beliefs and behavior that expressed themselves in Roseto's family-centered social life, absence of ostentation even among the wealthy, nearly exclusive patronage of local business, and a predominance of intra-ethnic marriages changed toward the more familiar behavior patterns of neighboring communities. Roseto shifted from its initially highly homogeneous social order—made up of three-generation households with strong commitments to religion and to traditional values and practices—to a less cohesive, materialistic, more Americanized community in which three generation households were uncommon and inter-ethnic marriages became the norm (Wolf & Bruhn, 1993). The "Roseto Effect" has been widely cited as evidence for the positive effects of social cohesion and social support on longevity (Egolf, Lasker, Wolf & Potvin, 1992).

In order to reexamine the possibility of bias in the mortality data due to the small population of Roseto (approximately 1,600 at the onset of the study in 1961), and to test the possibility that the relative differences in mortality rates from one decade to another were due to random fluctuations in the number of deaths in each town, a group of investigators from Lehigh University examined death certificates from Roseto and Bangor from 1935 to 1985 (Egolf, Lasker, Wolf, & Potvin, 1992). The examination of death certificates confirmed the earlier study, based on a shorter span of years, that the death rate from heart attacks was lower in Roseto than in immediately adjacent Bangor in three decades prior to 1965. Separate analyses of individual Rosetans who appeared in both the marriage license

(above) A three-generational dinner in Roseto; *(below)* a Rosetan graduation party (Photos by Remsen Wolff)

(above) Church in Roseto was both a religious and a social occasion; *(below)* the annual processional honoring Our Lady of Mt. Carmel (Photos by Remsen Wolff)

and death record data suggest that those who married non-Italians in the first several decades had a higher mortality rate than Italians who married other Italians (Lasker, Egolf & Wolf, 1994). The difference between the two communities was statistically significant despite the small number of heart attacks. The sharp rise in heart attacks that began to occur in the late 1960s involved mainly young Rosetan men and elderly women fits well with John Cassel's formulation regarding the effects of social change on the incidence of heart disease in populations (Cassel, Patrick & Jenkins, 1960).

Rosetans made several deliberate trade-offs in their desire to become accepted into American society and experience the benefits they perceived from being an American. Social change has its costs and benefits, some of which are not reversible. Rosetans made some choices that have weakened their basic values. The results of social change, whether spontaneous or devised, have had dramatic effects on community life and the individual lives of Rosetans (see Table 8.1). While Roseto exists today adhering to its values of faith, family, and friends it has the look and feel of its neighbor Bangor, a largely commuter community. Perhaps the most important lesson from Roseto for each of us personally is that close personal ties with others for whom we care and who care for us are important to our health and well-being (Bruhn, Philips & Wolf, 1982).

Creating Social Cohesion

Social cohesion is created; it is what happens when people share beliefs and values. Sharing a common purpose or destiny creates a bond between members of a community. Members invest in, and feel a sense of responsibility for each other's welfare. An essential factor necessary to create social cohesion is stability. If a community has a continual in-flow and out-flow of residents it is not possible for the interpersonal seeds of social cohesion to take root. Therefore, significant continuous social change is an enemy of social cohesion. On the other hand, social change can, in the form of crises or disasters, help to further strengthen already cohesive communities.

Given the prerequisites of a common purpose and relative stability it is important for members of the community to take risks in establishing personal ties by being open and honest in their communication with each other. Reciprocity must exist before trust can exist. Trust is the bedrock of social cohesion. Trustworthiness among members is a constant reaffirmation of the common beliefs and values of members.

A cohesive community is also a supportive community. Members help each other with unconditional acts of sharing as they experience the good and bad effects of life events. The community itself is a safety net. A

Table 8.1. Cultural Changes and Choices in Roseto

Roseto culture, pre–1965	Roseto values	Cultural change, 1965–present	Results
• Ethnic homogeneity	• Education of children	• Inter-ethnic/Inter-religious marriage	• New rules for success
• Intra-ethnic marriage	• Family/Friends	• Materialism (Upward social mobility)	• New definition of the good life
• Three generation households (many living together)	• Religion (Faith)	• Increased ties with those marginal to dominant group	• New meaning of satisfaction
• Dense social and organizational life (ethnic and church-based)	• Work ethic	• Fourth generation living and working outside the community	• Learn new ways of adapting to life and stress
• Predominately Roman Catholic	• Trust	• Smaller families	• More attention to wants than needs
• High degree civic-minded behavior	• Traditions	• Many small business closed	• Changing health status of individuals
• Strong communal help ethic	• Camaraderie	• Decreased civil and social participation	• Less egalitarian
• Strong work ethic	• Social support	• Theft	• More concern for personal safety
• Family-centered social life		• Lessened sense of community	
• High degree ethnic pride		• Shopping in businesses outside the community	
• Patronage of local businesses			
• Absence of crime			

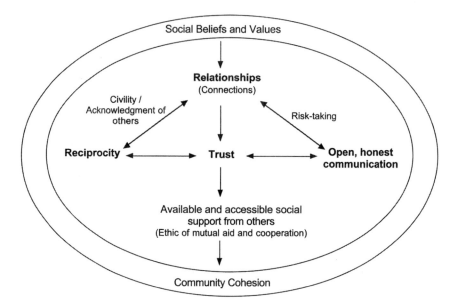

Figure 8.1. How Communities Create Social Cohesion

supportive community that practices the ethic of the collective good is cohesive (see Figure 8.1).

However, social cohesion is not a static characteristic. Community norms and values must continually be reaffirmed and strongly supported to withstand the challenges of generational change and forces outside the community that continuously test its cohesiveness. Perhaps the best example of tenacity in this regard is the Amish community in Pennsylvania. On the other hand, many of the ethnic communities in the United States that have attempted to select values of the dominant culture and meld them with their own have also ended up in weakening their community cohesion. Acculturation can make survival easier, but at a cost to social cohesion.

SUMMARY

Social support is necessary for healthy survival. Participation in social networks is necessary to enhance physical and mental well-being and to experience the benefits of being a social animal. Most individuals make choices about the conditions under which they will give and receive social support from others and how active they are in creating and participating in social networks. Social support is an aspect of life that is often ignored until it is needed. People view social support according to their experiences with it beginning in early life. Therefore, how important social support is, the ways it is expressed, and the appropriate contexts for showing it vary both culturally and individually.

Social networks have been shown to be beneficial to our health. Isolated persons are less healthy and more likely to die prematurely than connected persons. Social support and social networks work to affect individual health in two ways: 1) they can enhance health and reduce mortality, and 2) when illness strikes, they can ameliorate its effects. Several community studies have found that decreased social connections were consistent predictors of increased mortality for most causes of death. Even the perception of low social support was associated with the risk of premature death. Among ill people, investigators have found that social networks have the effect of reducing physical symptoms, especially those related to stress. Supportive relationships are thought to help people cope with their illness.

People with major psychiatric illnesses usually have weak or absent social ties even with family members. Individuals with less severe mental disorders tend to have social networks that are negative, unconnected and non-reciprocal. A major challenge in treatment is to help them establish healthy social networks. Social support has been shown to be a potent factor in the recovery and habilitation of patients recovering from heart attacks and heart surgery. Recovery appears to be faster and with fewer complications among patients with strong support systems.

Self-help and support groups are increasingly popular and useful ways individuals can access help and advice from others who have experienced similar situations. Self-help groups meet specialized needs such as grief, provide anonymity, are loosely structured, and can be utilized repeatedly, cost-free. Support groups are usually led by a professional mental health counselor who understands group dynamics and can deal with complications such as intense anger and suicidal threats or thoughts. Self-help and support groups help to fill gaps in the continuum of care that are often not offered as part of physician-centered care.

The ways in which social support and social networks relate to health have been studied at the community level. Some communities are healthier places to live than others. People living in closely-knit communities that share common beliefs and values tend to provide a collective and positive environment for dealing with the disruptions of stress and social change. Cohesive communities that practice the ethic of the common good have been shown to have lower rates of certain diseases and increased longevity. Investigators who have studied healthy egalitarian societies in different countries have found that social cohesion was a common characteristic. These communities had a strong community life, they had more social capital, they appeared to be caring, they restrained the values of the market and individualism, and people were involved in activities outside the home.

This kind of social fabric was found to be what provided a health advantage to a small Italian-American community in eastern Pennsylvania. This community, Roseto, was discovered in the early 1960s when a local physician observed few heart attacks in the community, especially among men, during a time in the United States when heart attacks among men were common. A study of death certificates from Roseto and several of its non-Italian neighbors verified the low Rosetan rates. Community medical clinics in Roseto and two of its closest neighbors, Bangor and Nazareth, focused on the numerous clinical risk factors agreed upon by most physicians as causes for heart attacks. Concomitant with the medical examinations of the community populations sociologists conducted interviews, observed the behavior of residents, learned about the cultures of the communities, and probed causes of death other than heart disease. Roseto was studied thoroughly as the study team followed residents, as well as those who moved away, over a period of 30 years. The team had predicted at the onset of its studies that, as Rosetans became acculturated, the heart attack rate would increase to the rate of the general United States population. The prediction was realized. As Rosetans became more American they traded many of their values that kept them cohesive for the values of middle class America, including their relative immunity from heart disease.

Social cohesion is a choice; it is created. It is an investment in the welfare of others. Usually social cohesion is an attribute of religious, ethnic, and small rural communities because these groups are more likely to control the pressures of social change to relinquish closely-held values for values commonly held in larger society. But communities do not have to be homogeneous in order to be socially cohesive. What is essential for community cohesiveness is a shared purpose, open and honest communication among members, reciprocity, and trust. Concern for one another is unconditional. Social cohesion is difficult to generate and sustain in a society that values individualism. It usually takes a disaster to experience social cohesion, and then only for a short time. Cohesive communities and their members have important lessons to teach us about the value choices they have made.

QUESTIONS FOR DISCUSSION

1. Do you think that social support is viewed differently by men and women? How do we learn our attitudes toward social support? What role does culture play in our use of sources of social support? Explain.
2. Is there such a thing as negative social support? If so, how might it work? Explain and provide examples.
3. In what ways can *perceived* social support affect one's health?
4. In what ways might self-help and support groups be more effective than a personal visit with a professional helper?
5. Do you think the people of Roseto, Pennsylvania were cognizant of the choices they made about their acculturation that led to changes in their health status? Explain.
6. How is social cohesion created? What are the factors that cause social cohesion to change? Do you think most small communities in the United States today are cohesive? Explain providing an example.

Chapter 9

The Social Internet
Cybercommunities

INTRODUCTION

The Internet as a Community

Our society has developed the belief that political, moral, and social problems are the result of a lack of communication, and that if we improve communication we will also solve the various problems that plague modern society (Wise, 1997). The Internet would enhance communication. It would result in a society free of the constraints of space and time and free us to engage with fellow humans (Jones, 1997). New communities would be constructed from communication rather than from physical proximity, which does not guarantee communication (Jones, 1997). These new electronic communities, according to Schuler (1996), would have a high degree of awareness, principles and purpose, focused around action. Communities would no longer be places to be, but groups of people seeking to achieve particular goals. Jones pointed out that this perspective puts a new spin on the modern nostalgia for community. Instead of criticizing the deterioration of community in modern society, he argued that the Internet would provide broader and more useful opportunities.

Jones (1995) suggested that, as community dissolves in the spaces we physically inhabit, we can socially create space through computer-mediated communication (CMC). We can customize our social contacts and move from place to place without having physically traveled. We can participate in interactive communities that are not of a common location, but of a common interest. Virtual communities, according to Jones, are passage points for collections of common beliefs and practices that unite people who are physically separated. Users of CMC become citizens of cyberspace.

There is considerable debate and disagreement about what citizenship in cyberspace means. Supporters of virtual communities point to the emotional support offered by electronic communication and the solidarity that emerges among its users. Detractors, on the other hand, see virtual communities as ersatz communities, and regard them as a symptom of the superficiality of modern society that individuals would find meaning in them (Komito, 1998). When discussing electronic communities, the term "community" acquires a number of different meanings. In some cases community means reciprocity and mutual assistance, in other instances it means the values and norms shared by individuals, yet in other situations, community is equated with a loose collection of like-minded individuals, and, finally, community can refer to the social relations that result when people who live in the same locality voluntarily interact over time. These meanings are often used interchangeably resulting in the confusing use of the term community.[1]

The Internet substitutes language for physical appearance. It is a silent world where all conversation is typed. To enter this world a person relinquishes both body and physical space and becomes a thing of words alone (Ruskoff, 1994). In that sense it is an imagined space where narrative is facilitated by discursive interaction and our imagination. Narratives are not communities, but they are artifacts of communities and do what communities do to maintain themselves over time. On the Internet we can imagine ourselves to be a part of a community based on our reading of a narrative. Frequent Internet users have been found to "feel" that a group and its messages "belong" to them. This creates an inversion of traditional community power and possession (McLaughlin, Osborne & Smith, 1995). Jones (1997) pointed out, however, it takes more than feeling to make a community. Interacting in the same place at the same time does not constitute a community. A person needs to be a part of imagined space. Aimless connectedness is of no greater benefit online that it is offline.

The sense of community and membership in one is rooted in the actions of the users. The Internet is not a social world unto itself, it is part of the real world which we share with others and where we have social connections. Wherever we go or whatever we do in the world we take these connections with us. The Internet permits us to take our primary identity with us. We can disguise it or underwrite it as our real self. The Internet is the ultimate tool for manipulating the environment to create our identity. Virtual environments are valuable as places where we can acknowledge our individual diversity, and a resource for self-reflection and self-transformation, but upon returning to the real world we need to be able to authenticate our real selves, solve real problems and build better offline communities (Turkle, 1996).

Defining Online Communities

There have been many characterizations of online communities, but the most frequently cited and accepted definition is that provided by Howard Rheingold. He wrote: "Virtual communities are cultural aggregations that emerge when enough people bump into each other often enough in cyberspace. A virtual community is a group of people who may or may not meet one another face to face, and who exchange words and ideas through the mediation of computer bulletin boards and networks" (Rheingold, 1994, pp. 57–58).

Online community has also become a blanket term to describe any collection of people who communicate online (Preece, 2000). Sociologists make distinctions between groups, networks, and communities. A group has clear boundaries that determine membership. It is a special kind of network whose members are highly interconnected. An example of a group is a special interest group that has a narrowly defined purpose and attracts members sharing that interest. Online groups may remain groups and never become a community as long as group members fulfill their roles in meeting group goals.

Networks involve relationships or connections that can cross boundaries. Groups can become networked, for example local groups interested in antique cars can become connected to form a statewide network. State networks can be linked to form a national network. Linkages can also be made to groups in other countries. Networks can vary in size, complexity, and density. Community connotes the strength of relationships in networks. Sociologists can map and determine the strength of relationships using the technique of network analysis. The aim of social network analysis is to describe why people communicate individually or in groups and to understand the patterns of relationships that people have online. Sociologists have identified characteristics of relationships that are weak and those that are strong. Weak and strong relationships explain how people get their needs met, how information and other resources flow through the network, and therefore, what shapes social networks (Granovetter, 1973).

More and more people are going online in search of social support and companionship as well as to get information. Many online relationships show strong ties similar to offline relationships. In fact, some online relationships endure when they would otherwise flounder because of geographical distance. Studies have reported that some Net users regard their closest friends as members of an electronic group whom they have never seen (Hiltz & Turoff, 1993). Also, the longer people stay in contact online, the stronger their ties tend to become (Walther, Anderson & Park, 1994).

As we participate in online experiences, it is important to keep in mind our ties to the real world. Putnam (1995) said that, because technology enables people to get their needs met without leaving their homes. Consequently, it is suggested that as Americans choose to spend more time physically alone, many are becoming lonely, and are becoming less involved in strong relationships. In other words, strong ties may be getting substituted for many weak ties (Preece, 2000).

THE SCOPE AND EFFECTS OF INTERNET DIFFUSION

The Scope

In 1999 the Pew Charitable Trust funded a series of studies to explore the social impact of the Internet on American life (www.pewinternet.org). Surveys have been completed on over 12,000 Americans age 18 years and older who provided answers to questions by telephone.[2] The investigators have found that on an average day 64 million Americans will use the Internet, almost one half of the 149 million persons of all ages with online access. More than 60 percent of adults use the Net at least once a week. They usually read e-mail, read the news, and window-shop online. Results showed that people are using the Internet to expand their social world. Internet use has become the norm and people now expect other people and institutions to be online. The Internet, which once was predominately white and male, is increasingly becoming available, accessible and affordable to more Americans.[3] The project team also learned that experience online makes a difference in what you do online. Those who have more than three years experience have a different profile than those who have less experience. More experienced users do more, spend more, and use the Net more for everyday activities such as banking and paying bills. Some of the project's other findings include:

- More women than men are now online.
- More than 85 million Americans belong to some kind of online group.
- People use the Net in different ways. Women use it differently than men, blacks use it differently than whites, and Europeans use it differently than Americans.
- People bring their offline lives online.
- People use the Net to further interests they already have.
- The Internet equalizes the power differential between individuals and institutions.
- The use of e-mail helps people build their social networks by extending and maintaining friend and family relationships.

Howard and his colleagues (2001) used data from the Pew survey to build a typology of Internet users based on answers to two questions: How long have you had Internet access? And, how frequently do you log on from home? By focusing on these questions about experience levels and frequency of home use the investigators gained insights into user's willingness to be innovative and the degree to which they have embraced Internet tools at home. Howard and his team developed four broad categories of Internet users.

Netizens comprise 16 percent of the adult Internet population and eight percent of the adult United States population. They obtained access more than three years ago and say they go online from home every day. They have incorporated the Internet into their work lives and home lives; are comfortable spending money online; use the Internet to manage their personal finances; use e-mail to enhance their social relationships; and are the most avid participants in Web activities on an average day.

Utilitarians comprise about 28 percent of the adult Internet population and 14 percent of the adult United States population. They obtained access less than three years ago but also log on from home every day. Compared to Netizens, members of this group are less intense in their use of the Internet, express less appreciation for what the Internet contributes to their lives, are less likely to spend and manage their money online, and are less active in accessing the Web's content. The Internet is a tool for them and they see it as less useful and entertaining than Netizens do.

Experimenters comprise 26 percent of the adult Internet population and 13 percent of the United States adult population. They accessed the Web about a year ago and say they go online from home every day. They basically use the Web to retrieve information.

Newcomers comprise 30 percent of the adult Internet population and 15 percent of the United States adult population. They accessed the Web less than a year ago. This group shows the characteristics of apprentices. They play games, browse, participate in chat rooms, get information about hobbies, and listen to and download music. Usually newcomers have access at only one place—work or home.

As the Internet grows, there has been considerable interest in the question of whether Internet use encourages social connectedness or social isolation. Respondents to the Pew surveys said that the Internet allows them to stay in touch with both family and friends, and in many cases, extend their networks. A sizable majority of those who e-mail relatives said that it increases the level of communication between family members. About 59 percent of those who e-mail to communicate with their families say they communicate more often, and 60 percent of those who e-mail friends said that they have increased their communication. Thirty-one percent of family e-mailers said that they have started communicating with a family member that they had not contacted much before.

The Effects

The Pew findings suggest than online tools are more likely to extend social contact rather than detract from it. However, the availability and accessibility of the Internet is unevenly distributed across the United States. Regional variations reflect differences in education and income. The race, age, and gender of users also show regional differences. Each region of the country has its own online character. Therefore, conclusions about the positive and negative effects of the Internet must be assessed considering different social and cultural environments and the social and demographic characteristics of the people residing there.

Furthermore, the nature of the Internet is changing and the nature of these changes affects utilization. A recent survey carried out by the Pew Project on spam indicates that spam is beginning to undermine the integrity of e-mail and degrade life online. Some e-mailers said that they are using electronic mail less now because of spam. More people are reporting that they trust the online environment less. Increasing numbers of users state that they fear they cannot retrieve the e-mails they need because of the volume of spam. They also worry that their important e-mails to others are not being read or received because the recipients' filters might screen them out. Users are increasingly complaining that spam has introduced uninvited, deceptive, and offensive messages into their personal lives.

Other surveys on the social effects of the Internet have yielded findings which both agree and disagree with those of the Pew Project. The first national random study of the social consequences of the Internet was developed by James Katz and Philip Aspden (1997). This project, known as Syntopia, began a series of surveys in 1995, 1996, 1997 and 2000 to use national random telephone survey methods to track social and community aspects of Internet use, and to compare users and non-users (Katz & Rice, 2002). Their conclusions did not support arguments about negative effects of the Internet that have generally been reported. Their findings were that this new technology has substantial benefits to society. They found that Internet usage was becoming more equally accessible and widely used, that it is associated with increased community and political involvement, and is associated with significant and increased online and offline social interactions.

How does the Internet affect social capital in terms of social contact, civic engagement, and a sense of community? Does online involvement increase, decrease, or supplement the ways in which people engage? These questions were addressed by Quan-Haase and her colleagues (2002) in a 1998 survey of North American visitors to the National Geographic Society Website. These researchers found that online social contact supplements the frequency of face-to-face and telephone contact. Online activity also supplements participation in voluntary organizations and politics. Frequent e-mail users had a greater sense of online community, although their overall sense of community is similar to that of infrequent e-mail users. The evidence suggested that as the Internet is incorporated into everyday life, social capital will be augmented and geographically dispersed.

Nie and Erbring (2000) surveyed 4,000 Internet users online and asked how the Internet had changed their lives. Most reported no change, but heavier users reported declines in socializing, media use, shopping, and other activities. Nie and Erbring viewed the substitution of e-mail for telephone contact by heavy Net users as part of their loss of contact with their social environment. By contrast, Lin (2001) regarded online communication, including e-mail, as markedly expanding one's social capital. More recent surveys have shown that Internet users have higher levels of generalized trust and larger social networks than non-users (Uslaner, 1999; Hampton & Wellman, 2000; Cole, 2000). Results from these surveys also suggest that Internet use serves to complement rather than substitute for print media and offline socialization. A detailed time diary study also found Internet users to be no less active media users or offline socializers than non-users, though users did less housework, devoted less time to family care, and slept less (Kestnbaum, Robinson, Neustadtl & Alvarez, 2002).

Kraut and his associates (1998) examined the social and psychological impact of the Internet in 73 households during their first one or two years online. They found that the greater use of the Internet was associated with declines in social involvement as measured by communication within the family and the size of people's local social networks, and with increases in loneliness. Greater use of the Internet was also associated with increases in depression. These investigators concluded that using the Internet adversely affects social involvement and psychological well-being. Yet, as the researchers followed their sample they discovered that, except for increased stress, the negative psychological effects disappeared. They attribute this change to the increased experience and competence of the users.

An innovative study that used special use-logging software to compare the online behavior of experienced and novice Web users reinforces the notion that the effect of Internet use may vary with user competence. Compared to experienced Web users, novices engaged in more aimless surfing, were less successful in finding information, and were more likely to report feeling a souring of affect over the course of their sessions. Their negative reactions reflected the sense of frustration and sense of impotence of the inexperienced user without immediate access to social support (Neuman, O'Donnell & Schneider, 1996).

William Galston (2000) posed the question, "Does the Internet strengthen community?" Galston pointed out that this question is similar to the question raised in 1952, "What are the social consequences of television?" He noted that in both instances the diffusion of television and the Internet was moving faster than research about their effects, and conclusions that might have been drawn from research carried out early in the diffusion of these media would probably be antiquated a few years later. Galston stated that Americans are looking for ways of reconciling the desire for autonomy and connection. The Internet is appealing because it is a voluntary community that links us to others by choice, however, the entrance and exit to online groups to fulfill emotional and utilitarian needs are not always cost-free. The long-term social effects of the Internet will require longitudinal research.

DiMaggio (2001) summarized five points from the research to date. First, the Internet has no intrinsic effect on social interaction and civic participation. Second, Internet use tends to intensify already existing inclinations toward sociability or community involvement, rather than to create them. Third, we need to know more than we do about the qualitative character of online relationships. Fourth, we know that virtual communities exist in large numbers, but we know little about their performance such as factors that contribute to making a virtual community effective. Fifth, we need more systematic studies of how civic associations and social movements use the Internet so that we can move beyond single cases to understanding the institutional conditions that encourage or discourage successful exploitation of this technology.

COMMUNITY NETWORKS

Wellman (2001) argued that the Internet has contributed to a shift from a group-based to a network-based society that is decoupling community and geographic propinquity. Communities are about social relationships while neighborhoods are about boundaries (Wellman, 1999; Wellman & Gulia, 1999). Most social ties today are not local neighborhood ties as they were in past decades. Wellman's (1982) study of East York, a borough of Toronto, showed that a quarter of the neighbors had ties with people they said they would not choose to know better. A neighborhood is not automatically cohesive because people live close to one another. A neighborhood is best characterized as a *potential* community. A functional community is what people do for each other not where they live. Communities are where people get their personal needs met. This is not to say that the traditional neighborhood has become extinct, rather its boundaries have been broadened by social change, especially the Internet. Individuals now are members of multiple communities that ignore the constraints of space and densely knit solidarity groups. Technology tends to foster specialized relationships so that except for family and a small group of friends, members of a Net community only know special characteristics about each other. But neighborhood and kinship ties are only a portion of people's overall community networks (Smith & Kollock, 1999). People must maintain a variety of different networks of social relationships to meet their needs. Even the best electronic group can not always satisfy the needs of all of its members so some members may supplement virtual help with a real-life self-help group. The important point is that Internet users maintain a variety of portfolios of social ties, which vary by size, complexity, intimacy and interests. Some users can, for example, obtain what they need from a therapy group online, while other users may need additional real life meetings.

Networks are linkages. The characteristics of linkages may be used to interpret the social behavior of the people involved. People who are linked together need not necessarily be individual persons. They may be families, various work groups within a corporation or work groups in the same corporation but living in different countries. Most linkages are with individuals but the individuals may represent larger units of which they a member. Linkages can be direct or indirect. For example, a person's job may link her indirectly through cc or bcc with individuals and networks they may not be in contact with directly. This is especially true in matrixed organizations. There are some networks we are members of because we hold a position of power and decision-making in an organization.

Our behavior in networked communities is greatly affected by whether we have the protection of anonymity. Users of computer-mediated communication often cite anonymity as one of its attractive features. It has been found that electronic meetings between members of business organizations who know each other and bound by status and hierarchy, are more open and innovative when suggestions are anonymous (Dunlop & Kling, 1996). On the other hand, the leveling of status differences in an electronic group makes consensus more difficult to achieve. It may change the character of interactions between males and females and promote the consideration of minority viewpoints. For people with restricted lives, electronic systems may provide avenues to expand their social circles. Online friendships often develop that might have not begun had age, sex, race and appearance been initially evident.

THE VIRTUAL ORGANIZATION

An experiment conducted by the Rand Corporation demonstrated that peripheral people who communicated electronically became better integrated into the organization. Eveland and Birkson (1988) created two task forces, each composed equally of recently retired employees and employees still at work but eligible to retire. They were given identical tasks of preparing reports for Rand Corporation on retirement planning issues. One group had full conventional office support. The other group had, in addition, networked computers with e-mail and routine office software. Structured interviews were conducted four times during the year-long project. In addition, e-mail activity was logged for the online group. Both groups produced effective reports, but they differed in the kinds of work they produced, the group structures that emerged, and evaluations of their own performance. The electronically supported group developed a structure different from the standard group. The standard group had a consistent set of leaders, while the electronic group had a fluctuating leadership pattern. The electronic group allowed different people to work at different times of the day according to their own schedules and enabled retired members to take an active role in the project. The electronic group maintained a higher degree of contact than the standard group. Members of the electronic group also were more involved in the work of the group and were more satisfied with their outcomes. The research project provided evidence that both the outcomes and processes of cooperative work are directly affected by the tools participants have at their disposal. Electronic media can be especially effective in an information-intense work group.

Sproull & Kiesler (1991) found a similar story in a city government where over 90 percent of the city employees used e-mail routinely. The more they used it, the more committed they were to their employer. Computer communication reduced the status imbalance from subordinate to supervisor. There was, however, less commitment to using e-mail among the shift workers, supporting the idea that electronic mail can increase commitment among those employees who feel peripheral to an organization. There is some evidence that the greater the number of electronic groups a person participates in the more positive is the effect on their mental health (Thoits, 1983). Multiple group membership not only meets a variety of needs but provides a range of social support and creates feelings of inclusiveness.

Handy (1994) pointed out that organizations now need to be global and local at the same time, to be small in some ways and big in others, to be centralized some of the time and decentralized most of it. Organizations expect members to be more autonomous yet more of a team, have less face-to-face contact with each other and more by electronic communication, and to work on projects in clusters and with different groups in the same organization. This is what some have called "the virtual organization."

The virtual organization is not a place to go, but rather activities to be accomplished by electronic means. When we work with people we do not see and whom we do not know as persons, trust is difficult to establish. Organizations now create a sense of belonging to a virtual community rather than a sense of belonging to a place.

All members of a virtual organization need to share responsibility in following rules of trust and privacy. Information in virtual organizations cannot be directly checked with observed behavior, therefore there must be trust in the information members choose to share. An employee of a large international firm told how he worked daily at his computer together with a team comprised of decision-makers from several different countries. The team had never met face-to-face yet made key decisions by e-mail affecting the worldwide operations of the corporation. The team was leaderless with all parties carrying equal responsibilities. Their decisions were team decisions. The employee related that there had never been a question of distrust among team members over the years they had worked together.

Cooperation and Trust

Successful communities are established on cooperation and trust. Reciprocity is of central concern for communities despite the absence of social presence, anonymity, and the ability to leave a community. Cooperation is the outcome of the dilemma of what is best for the group and what is best for the individual. The social theorist, Robert Axelrod (1984), studied the nature of cooperation through a puzzle called the Prisoner's Dilemma. The puzzle offers imaginary choices facing a prisoner in cooperating with another prisoner in confessing to a crime and the implications for the length of their respective incarceration. Several conditions for cooperation from the Prisoner's Dilemma are relevant to establishing cooperation in online communities.

First, the chance of two individuals meeting again in the future must be high, otherwise people would take what they want from the community without worrying about the effects on others. Second, people must be able to identify one another so that everyone knows who is responsible for a given message or comment. Third, there needs to be a record of past behavior and the probability of future interactions, so that those who cooperate and those who do not can be separated out. The definition of acceptable behavior in a community will depend on the purpose of the community, the attitudes of the people who belong to it, and the rules by which the community operates.

When there is trust among people, relationships flourish. As Rheingold (1993) pointed out, meeting people online is the reverse of how we do so in person. In real life we meet people and get to know them, in virtual communities we get to know people and then choose to meet them. Online, trust is somewhat dichotomous: on the one hand, people feel freer to disclose personal details; on the other hand, lack of actual contact makes trust online fragile (Preece, 2000). Trust is the expectation that arises within a community of regular, honest, and cooperative behavior, based on commonly shared norms on the part of the members of the community (Fukuyama, 1995).

Shneiderman (2000) suggested a model for facilitating trust applicable to online communities. The model has three components: first, clarify the context in which interactions are to occur; second, make clear and truthful commitments; third, recognize that trust involves taking a risk. Encouraging community members to be responsible and reliable helps build trust; but first members must be made aware that trust is valued in the community (Goleman, 1995). The importance of trust is best illustrated online through the work of virtual teams.

Virtual Leadership

Leadership personalities emerge as group members began to assume responsibility for shaping the structure and normative behavior of the group. Moderators direct group activity and behavior, through facilitation, filtering messages, editing text, marketing and managing the membership list and preventing spam and personal attacks. Mediators help to settle disputes. Professional commentators help to guide discussion, provide facts, and provoke interaction. People can be as unpleasant online as they are offline; in fact, anonymity and the ease with which a person can leave a group may encourage group members to be more forceful in their negative comments than they would be in person (Sproull & Kiesler, 1991; Hiltz & Turoff, 1993). Being a moderator requires skill and experience, and it is time-consuming. Leaders of virtual groups are gatekeepers of sociability, that is maintaining a balance between setting policies and letting them evolve in the community. To protect moderators from criticism, most online communities make their moderation rules public (Preece, 2000).

Virtual Teams

A global virtual team is a boundaryless network organization where a temporary team is assembled on an as-needed basis for the duration of a task and staffed by members from different countries. Coordination is accomplished through trust and shared communication. Trust is key in preventing geographic distance from leading to psychological distance in a global team. Other ways to "check up" on trust such as direct supervision are usually absent.

Jarvenpaa and her colleagues (1998) studied in a virtual team setting, the effect of factors that have been identified as sources of trust in traditional face-to-face relationships. Seventy-five teams, consisting of four to six members (students) residing in different countries, interacted and worked together for eight weeks. The teams were charged with completing three tasks: two team-building exercises and a final project (developing a World Wide Web site) presenting information of interest to global information technology practitioners working in a global business setting. Students communicated solely through electronic means. The list processor archived mail messages and team members were sent an electronic survey to complete immediately following the second trust-building exercise. A second survey was sent to the team members the day following the completed final project.

The two-week trust-building exercises were found to have a significant effect on the team members' perceptions of the other members' ability, integrity, and benevolence, but they did not have a direct effect on trust. Team trust was predicted most strongly by perceptions of other team members' integrity, and less strongly by the perceptions of their benevolence. Members' own propensity to trust had a significant effect on team trust. High-trust teams were pro-active. They showed a high level of optimism and excitement, task orientation, rotating leadership, good time management, a clear sense of task goals, and high levels of individual initiative and accountability. The three high-trust teams also exhibited a form of "swift trust," that is, members acted as if trust was present from the start. Swift trust enabled members to take action, and this action helped to maintain trust and deal with uncertainty, ambiguity, and vulnerability while working on complex interdependent tasks with strangers in a situation of high time pressure. Yet, swift trust appeared to be fragile and temporal. In swift trust, unless one trusts quickly, one may never trust at all. In a second study, Jarvenpaa and her associates (1999) found that only four out of 29 teams shifted to a high-trust condition from a low-trust condition. The first e-mail messages by a team appeared to set the tone for how team members interrelated. The adage "You can never give a second first impression" seemed to apply to electronic impressions as well.

The results of these studies suggest that trust might be imported in global virtual teams, but it is more likely created by communication behavior established in the first message. Communication that rallies around a project and tasks appears to be necessary to maintain trust. Social communication that complements rather than substitutes for task communication may strengthen trust. Finally, initial behavior such as member's verbalizing their commitment, excitement, and optimism and their own propensity to trust has an effect on establishing team trust (Lipnack & Stamps, 1997).

THE VIRTUAL SELF

Online Personas

Social theorists believe that physical bodily interaction with objects and people is necessary to develop a sense of self. Eliminating physical contact by socially interacting in electronic space raises the issue of how people present themselves to each other. People represent themselves more favorably online, representations that are often not borne out in real life (Preece, 2000). Barnes (2000) reported the results of a study of messages exchanged by members of a virtual community before and after they met face-to-face. Barnes found that in addition to group beliefs they shared individual ideals. Individuals believed that the bonds of virtual friendship would not change when they met face-to-face. They thought that replacing the imaginary images of others with real life experiences would strengthen their commitment to the community. They believed that the written verbal messages shared over time were stronger than visual first impressions.

The decision to meet face-to-face changed this virtual community. After three years online members felt a need to meet each other in person. Barnes found that a face-to-face meeting created anxiety for people who believed that their physical appearance would not match their online persona. To alleviate these fears, the group created the myth that physical appearance and real personalities would not interfere with established friendships. Contrary to belief, in-person personalities did alter their relationships. Barnes explained that when virtual friends become real there is a level of disillusionment because messages do not reveal the whole person. But members decided to find out more information about one another. They tried to explain themselves often through private conversations, writing biographies, and describing each other to the entire community. During this process the community became divided between those who met in person and those who didn't. As a result the community changed and began to disintegrate.

To keep the group together a moderator began to act as a therapist to help the community face the differences between virtual and real friendships. But changing the context of members' relationships changed their relationships. The face-to-face meeting changed how the group interacted when they returned to their virtual community.

Other studies of online personas have shown that filtering out social cues impedes normal impression development. First impressions are developed in face-to-face conversations, primarily from nonverbal cues–physical appearance and attractiveness, race, age, and gender–especially are powerful social markers. The more people discover they are similar to each other, the more they tend to like each other, and disclose about themselves. Self-disclosure reciprocity is powerful online. Anonymity can encourage people to disclose more about themselves as in a support group. However, electronic communication, in general, tends to retard impression development and the formation of relationships except among experienced users who know ways to deal with the absence of visual cues (Rice & Barnett, 1986).

In some online environments responses to men are different from those to women. Often a first question asked of a newcomer is their gender. Consequently, women frequently disguise their gender so they can maintain their freedom in the electronic world (Preece, 2000). Some people like to explore changing their persona to see how people treat them. Both men and women are known to switch genders in order to explore what life is like as the other sex.

Many researchers have observed empathy online. Empathy is knowing what the other person is feeling. Empathy depends heavily on nonverbal communication such as body language and gaze. The more similar people are the less they have to look for overt social cues. Empathy can be conveyed online by the choice of words, punctuation, and the frequency of messages. Empathy is a powerful force online, especially in establishing trust and in health communities (Preece, 1999). As Preece (2000) has pointed out, a virtual hug, shown in the form of parentheses . . . ( ), is not as warm or satisfying as a real hug, but it does communicate a feeling among people separated by distance.

Waskul and Douglass (1997) studied the emergence of self in online chat. The anonymity of online interaction allows people the option of being anything they want to be. Categories of personhood such as race, gender, age, physical appearance and socioeconomic status, all become labels to interact with. In chat environments, categories of personhood can be real or altered through one's online presentation of self. Many users report that this is a liberating experience of free expression. A cyberself emerges in the context of chat environments through interaction with others. Participants regard these cyberselves as real elements of who they are. On the other hand, the ability to be anything implies that all claims of selfhood are potentially suspect. There is no way of sifting the real from the fake. In addition to the opportunity to present an alternative image of oneself, users can have up to four screen names. This provides the opportunity to construct multiple anonymous cyberselves. It has been found that teenage girls and women of all ages are more likely to maintain multiple online personas. There is some concern that this behavior leads to dysfunctional communication networks. Turkle (1995) states that chat participants are "reality hackers"—people struggling to do what they have always done: to understand themselves and their world using whatever materials they have at hand.

Humans communicate by playing roles that they consider appropriate for a time, place, and situation whether face-to-face or online. According to Wallace (1999), everyone on the Net creates an online persona, whether they realize it or not. Sending e-mail, creating a homepage, building a Web site, participating in discussion groups all contribute to the impression people form about us, our organization, or business. Some people become disinhibited by the Net because the usual social constraints are lowered. Many people show more self-disclosure than they would in face-to-face settings; some also show verbal aggression in flame wars or by sending harsh e-mails.

Technology makes it easier to bring out the best and the worst in human behavior. The Internet is merely an intermediary for the behavior of the user. Therefore, technological applications are not ethically neutral. How we use the Internet raises many ethical and social issues about its governance, the rights of users, and the Net's future development (Ladd, 1989).

INTERNET ETHICS

Ethics refers to the rights of others and to the rules that define how we should behave when our behavior affects others. Currently the Internet is self-regulated by users and information and network service providers, however, some material on the Internet pushes the boundaries of the freedom of speech by violating people's privacy and moral standards and has raised issues regarding Internet conduct and regulation. Vint Cerf, (1994) President of Internet Society, explained that the Internet has evolved rapidly from a university and industrial owned and operated research and education enterprise, to a shared global information infrastructure. However, our views about the Internet's use and abuse have not kept pace with this technology.

Computer ethics as a field of study has a short history. In 1950 MIT Professor Norbert Wiener published the first computer ethics book, *The*

Human Use of Human Beings, which laid a foundation for computer ethics. Computer ethics remained undeveloped and unexplored until the mid 1960s when computer invasions of privacy by government agencies became a public concern. By the mid 1970s new privacy laws and computer crime laws had been enacted in the United States and Europe, and organizations of computer professionals were adopting codes of conduct for their members. Since 1985 the field of computer ethics has grown to encompass university courses, research centers, conferences, articles, textbooks, and journals.

Computer ethics thinkers offer two very different views of ethical theories related to the Internet. One group sees computer technology as ethically revolutionary, requiring us to reexamine the foundations of ethics. A second group sees computer ethics as simply old ethical questions with a new twist. Social and behavioral scientists have concerns about the gap between those people who have access to computers and those who do not. While there is advocacy for universal access to the Internet this raises the question of who will pay for such access. There is also concern among social and behavioral scientists about creating addictions to Internet gaming and casino gambling. The American Psychiatric Association issued an advisory to parents noting that there has been a growth in gambling opportunities for children and teenagers who can link to gambling sites from game sites, lured by gifts and discounts. About 10 to 15 percent of young people surveyed in the United States and Canada report having experienced problems related to gambling.

But most of the public's concern about the Internet focuses around other issues, including privacy, censorship, piracy and plagiarism, security, and e-commerce and advertising. Should people be able to exchange copyrighted material over the Net without compensating the author? To what extent should companies be allowed access to and monitor employee communications and downloads? How will we protect computer networks, host systems, personal computers and laptops from break-ins, and the invasion of personal privacy?

As a society we are in the early stages of developing constructive models of ethical conduct for the Internet. Developing an ethical culture for the Internet revolves around answers to two basic questions, how is the Internet to be used and how will it be regulated? Currently community norms and user etiquette is determined by the people and sites we associate with on the Net. The Internet, similar to television, has markedly changed human relationships in a short period of time. We ultimately face choices about the new technologies we create–do we let technology shape the quality of our lives or do we shape technology to yield the effects we desire?

SUMMARY

The Internet has facilitated communication across cultures worldwide with minimal constraints on its applications. The Internet has connected people with each other who would not have met otherwise, it has enabled geographically separated family and friends to maintain their connections, it has supplemented face-to-face communications, and it has become a necessity in conducting business for globally dispersed corporations. The Internet has, to a great degree, replaced traditional communities of place with numerous types of electronic or virtual communities. We can imagine ourselves as being part of a community wherever we live and work. The Internet enables us to take our real self and disguise it, endorse it, or create a new identity.

There are conflicting views of the effects of the Internet much like the views of the effects of television as it has evolved to dominate our daily lives. Since Internet technology and the innovativeness of its users continue to change at a rapid pace, it is difficult to study the effects of a moving target. Most all of the studies conducted on the effects of the Internet have utilized telephone interviews to obtain large samples. The time of these surveys, the time-limited nature of telephone interviews, the honesty of the respondents are all factors which affect the results of studies. These factors account for differences in the positive and negative views of Internet technology from study to study. Overall, to date, the Internet is seen as a positive augmentation to everyday life, but there are aspects of the use of the Internet that cause concern such as the digital divide, issues of security, privacy, regulation, piracy, and e-commerce and advertising. There is special concern about the negative aspects of the Internet on young people and its seduction into addictive maladaptive habits. The ethical and social issues of Internet usage confront nations worldwide to make choices about this new technology we have created. Will the Internet be a tool to use within the constraints of ethics and etiquette or will we let the Internet evolve as we adapt to it?

QUESTIONS FOR DISCUSSION

1. What are factors that could influence the increased or decreased use of the Internet in the future? Discuss.
2. Contrast the differences in establishing trust between individuals from different cultures on the Net and in person.
3. Explain the statement "the Internet is merely an intermediary for the behavior of the user."

4. Should ethics on the Internet differ from ethics in everyday life? What are informal and formal ways of overseeing the boundaries of ethical behavior on the Internet?
5. What are the limits of the Internet in facilitating a greater understanding of world cultures?
6. What are the motivations for Net users to take on contrived online personas? What are ways to detect contrived personalities in person that can't be used on the Net?

Chapter 10

Solitary Communities
Disconnecting from the Common Good

INTRODUCTION

A community is a place to become self-fulfilled, so in an age of self-interest we take community with us wherever we go. Community is no longer based on locale, but it is a product of our interactions. Technology enables us to connect and disconnect with people in a world of matrixed relationships. According to Gergen,[1] new communities can form wherever communication links can be made. He pointed out that the face-to-face interaction of traditional communities might seem more natural or real, however, in a post modern age when people's self-interest outweighs their interest in others, it is less feasible to create and maintain traditional communities. The ubiquitous cell phone is evidence of people's disinterest in leaving their private worlds to interact with each other.[2]

While we are more available to communicate, Isaccs (1999) said ".... we are not necessarily any more capable of sharing understanding, insight, wisdom, or our hearts" (p. 389). Indeed, Peter Berger[3] wrote that technology brings about an anonymity and meaninglessness in social relations. We have become so attracted to time and task-driven connections that lead to short-term outcomes that there is an impatience with devoting time and effort to building people-driven networks.

We have become a nation of solitary communities. The individualization of community has resulted in limited interest in becoming engaged in other people's communities except for purposes of expediency. Accountability, trust, and commitment are limited to the radius of individualized communities; this fragmentation falls short of embracing a more encompassing societal good. The common good depends on the involvement of

233

everyone to achieve mutual benefits. Everyone committed to their own in-dividual or solitary community promotes their own good. Protecting one's personal good has become more important than promoting the common good.

"The common good" has the good feeling associated with apple pie and motherhood, however, the common good involves more than ran-dom acts of kindness. If asked, most people in our country would affirm that they believe in and work for the common good. We make pledges to uphold the common good in the mission statements of organizations, in advertisements upholding the rights of customers, patients, and clients, in commitments to abide by affirmative action laws. Our "public language" is that we endorse the moral principles of the common good. However, as mentioned in Chapter 1, Alan Wolfe (2001) found in his recent sur-vey of moral attitudes in the United States, when a moral decision has to be made most people do what they individually consider to be the right thing.

One of the shortcomings of a society that has become a collection of solitary communities is that political leaders and public policy makers find it difficult, and sometimes impossible, to generate a consensus or reach a compromise on major issues facing our society. Instead of dialogue about differences various communities of interest assert their rights to differ and act to delay, detour, or disengage from working toward a common resolu-tion. As a consequence, our society has failed to move forward on ways to cope with several major problems that affect all its citizens. As commu-nities have become more individualized our style of communication has become more specialized.

COMMUNICATION IN SOLITARY COMMUNITIES

As we discover new and faster ways to interact with each other, we seem to know less about each other as persons. We have become time dependent and task-driven, impatient with process, especially with other people who become obstacles to our success. People are viewed and treated as liabilities rather than assets. We have eagerly acquired technological de-vices to minimize time-demanding face-to-face encounters. Our styles of communication reflect the value shifts that have occurred over the past sev-eral decades. Two different styles characterize communication in our soci-ety today. One style, outcome-oriented and technology-driven, is the most prevalent; the other, process-oriented and people driven, is less common. There is a need for both styles, but the outcome-oriented and technology-driven form is valued and rewarded more in society today.

Outcome-Oriented Communication

Outcome-oriented communication is time and task dependent. This is typical of business conversations where people are expected to be direct, demanding, and decisive. Tasks and goals are usually tied to time deadlines so that there is usually pressure to make decisions expediently. The outcomes of most conversations have personal repercussions in the form of bonuses, salary raises, and promotions. Everyone is driven by a bottom-line. Singer (1995) refers to this as "what's in it for me." Outcome-oriented communication is usually constrained by rules, procedures, or boundaries, which help the parties involved to control the outcome. The use of technology is essential in being accessible and available in a time and task-oriented society. Sociability and affability are not considered essential in arriving at an outcome.

Outcome-oriented communication is not limited to business conversations. It is an "in your face" "I win, you lose" style found in many conversations on sidewalks, in shops, and restaurants everyday in which people challenge other's commitment and responsibility, and cynically demand the specific outcome they expect. Our society's orientation to time and task does not permit us to know the motivations and values of people as persons. People are viewed as obstacles to reaching outcomes that we believe are important to our own success. The expediency and efficiency of technology helps to focus the purpose of communication and minimizes the time spent in the cordialities expected in face-to-face interaction.

Process-Oriented Communication

Process-oriented communicators also value achieving outcomes, but do so by working with people face-to-face and using technology when necessary. There is an emphasis on collaboration and team-work. Input and the involvement of others are encouraged. How the outcome is reached is as important as the final product itself. Process-oriented communicators benefit from non-verbal communication. And they are more likely to take time to get the big picture rather than focus only on the outcome. In communicating with people there are certain to be disconnects despite the style. However, the process-oriented communicator uses cues gathered in person as helpful information for subsequent encounters. The greatest obstacles in process-driven communication are rigid boundaries, rules, procedures, and time pressures that limit the flexibility to adapt to individual circumstances.

Communication styles are important because they convey persona, values, and expectations. Organizations and businesses attract and select the type of communicators who they want to represent their persona. Most conflicts are due to failed efforts to communicate. The opportunities for failed communication to occur increase as communities of self-interest become more specialized and outcome-driven. When conflict and failed communication occur in outcome-driven organizations technology is usually blamed. It is easier to blame a computer than a person; it protects the organization's persona and obscures sources of accountability and responsibility. When communication failures occur in a process-driven organization the organization's persona is enhanced when the responsible parties are held accountable and responsible, and are given the opportunity to correct the problem. Process-oriented communication should be more, not less, important in a society of self-interests.

Disconnectedness can be a consequence of failed communication for both individuals and communities. There are forces that can create or enhance disconnectedness on a societal level that affect all citizens and there are forces that are unique to specific communities or individuals. The greater connectedness between nations means that both natural events and those instigated by man create continuous change. Nations differ in the types of changes they experience at different points in their lifecycles as do communities of self-interest and individuals. There are many ways that people can become disconnected in our society. Some of the more pervasive ones are discussed here.

SOURCES OF DISCONNECTIONS

Fear

One of the general sources of disconnection in our society comes from fear. Glassner (1999) studied what he called "the culture of fear" in our country by examining news stories, television transcripts, and research studies. He concluded that Americans are afraid of the wrong things. He emphasized that we magnify our fears about problems that are relatively minor and neglect major problems such as poverty and social inequalities. Glassner suggested that we need to learn to doubt our inflated fears. False and overdrawn fears can cause hardships; valid fears can prepare us for danger. While news media are usually criticized for creating unnecessary fear, Glassner also includes a wide array of groups such as advocacy groups, religious sects, political parties, and groups that benefit from the products and services that they sell to increase our sense of security.

Fear is a part of the way of life of the world and of our society. It is a matter of deciding which fears are real and which ones have personal consequences. For example, information provided to the public from different research studies about the negative health effects of different foods is frequently contradictory. Recently, researchers found that salmon raised on farms are given food that is high in cancer-producing toxins. Investigators advised that farm-raised salmon should not be eaten more than once a month. Representatives from the salmon industry said that the risks of cancer were exaggerated. And physicians advise that Omega 3 contained in fish is beneficial in preventing heart disease. The public is left to choose among these fear alternatives. Contradictory messages cause people to doubt fear so they discredit sources of fear and ignore their warnings.

There are specific fears that threaten one's self-interests. The more personal the fear, the more people tend to take action by disconnecting, withdrawing, changing their lifestyles, and acquiring skills and resources to defend themselves. Therefore, homicides in one's neighborhood generate a higher level of fear than news reports of serial murders in a city thousands of miles away. Levels of fear can change, for example, the color-coded index of terror alert controlled by the Office of Homeland Security is a barometer of the level of the government's fear of a terrorist attack, but unless there are specific locations given, people cannot personalize the fear so they are encouraged by the government to go about their business as usual until advised otherwise.

Fear and its friends, distrust, dishonesty, and opportunism, now cause Americans to look over their shoulders more than they look in each other's eyes. Fear has caused us to re-direct our societal priorities so that we spend more time and resources safeguarding our security. Security concerns have created social distance between people and dampened their cordiality. We now fear what a person might do, we avoid unnecessary communication, and withdraw to the security of what we can control.

Distrust of Institutions

According to Bok (1978), "Trust in some degree of veracity functions as a *foundation* of relations among human beings; when this trust shatters or wears away, institutions collapse" (p. 31).[4] Distrust is a word we commonly hear when people discuss their experiences with government and politics, health care providers and insurers, education, Wall Street, religion, corporate business and law. Distrust is a symptom of the loss of integrity and a disregard for the common good.

Several writers have described how the common good has been replaced by an ethic of individual rights where everyone does what they consider to be the right thing. The decline of collective responsibility and the rise of individual responsibility are evidenced in distrust. The common good raises the ante for everyone. Everyone doing the right thing raises the ante for oneself. The sociologist, M. P. Baumgartner (1988) found adisturbing unwillingness of people to make moral claims on one another. Most people did not feel it was their place to express their convictions when someone did something that was wrong.

In a time and task-driven society the final outcome and the benefits that accrue to the individual achieving it is what counts. Contributing to the common good yields rewards only to an individual's conscience. The common good and the ethical and moral standards it provides are unacknowledged by many in society and justified by them as "this is business, we have to do what our competitors do." To have achieved a favorable bottom-line is considered to have acted accountably and individuals who realize the bottom-line are generously rewarded and upheld as models by their leaders. Distrust comes into the picture when clients, patrons and investors learn that legal and ethical infractions were knowingly engaged in by leaders and their teams who acted to "cover up" traces of their criminal behavior.

There are numerous examples of scandals in institutions in our daily newspapers, the most recent of which include the greed of corporate CEOs and of brokers, the abuse of children by clergy and teachers, the abuse of patients by doctors, the misuse of funds by government officials, and the exorbitant fees charged by lawyers in the tobacco settlement lawsuits. Trust, like fear, is built on individual experience. We talk about fear and trust to compare and learn from other people's experiences. Trust is what is needed during periods of change and transition, when there is not enough confidence to predict behavior or outcomes. Trust is what we need when we interact with people, especially strangers. Fear and trust go hand in hand and reinforce each other. A high titer of fear and distrust encourage people to disconnect from each other.

Anger at Inequalities

People become frustrated and angry when they are blocked from achieving outcomes for themselves and when they see others successfully achieve the same outcomes using illegal and unethical means and without consequences. Anger is an increasing behavioral response in our society today; people sense threat in much of their environment on a daily basis. Aggression is a competitive response in the form of asserting oneself, or making one's views or opinions known. It can be positive, especially in a time and task-oriented society, but it has the potential for escalating into violence and doing harm or damage to others. People seem to be riding the fine line between being aggressive and being violent.

Anger and depression are emotions commonly seen together in the same person in our society today. Depression is the experience of an emotional loss and characterized by a sense of hopelessness, or as anger toward another that is turned inward to ward off its painful consequences. Depression affects more than 19 million Americans. It is estimated that as many as one-third of office visits to physicians involve depression. Depression and anger are emotions that occupy the whole body, complicating existing health conditions and triggering the onset of new ones.

Despite the fact that the incidence of violent crime in the United States has statistically decreased, the United States remains one of the most violent societies in the world. Interpersonal violence has invaded all facets of life, reaching what public health experts now conclude is an epidemic (Cohen & Swift, 1993). Cohen and Swift argue that violence is learned, therefore it can be prevented. They identified three root causes at the societal level that generate violence in the United States:

1. Depressed economic conditions; unemployment and underemployment[5]
2. Oppression resulting from feelings of inequality and powerlessness including sexism, racism, and various kinds of discrimination
3. Home environments that are unsupportive and abusive, where there is a sense of isolation, and fear for one's safety

They also identified six risk factors at the community level that are factors that enable violent behavior: 1) the availability of guns; 2) the sensationalization of violence in the mass media; 3) alcohol and drugs; 4) incarceration as a training ground and communication center; 5) experiencing and witnessing violent acts; and 6) lack of community services and community participation in providing buffers against violence. Cohen and Swift stressed that most violence prevention efforts have been conducted at the grass roots level with small community agencies providing leadership. Most large social institutions have either ignored violence as an issue or encouraged retribution. Ironically, much of the anger people feel is directed toward institutions that are blamed for helping to create the inequalities. People who are angry because they feel victimized by society's institutions are unlikely to respond positively to efforts by these institutions to rehabilitate them for their violent misdeeds. Therefore, the cycle continues. Feeling victimized generates anger, the lack of change breeds violence, those who act violently are punished, and those who are punished become more angry.

Changes in Institutional Boundaries

Boundaries set limits, restrict access, and control behavior. There have always been ways of controlling behavior in health care through accessibility, availability, and affordability. With managed care these methods have become more bureaucratized and rigid. Before managed care people could choose and access both primary care providers and specialists with relative ease. As public policy makers became concerned with the rising costs of health care, especially specialty care, cost controls were initiated. As the government and insurance companies have managed health care costs, they have also gained greater control over who can have access to certain providers and their services. In addition, the funders of health care have influenced how health providers practice their professions. For example, physicians and patients are forced to relate to each other in a narrower range and more of physicians' actions are being dictated and standardized. The problems and issues discussed by physicians and patients are largely limited by what is reimbursable.

Rigid boundaries help to control financial costs, but many social inequities related to health status and health care have not changed as a result of managed care. Our society's approach to health care is still multitiered; a minimum level of services is available to patients in the lowest tier. Depending on one's ability to pay, a person can receive the best health care in the world or not fare as well as one's contemporaries in Europe. National health care costs are projected to reach 16.2 percent of the Gross Domestic Product by 2008 and continue to rise despite managed care. More than 44 million Americans have no health insurance. Many senior citizens obtain their prescription drugs from Canada or Mexico where they are from one-half to two-thirds less than in the United States. Uninsured citizens are usually financially poor; subsistence needs preempt those of health even when there are severe symptoms so health care is usually a catastrophic event.

Managed care encourages a fragmented approach to health care. A patient becomes a series of problems, some of which are reimbursable and others not; the priority of managed care is to diagnose and treat reimbursable conditions. Rigid boundaries are not conducive to building partnerships or teams. More than one-half of the households in the United States changed physicians during the past two years chiefly because people were not happy with their physicians. Health Maintenance Organization representatives advise clients to select a primary care physician from a list of participating providers about whom the client knows little. So if a client selects a physician from the list and is not satisfied with his/her services, they can change physicians up to eight times a year—not a way to build a meaningful physician-patient relationship! The virtues of trust and loyalty valued in this relationship in the past have been replaced by what is expedient and self-serving.

More health care decisions are being made by insurance companies. What insurance companies are willing to reimburse ties the physician's hands; diagnoses are often stretched to enable patients to receive reimbursable care. Knowing this, insurance companies require more documentation from physicians rigidifying their boundaries of control.

Health care has become an increasingly tough culture. Cultures can be judged as tough or easy depending on the ways and means they provide for their members to meet their needs. The core of a culture is its set of values. The value driving managed care is cost control; the value that health professionals emphasize is providing quality care to the sick. The values of health care managers conflict with those of the providers; the patient is in the middle. There is no evidence that either managers or providers will change their values or become more flexible in negotiating their respective boundaries, although a recent Institute of Medicine panel has recommended for the first time that the government provide universal health insurance by the year 2010.

While the boundaries of health care have become more rigid over the past several decades, the boundaries regarding marriage and family have become more flexible. People are postponing marriage until their midtwenties. People are divorcing more often; about one-half of all marriages end in divorce. The proportion of unmarried adults has increased with an estimated 80 million single adults 59 percent of whom have never married. As the stigma against divorce, cohabitation, and single parenthood lessens, marriage becomes less attractive. Growing economic independence has made marriage less obligatory for women. There are also more options for those who marry and change their minds. No-fault divorce has allowed one parent to leave the other without an established cause.

As attitudes and expectations regarding marriage have changed so have the boundaries that characterized the traditional nuclear family. There are fewer two-parent families; fewer two-parent families with children; more single parents; more single parents with adopted and step-children; and more racially mixed families. The definition of "a family" is now whatever people (partners, friends, or lovers) choose to call their living arrangement. Greater flexibility in the boundaries of marriage and family has enabled choices about what is right or wrong to become more individualized. Choices people make regarding marriage and family are not limited to those two spheres of behavior, but have spill over effects to religion, politics, education, law, government, health care, and the military, for example the effects of the legalization of same sex marriages. As the reader might surmise, changes in the boundaries of marriage and the family are highly emotional and anxiety-producing public issues. Since people's attitudes toward sexuality, marriage, and parenthood are the expression of their core values that define their personhood, their attitudes, much less their values, are unlikely to change. Therefore, one of the most polarizing and irreconcilable issues in our society today is related to the changing boundaries of marriage and family, best exemplified by the Pro-life, Pro-choice organizations.

Domestic Migration

One of the reasons people disconnect is because they move. Approximately 43 million (17 percent) of Americans change residences annually; half lived in their homes five years or less. According to Census 2000, the highest levels of migration were in the south while the lowest levels were in the Northeast.[6] Why do people move? Most social scientists agree that there are a combination of economic and noneconomic reasons for moving that vary depending on the time period and age of the movers.[7] Interregional moves are more likely to be job-related, while intraurban moves are more likely to be housing related. The highly educated are more likely to move for work-related reasons, especially for long-distance moves. People with less than a high school education are more likely to move for housing-related reasons. Lower income groups were more likely than higher income groups to move for family reasons.

The distance of a move is strongly related to the reason an individual moves. Socioeconomic characteristics are related to the reason for moving with lower education and income groups more likely to move for family reasons and less likely to move for work-related reasons than higher education and income groups.

Geographic mobility is disruptive; it involves disconnections and reconnections between individuals, organizations, and social networks. When children are involved breaking connections with school and peer friendships is usually traumatic. The effects of frequent mobility on psychological and physical health depends a great deal on the personalities of the people involved, their previous experience with moves, and available sources of support, such as the extended family.

RECONNECTIONS

All people experience disconnections and reconnections in relationships as they progress through life transitions such as leaving home, changing friendships, jobs, and places of residence, having children and acquiring grandchildren, the death of friends and family members, retirement, and possibly personal injury and illness. Life changes have been associated with the onset of illness. Research has shown that the accumulation of life change precedes the onset of illness: the greater the magnitude of life change, the greater the risk of illness, and furthermore, the greater the seriousness of the illness (Masuda & Holmes, 1978). The relationship between life change and illness onset persists across cultures, although people in different cultures may differ in the weight they attribute to various life changes.

The key point is that changes in personal relationships can have helpful or hurtful effects on our well-being individually and collectively. The stronger our social networks the more support we will have available to help us cope with change. When social networks are weak or absent, and we have to cope alone, the effects of change can be overwhelming, causing some people to "give up" or "drop out." It would be expected that support systems are less available in a society of self-interest, and if and when they are available, there might be a reluctance to access them.

In our society, characterized by frequent social change, it is difficult to reconnect. By 2050 it is predicted that 25 percent of Americans will move annually; most current movers have lived in their homes five years or less. As Putnam found, people who know or expect that they are going to move do not invest time to become socially or civically engaged. Therefore, support for many people is what they can receive by phone or mail. Furthermore, reconnections take time to develop; many people choose "convenience friendships" instead.

Some people live their lives around disconnections and reconnections as a result of their choice of personal habits such as alcohol and drug abuse. Alcohol and drug abusers experience many negative life changes both preceding and subsequent to their addictions. These may include abuse, poor citizenship in school, encounters with the law, separation or divorce, job changes, periods of unemployment and homelessness, incarceration, hospitalization for their addiction and associated illnesses, and social rejection. Addicts learn to cope with their addiction and social disconnectedness by moving on and attempting to establish new connections, usually to sustain their lifestyles. Should they be successful in connecting with intervention and self-help groups they may be able to successfully reject their old connections for new connections to healthier communities. Alcoholics Anonymous and Alanon are communities of self-interest; peers helping peers to provide on-going social and emotional support for each other in order to successfully live in a society where individualism is valued and rewarded.

Whether by choice or due to life circumstances some people become permanently disconnected from society, indeed, society may have marginalized and negatively labeled them. Others, through their recidivism, have indicated their disinterest in establishing socially acceptable reconnections. Lifestyles of disconnectedness are very difficult to change; recidivism is about 50–50 for many addictions and for criminal behavior.

Yet, there are some successes such as The Greyston Bakery Story (www.greystonbakery.com). In 1982, a Zen Buddhist meditation group led by a former aerospace engineer, Bernard Tetsugen Glassman, borrowed $300,000 to open a small storefront bakery in the Bronx, that it was hoped would become profitable enough to free up its members from their usual jobs. They would earn their own daily bread by turning out muffins, scones, and cakes for the neighborhood and for upscale restaurants in Manhattan. After realizing this goal and moving to Yonkers, the group decided to hire the chronically unemployed and give them on-the-job training as well as paychecks. Today, Greyston Bakery has been transformed into a gourmet wholesale-retail bakery whose cakes and tarts have been served at the White House. The Bakery generates more than $3.5 million in revenues and employs 55 people. The Bakery makes more than two million pounds of brownies a year for Ben and Jerry's ice cream, has developed brownies free of genetically modified organisms (GMO-free) for Europeans, and Kosher brownies for Israel. Greyston Bakery has outgrown its current home and is building a larger, more modern facility. The Bakery is a revenue producer for Greyston Foundation, which is an integrated system of non-profit and for-profit organizations. The Foundation is a $14 million organization of 180 employees that provides jobs, housing, social services, and health care to more than 1,200 low-income residents of Yonkers.

Recognized as a pioneer in social enterprise, Greyston uses entrepreneurship to solve the problems of the inner city. Greyston's human services help residents achieve personal and economic self-sufficiency. The services are intensively targeted to the formerly homeless families living in Greyston's supportive housing. Greyston emphasizes the importance of employment and helps individuals identify a path towards greater independence and remove obstacles in the way of personal success. As the CEO of Greyston said, "We have a double bottom line."

COMMUNITIES OF THE FUTURE

Frances Hesselbein (1998) has said that the community of the future is "a dream that lies before us" (p. 177). Futurists state that there is a need for different structures for community, but that these structures need to embrace diversity and differences and at the same time build partnerships that enhance interdependence and cohesiveness. Self-interest or solitary communities meet the needs of some people, but the strongest societies are those that create opportunities for all citizens to connect and find areas of common interest (Morse, 1998). Robert Putnam and Lewis Feldstein (2003) endorse "better together" as the theme for communities of the future. They studied twelve communities that were working to solve specific problems and advocate that "better together" demonstrates that bringing people together by building personal relationships remains one of the most effective strategies to build social capital at the individual, community, and societal levels. Some observers, researchers, and futurists propose that what we need first are visionary leaders whose priorities are to set goals to improve the quality of life for everyone so that local communities can collaborate in meeting both local needs and contribute to a societal common good. Then, according to Wilkinson (1996), there will be fewer fault lines in the "moral community" because people will have a sense of purpose and direction from a set of values they can share despite their differences.

SUSTAINABLE COMMUNITIES

In the 1980s a Healthy Communities movement was inspired by Drs. Len Duhl and Trevor Hancock and first implemented by the World Health Organization to bolster the quality of life in European cities. (www.healthycommunities.org). The movement spread to the United States in 1988, where, now in its second decade, it has involved more than 1,000 cities which have built partnerships at local, state and regional levels to take actions to improve the economic health, environmental quality, and social equity of cities and communities. Effectiveness is being measured by citizen's reports of improvements in social cohesion, trust, and a sense of community and tangible progress is assessed by reduced crime rates, lower teen pregnancy rates, declining numbers of HIV infections, and improved cardiovascular health.

As Healthy Communities gained momentum across the United States Duhl and two colleagues Tyler Norris and Mary Pittman (2000) created a national network of community and organizational leaders that led to the formation of the Coalition for Healthier Cities and Communities.[8] The coalition brings together local, state and national organizations to form linkages to resources, a public policy voice, and provide the facilitation of the Healthy Communities efforts. In 1999, the coalition conducted more than 300 dialogues engaging 4,000 people in the United States to stimulate action. The dialogues identified seven characteristics of a healthy community. A healthy community:

- Participates in ongoing dialogue among residents to build relationships and a shared vision of what a community is, what it should be, and how to get there.

- Generates leadership with the community, encourages facilitation, collaboration, coalitions, and partnerships.
- Shapes its future based on a shared vision of the community.
- Embraces the diversity of its citizens.
- Gathers information about its assets and needs.
- Connects people to community resources.
- Creates a sense of responsibility and belonging among its residents.

To be healthy and vital communities of the future need to be both environmentally and socially sustainable. This does not mean that sustainability is in opposition to change, but rather that change is anticipated, planned for, and directed as much as possible. Change usually needs to be created to serve a purpose. For example, California Smoke-Free Cities initiative led to the passage, in 1994, of a state law that banned smoking in all workplaces including bars.

Creating social sustainability in communities is challenging because many of our social problems are tied to closely held values which people are often reluctant to change. Yet, many communities have been successful with the assistance of the Healthy Communities process.

However one might envision future communities, one thing is certain; we need to become involved in shaping them. Communities are no longer stable nostalgic places that we can return to when we feel lonely or homesick, they are dynamic sets of relationships between people—some are in real places, others are virtual, and still others are mobile. We create our connections and disconnections with others by the kind of lifestyle we choose, in our participation in our community, and through our contribution to the common good.

SUMMARY

Human relationships can be grouped into three levels, interactions, connections, and attachments. In our society we seem to have fewer and less meaningful attachments and connections with others. We seem to have detached from the common societal good and disconnected from relationships that help to promote it. In essence, we interact in solitary communities with people like ourselves who have few, if any, commitments to each other. Even our cursory daily interactions with others have become uncivil and project our attitudes of cynicism and distrust. Communities have become utilitarian rather then nostalgic places.

There are pervasive societal factors that have contributed to our changing views of community and to our general disconnectedness. One of the general sources of disconnection in our society comes from fear. We have developed a "culture of fear," reinforced by threats of terrorism, that has created social distance between people. We fear what a person might do, we avoid unnecessary communication, and withdraw to the security of what we can control.

A second factor contributing to our disconnectedness is the distrust of institutions. There are numerous examples of scandals in our social institutions and cover ups of criminal behavior that have fostered cynicism and distrust. Fear and distrust go hand in hand and reinforce each other. A high titer of fear and distrust encourage people to disengage from each other.

Third, there is considerable anger at social inequalities that continue to exist in our society. Anger is commonly expressed in interpersonal violence which has reached epidemic proportions. Root causes of violence include depressed economic conditions, unemployment and underemployment; oppression from feelings of inequality and powerlessness; and home environments that are unsupportive and abusive.

Changing boundaries in institutions, especially marriage and the family, have created a great deal of anxiety and polarization in our society. While the boundaries of marriage and the family have become more flexible the boundaries in health care have become more rigid.

Finally, domestic migration is a reason many people disconnect in our society. About 17 percent of the population changes residences annually with this number increasing to 25 percent by the year 2050. While the reasons for moving may be positive, moving is disruptive, especially for children. In anticipation of moving many people don't bother to become involved in their communities.

Many people reconnect following life events or crises that have disrupted their connections. Other people choose lifestyles that are characterized by frequent periods of disconnectedness, such as alcohol and drug addiction. There are many positive examples of businesses and institutions that sponsor initiatives to help disconnected people reconnect with society.

What will communities in the future look like? There are social movements like the communitarian movement and the healthy cities and communities movement that are attempting to swing the pendulum from "me-thinking" to "we thinking" and reestablish a concern for a common good. There are efforts throughout North America to create an awareness and action groups to create sustainable communities. We create our connections and disconnections with others by the kind of lifestyle we choose, in our participation in our community, and through our contribution to the common good. Hopefully more citizens will become active in shaping the communities they will live in during the 21st century.

QUESTIONS FOR DISCUSSION

1. In what ways do people work for "the common good"? What are some of the principles that underlie the common good in the United States?
2. Give some examples of outcome and process-oriented communities from your own experiences. Which type do you relate to the best? Discuss.
3. Mention other sources of disconnectedness in our society in addition to those in the book.
4. How does immigration contribute to both connectedness and disconnectedness?
5. Have you experienced disconnections in your life? Did you choose to reconnect? Why or why not?
6. Mention other examples you know of, in addition to the Greyston Bakery Story in the book, that illustrate how businesses and organizations can help in reconnecting individuals who are socially excluded or marginalized in our society.
7. What are your thoughts about what communities of the future should be like?
8. What might a socially sustainable community look like?

Notes

Chapter 1: Social Connections

1. Drawing on data from the 1987–1988 wave of the National Survey of Families and Households, Eggebeen and Knoester explored the effects of a range of fatherhood experiences on the lives and well-being of men. They found strong evidence that fathers differ from nonfathers in their social connections, family relationships, and work behavior. See Eggebeen, D. J., & Knoester, C. (2001). Does fatherhood matter for men? *Journal of Marriage and Family, 63,* May, 381–393.

2. In her book, *Party of one: The loner's manifesto* (New York: Marlowe & Co.), Anneli Rufus (2003) delivers an argument in praise of loners. Assembling evidence from diverse aspects of culture, Rufus says that loners are a vital force in world civilization rather than people who need to be "fixed." She rebuts the prevailing notion that aloneness is indistinguishable from loneliness, and the only experiences that matter are shared ones.

3. In his book, *How to break your addiction to a person.* New York: McGraw Hill. Howard M. Halpern (1982), deals with the opposite problem of the failure to attach to key persons. He discusses "attachment hunger" in which individuals become so attached to another person that it becomes disabling and destructive. He suggests the value of friends and a supportive network during the process of breaking addictive relationships.

4. See Bell, C., & Newby, H. (1974) (Eds.), Introduction in Bell, C. & Newby H. *The sociology of community: A selection of readings* (pp. xlii–lii). They are critical of the lack of a theory or accepted definition of community despite hundreds of community studies. In the same volume, Margaret Stacey (pp. 13–26), strongly asserted that confusion over the concept of community has led her to refuse to use the word. G. A. Hillery (1955), in Definitions of community: Areas of agreement, *Rural Sociology, 20,* 111–125, set out to identify areas of agreement among the many definitions of community and uncovered 94 definitions. Among the many different definitions that have been offered, three characteristics are mutually agreed upon as a minimum, namely locale, common ties, and social

interaction. Yet, as Jessie Barnard pointed out, this definition is deceptive because there are two different concepts; "community" emphasizes social interactions and "the community" stresses locale (see *The sociology of community* by
Jessie Bernard (1973), pp. 3–14). The concept of neighborhood is often used
interchangeably with notions of community. Some authors have suggested
that neighborhood is a subunit of community; others state that neighborhoods
create community. See this discussion in Jeffres, L. W. (2002). *Urban communication systems: Neighborhoods and the search for community.* Creskill, NJ: Hampton
Press, Chapter 1. Although the notion of "community" enjoys the dubious
distinction of one of the most frequently and variably used terms in social
science, there is relatively standardized rule-of-thumb methodology used in
studying communities ranging from participant observation through interviews and/or questionnaires to the analysis of documents. The most common
reason to conduct a community study is to analyze particular behaviors and organizational patterns against a context or setting, which communities provide.
See E. Knop (1973), The concept of community: Cross-cultural perspectives.
The Rocky Mountain Social Science Journal, 10, 2, 121–129.

5. Several authors have suggested that community is a problematic term because
of difficulties in defining it (Note 1). But Paddison (2001) points out that there
are other reasons why community is problematic arising from the assumption
that it is inclusionary. How the boundaries of a community are defined determines who is included or excluded. Because of their inclusionary nature we
tend to think of communities as a good thing. Yet, there can be divisions and
conflicts within a community. Therefore, viewing a community as a functioning unit is somewhat idealistic, concealing divisions within it. See Paddison, R.
(2001) Communities in the city in Paddison, R. (Ed.), *Handbook of urban studies*
(pp. 194–205), Thousand Oaks, CA: Sage. Even within seemingly homogeneous communities there is always a basis for exclusion. For example, a gentile
woman told the author of her conversion to Judaism, but after her baptism and
receiving her Jewish name, was excluded from many social activities held by
members of the temple following several personality clashes emanating from
her abrupt, brash style of interaction. The woman felt that she had demonstrated her commitment to Judaism, and was disappointed that members did
not accept her "as one of them." She was confused about whether her exclusion
was her personality, or her not really being Jewish, or both.

6. The economic expansion of the 1990s greatly benefited rural economies, raising
earnings, increasing income, and reducing poverty. Rural areas attracted both
urban residents and immigrants; almost eight percent of nonmetro counties,
many in the West, increased in population at more than twice the national
average. The back-to-the-country movement is made possible by new communication technologies. Manufacturers, in search of lower costs and cheaper but
educated labor, can find those advantages outside of urban centers. See Baldauf,
S. More Americans move off the beaten path (1996, August 7) *Christian Science
Monitor,* p. 1, p. 4 and United States Department of Agriculture, Economic Research Service, *Rural America at a glance,* Rural development research report
No. 94-1, September, 2002.

7. Also see, Putnam, R. D. (Ed.). (2000). *Democracies in flux: The evolution of social capital in contemporary society*. New York: Oxford University Press. Putnam assembled authors from eight post-industrial democracies to examine the causes for changes in social capital in their countries from the end of World War II to the end of the 20th century. Several common threads were identified in social capital in the countries over the past several decades, including declining electoral turnout, declining public engagement in political parties, declining union membership, and declining church attendance. According to Putnam, the most important common thread in all of the countries was the growing inequality in the distribution of social capital within each country.

8. Three sociologists offer differing critiques of Putnam's, *Bowling Alone* in a symposium, *Contemporary Sociology* (2001), *30*, 3, 223–230.

9. Some authors who believe our core values as a society remain unchanged and take exception with many of the views of authors in Note 8 are: Ladd, E. C. (1999). *The Ladd report*. New York: The Free Press; Lin, N. (2001). *Social Capital: A theory of social structure and action*. New York: Cambridge University Press; Skocpol, T. (1997). Building community top-down or bottom-up? *The Brookings Review*, *15*, 4, 16–19; Samuelson, R. J. Bowling alone is bunk (1996, April 10). *The Washington Post*, p. A19. Lears, J. No there there. (1997, December 28). *New York Times Book Review*, p. 9.

10. Some authors who talk about the loss of social capital, loss of community and loss of virtues are: Singer, P. (1995). *How are we to live?* New York: Prometheus Books; Putnam, R. D. (2000). *Bowling alone: The collapse and revival of American community*. New York: Simon & Schuster; Etzioni, A. (1993). *The spirit of community: The reinvention of American society*. New York: Simon & Schuster; Fukuyama, F. (1999). *The great disruption*. New York: The Free Press; Fukuyama, F. (1995). *Trust: The social virtues and the creation of prosperity*. New York: The Free Press; Purdy, J. (1999). *For common things: Irony, trust and commitment in America today*. New York: Vintage Books. Myers, D. G. (2000). *The American paradox: Spiritual hunger in an age of plenty*. New Haven, CT: Yale University Press; Howard, P. K. (2001). *The lost art of drawing the line: How fairness went too far*. New York: Random House; Howard, P. K. (1994). *The death of common sense: how law is suffocating America*. New York: Warner Books; Oldenberg, R. (1997). *The great good place*. New York: Marlowe & Co; Carter, S. L. (1998). *Civility: Manners, morals and the etiquette of democracy*. New York: Basic Books. Galston, WA (1996). Won't you be my neighbor? *The American Prospect* May/June, 26, 16–18. Bellah, R. N., Madsen, R., Sullivan, W. M., Swidler, A., & Tipton, S. M. (1985). *Habits of the heart: Individualism and commitment in American life*. Berkeley: University of California Press.

Chapter 2: Conceptions of Community: Past and Present

1. For an excellent discussion of the two main controversies over territorial grounding and the range of functions that have divided theoretical research on community into four main research traditions see Effrat, M. P. (1974).

Approaches to community: Conflicts and complementaries. In Effrat, M. P. (Ed.), *The community: Approaches and applications* (pp. 1–32). New York: Free Press. Also see Berger, B. M. (1998). Disenchanting the concept of community. *Society, 35*, 2, 324–327. Kasarda, J. D., & Janowitz, M. (1974). Community attachment in mass society. *American Sociological Review, 39*, 328–339. Etzioni, A. (1995). The attack on community: The grooved debate. *Society, 32*, 5, 12–17. For a discussion of the forms of community that are best suited to the modern world see Brint, S. (2001). Gemeinschaft revisited: A critique and reconstruction of the community concept. *Sociological Theory, 19*, 1, 1–23.

2. For more information on "the new urban sociology" see Gottdiener, M. (1994). *The new urban sociology*. New York: McGraw Hill; Gottdiener, M., & Feagin, J. (1988). The paradigm shift in urban sociology. *Urban Affairs Quarterly, 24*, 163–187.

Chapter 3: Common Ties: Immigrant and Ethnic Communities

1. See Glazer (1975). *Affirmative discrimination: Ethnic inequality and public policy.* New York: Basic Books. And also Lipset (1963). *The first new nation*. New York: Basic Books, especially Chapter 2 for a discussion of the history of the emergence of ethnic patterns in the United States.
2. Immigration and Naturalization Service, Office of Public Affairs, February 7, 1997 and August 30, 2002. Smith, J. P. & Edmonston, B. (Eds.). (1997). *The new Americans*. Washington, DC; National Academy Press state that the United States will see an influx of 45 million immigrants between 1995 and 2050. By 2050 the white population will decrease to 51% while the black, Asian, and Hispanic populations will increase by 14%, 8%, and 26% respectively. The proportion of the United States population with multiple ancestry will increase and the social meaning of ethnic and racial lines will become increasingly blurred.
3. Of course many people insist that they are "just Americans," even when they obviously speak a foreign language. Most Americans deny that their national origin makes them unique, claim "no special comfort around their ethnic fellows," deny any ethnic pride, and apparently prefer that ethnicity "remain on a 'team sport' level of identification." It is something to root for, but not at a level where it affects important decisions. See Diane Barthel (1978), "The role of ethnicity" pp. 92–116, in Coleman, R. P. & Rainwater, L. with McClelland, K. A. (Eds.), *Social standing in America: New dimensions of class*. New York: Basic Books.
4. There is some debate about the concept of "enclave." Portes and Jensen state "enclaves do not emerge merely by residential concentration—a pattern common to all immigrant groups—but by the exceptional rise of a number of integrated ethnic firms without a metropolitan area that provide employment for a sizable proportion of workers from the same minority. The phenomenon must be examined on the basis of information on firms and labor markets, not housing." See Portes, A. & Jensen, L. (1989). What's an ethnic enclave? The case for conceptual clarity. *American Sociological Review, 52*, 768–771.

5. The decline of political participation in the United States is most serious in the central cities where the lowest levels of political engagement can be found among new immigrants, poor African Americans, Latinos, and Asian Americans. In recent years citizenship applications have increased although citizenship among new immigrants remains low, and those immigrants who become citizens are generally less likely to vote than native-born Americans. Latinos and Asian Americans, even those born in the United States, have shown a pattern of low voter turnout. Voter turnout in the African American community has also been low relative to voter turnout for white ethnics, especially in the absence of black candidates on the ballot. See Fuchs, E. R., Shapiro, R. Y., & Minnite, L. C. Social capital, political participation, and the urban community. In Saegert, S., Thompson, J. Phillip, & Warren, M. R. (Eds.). (2001). *Social capital and poor communities* (pp. 290–324). New York: Russell Sage Foundation.

6. See Driedger, L. (1995). Alert opening and closing: Mennonite rural-urban changes. *Rural Sociology, 60*, 2, 323–332. He found, in survey samples in the United States and Canada, that Mennonites are becoming more urban, professional, and mobile. Half of North American Mennonites now live in the city and many are adjusting by maintaining theological beliefs, morality, religious practices, and in-group identity of traditional rural communities. At the same time they are opening up to the larger political society, including its social concerns and greater church outreach. Rural and urban Mennonite communities are in continual communication with relatives, communities and conferences where rural-urban concerns are debated, and where they work together in numerous projects of outreach. Thus, rural Mennonite values continue to influence individual and community decisions, while Mennonites bring their more open outreach expertise and experiences to these same contacts and settings. In contrast, the Shakers, who during the 1840s numbered about 6,000 in the Northeastern United States, have not made attempts to adapt to larger American society. Primarily due to their practice of celibacy there are only eight members remaining in Sabbathday, Maine. Chura, W. How the Shakers keep it simple (1995, July) *U.S. Catholic*, p. 37.

7. According to Lin, J. (1995). Ethnic places, postmodernism, and urban change in Houston. *The Sociological Quarterly, 36*, 4, 629–647, preservationist activists and ethnic "place entrepreneurs" have used the symbolism and sentiment of ethnic culture to stimulate neighborhood revitalization and urban tourism in Houston.

8. There is evidence that the psychological health of sojourners is poorer than other types of immigrants. See Zheng, X. & Berry, J. W. (1991). Psychological adaptation of Chinese sojourners in Canada, *International Journal of Psychology, 26*, 4, 451–471.

9. For example, the "Talking Circle" in Alaska Native culture offers a context for sharing with the rest of the village. The belief is that only by coming together as a circle can cultural consciousness emerge and threats to the culture be overcome. A Talking Circle was formed in the Native Village of Eyak in Prince William Sound, Alaska to reduce community social disruption and promote local cultural mobilization following the Exxon Valdez oil spill.

See Picou, J. S. (2000). The "Talking Circle" as sociological practice: Cultural transformation of chronic disaster impacts. *Sociological Practice: A Journal of Clinical and Applied Sociology 2*, 2, 77–97. Similarly, the American Indian "powwow" has long been viewed as an index of community solidarity. As the American Indian population has become more urbanized and acculturated the powwow has become a popular national circuit involving Indians and non-Indians. Powwows are expressions of Indian identity and ways of forging and displaying group solidarity. See Eschbeah, K. & Applbaum, K. (2000). Who goes to powwows? Evidence from the survey of American Indians and Alaska Natives. *American Indian Culture & Research Journal 24*, 2: 65–83.

Chapter 4: Fragmented Ties: The Poor and the Homeless

1. See Martin, L., & Hotten, J. C., Editor and Translator, (1932). *The book of vagabonds and beggars*. London: The Penguin Press. *The liber vagatorum: Der betler orden* first appeared in 1509. After 18 editions Martin Luther wrote a Preface for the book in 1528, and in 1860 it was published as *The book of vagabonds and beggars with a vocabulary of their language and a preface by Martin Luther.* The book describes the manners and customs of vagabonds of Central Europe before the Reformation. It is estimated that toward the end of the Middle Ages a town like Augsburg contained 3,000 poor. In 1531 it was customary that those receiving alms be registered. The parish priest read from the pulpit a list of worthy alms seekers so that the congregation might know which of the poor were worthy of alms. Luther explains that he wrote a Preface "so that men may see and understand how the devil rules in the world; every town and village should know their own paupers and assist them. Outlandish and strange beggars should not be bourne with unless they have proper licenses and passports."

2. In 1995, the National Academy of Sciences suggested new ways to measure poverty. If the Census Bureau revises its definition of poverty according to these suggested definitions, another 46 million people will be recognized as living in poverty. See Millions more may fall below poverty line (1999, October 18). *Providence Journal*, pp. A1, A7. Also, United States Census Bureau (2000) *Poverty in the United States: 1999 Current Population Report.* Series P60-210, Washington, DC: United States Government Printing Office.

3. The oldest statistical study of homelessness in the United States is McCook, J. (1893). A tramp census and its revelations. *Forum*, (August 15), 753–761 as cited by Caplow, T. The Sociologist and the homeless man. In Bahr, H. M. (Ed.). (1970), *Disaffiliated man: Essays and bibliography on skid row, vagrancy, and outsiders* (pp. 3–12). Toronto: University of Toronto Press.

4. The idea of a social report on the nation's health is not new. President Herbert Hoover commissioned a President's Committee in 1929 to analyze significant societal trends in order to provide a basis for policy in the second third of the 20th century. This led to the two volumes titled *Recent social trends in the United States* published in 1933. The United States Department of Health, Education, and Welfare published *HEW Indicators* and *HEW Trends* from 1959–1966. In

1965 the Russell Sage Foundation commissioned a study of social change and social indicators published in 1968 as *Indicators of social change: Concepts and measurement*, edited by E. B. Sheldon and W. E. Moore. In a 1966 message to Congress, President Lyndon B. Johnson directed the Department of Health, Education, and Welfare to explore ways to improve the nation's ability to chart its social progress. On January 20, the last day of Johnson's administration, Wilbur Cohen, Secretary of HEW, released a document titled *Toward a social report*, which was the first step in establishing a set of social indicators for measuring the performance of the society in meeting social needs. The social report was not followed up by the Nixon or subsequent administrations. See Bell, D. (1969). The idea of a social report. *The Public Interest* 15 (Spring), 72–105, also Kristol, I. In search of the missing social indicators. *Fortune* (1969, August 1), 168–169. The need for a social report on the nation's health emerged once again in the early 1990s.

5. See Bennett, W. J., & Nunn, S. (1998). *A nation of spectators: How civic engagement weakens America and what we can do about it.* College Park, MD: University of Maryland, for Final report and The Index of National Civic Health.

6. Also see Sampson, R. J., Raudenbush, S. W., & Earls, F. (1997). Crime: A multilevel study of collective efficacy. *Science* 277 (August 15), 918–924.

7. Also see Conley, D. (1999). *Being black, living in the red: Race, wealth, and social policy in America.* Berkeley, CA: University of California Press, and Anderson, E. (1990). *Streetwise: Race, class, and change in an urban community.* Chicago: University of Chicago Press.

Chapter 5: Communities in Crisis: Reconnecting Frayed Social Ties

1. Historically studies that included social factors in research designs on community disasters began with Eric Lindemann's landmark study of the Coconut Grove fire in 1942 in Boston's theater district, Lindemann, E. (1944). Symptomotology and management of acute grief. *American Journal of Psychiatry, 101,* 141–148. He continued to follow the survivors of the fire documenting his neuropsychiatric observations, Cobb, S., & Lindemann, E. (1943). Neuropsychiatric observations during the Coconut Grove Fire. *Annals of Surgery, 112,* 814–824. In the 1960s a longitudinal study of the social and psychological consequences of Hurricane Audrey was published by the National Academy of Sciences, Bates, F. L., Fogelmen, C. W., Parenton, V. J., Pittman, R. H., & Tracy, G. S. (1963). *The social and psychological consequences of a natural disaster: A longitudinal study of Hurricane Audrey.* National Research Council, Disaster Study 18, Washington, DC: National Academy of Sciences. Since then many books and articles have been written about the social and emotional responses to numerous natural and man-made disasters including the Holocaust, Hiroshima, cyclones, tornados, earthquakes, oil spills, mass shootings, mine disasters, floods, nuclear accidents, and terrorist attacks. See Hobfoll, S. E. & de Vries, M. W. (Eds.). (1995). *Extreme stress and communities: Impact and intervention.* Dordrecht: Kluwer.

2. The trauma of being forced to lose "one's place" has been documented by Herbert Gans (1982) and Marc Fried (1963) in the late 1950s and through the 1960s when The West End, an old Italian section of Boston, was displaced by urban renewal. It was common in The West End for people to constantly check and reinforce each other's behavior lest their social networks be disrupted. For this, surveillance of everyone by everyone was of prime importance. The physical environment of the area supported this lifestyle. People were living in high enough densities so that many related families could live near each other. People, by way of their residences, were close to many other people. The people never idealized the housing itself, but they valued the types of buildings, the layout of the streets, and the commercial land uses relative to each other. This combination brought people into frequent, spontaneous, and intense contact with their relatives. This voluntary ghetto was safe and clean, yet West Enders were forced to relocate. What was fascinating was the similarities of the areas to which they moved to The West End. While they dispersed widely, the concentrations that occurred were in parts of greater Boston known for high density and mixtures of land uses, such as the North End, Charlestown, Somerville, and East Boston. See Gans, H. J. (1982). *The urban villagers* (2nd ed.). Glencoe, IL: The Free Press and Fried, M. (1963). Grieving for a lost home. In Duhl, L. J. (Ed.), *The urban condition: People and policy in the metropolis* (pp. 151–171). New York: Basic Books.

3. We also use such distinctions as "before my heart attack" and "after my heart attack" or "before my divorce" and "after my divorce" to signal to others that changes in our behavior are related to a significant life event. These events are called "markers" by Goffman. We can "mark" boundaries, relationships, or provide a system of reference for change. See Goffman, I. (1971). *Relations in public*. New York: Harper & Row, pp. 41–44. This gives us a reason for making life changes as well as legitimizes these changes to others and will more likely elicit other's support and empathy. Life events permit us to re-organize boundaries and social relationships without negative sanctions. Seemingly the more disastrous or disruptive the event the greater latitude we have to "start over."

4. Couch & Kroll-Smith (1985) and Kroll-Smith & Garula (1985), studied a community where a disaster produced a conflict so severe that the conflict became the focal point rather than the disaster. Since 1962, a coal deposit below the town of Centralia, Pennsylvania has burned out of control, threatening 1,000 elderly and ethnically diverse residents with toxic gases, explosion, and land collapse. There have been disagreements over the best way to fight the fire, whether the fire is really under the town and which direction it is moving, and disagreements over health and safety questions. Anger has been directed inward at the community. Community violence has been common. The primary stressor has been community conflict. Couch and Kroll-Smith pointed out that divisions within Centralia correspond to existing neighborhoods and the conflict is the result of trying to achieve consensus within a community that has several communities of interest. The authors recreated a basis for community discussion of the crisis by holding neighborhood meetings rather than

meeting with the entire community. This helped to dissipate the hostility in the town. See Couch, S. R., & Kroll-Smith, J. S. (1985). The chronic technical disaster: Toward a social scientific perspective. *Social Science Quarterly, 66,* 564–575; Kroll-Smith, J. S., & Garula, S. (1985). The real disaster is above ground: Community conflict and grass roots organization in Centralia. *Small Town, 15,* 4–11.

Chapter 6: Communities of Exclusion and Excluded Communities: Barriers to Neighboring

1. While moral minimalism dominates the suburbs, Alan Wolfe found that moral freedom was dominant in his study of a cross section of the United States. He said, "morality is no longer a fixed star" rather it is how individuals interpret morality in the context of their unique experience with it. See Wolfe, A. (2001). *Moral freedom: The search for virtue in a world of choice.* New York: W. W. Norton, 2001.
2. Warren describes six neighborhood patterns based on three characteristics: interaction, identity, and connections. See Warren, D. I. (1978). Exploration in neighborhood differentiation. *Sociological Quarterly, 19,* 310–331.
3. See Weiss, M. G., & Ramakrishna, J. (2001). Interventions: Research on reducing stigma. Paper presented at *Stigma and Global Health: Developing a research agenda.* September 5–7, Bethesda: MD for an interesting discussion of stigma and why it is an important consideration for health policy and clinical practice.

Chapter 7: Connections of Faith: Religion as Community

1. For a discussion of the small group approach see Chapter 6 in Putnam, R. D. & Feldstein, L. M. (2003). *Better together: Restoring the American community.* New York, NY: Simon & Schuster. Also, Wolfe, A. (2003). *Real religion: How Americans actually live their faith.* New York, NY: Free Press. Wolfe drew parallels between the salon experience and modern church groups. He said that people are seeking more intimate forms of religious fellowship, bible study, self-help, which offers non-judgmental discussion in a non-competitive environment.
2. Churches have filled the socialization gaps that schools and families often fail to address, especially information, discussion and counseling related to sex, drugs, parenting practices, blended families, and problem-solving skills.
3. The exception to this trend is the black church. See Franklin, R. M. (1994). The safest place on earth: The culture of black congregations. In J. P. Wind & J. W. Lewis (Eds.). *American congregations,* Vol. 2 (pp. 257–284). Chicago, IL: University of Chicago Press.
4. The term *religiosity* (or "being religious") refers to an individual or group's relationships with a supernatural power. Religiosity has two aspects: 1) a personal belief that involves activities such as prayer and meditation, and 2) an organizational or group aspect that involves other people such as in worship and

service projects. Religiosity differs from *spirituality*, which is a person's search for the meaning and purpose in life in general.

5. For an informative article by skeptics on the association between religion/spirituality and health see Sloan, R. P., Bagiella, E., & Powell, T. (1999). Religion, spirituality, and medicine. *Lancet*, 353, 664–667 and a rebuttal by Koenig, H. G., Idler, E., Kasl, S., Hays, J. C., George, L. K., Musick, M., Larson, D. B., Collins, T. B., & Benson, H. (1999). Religion, spirituality, and medicine: A rebuttal to skeptics. *International Journal of Psychiatry in Medicine, 29*, 123–131.

6. See Queen, E. L. (Ed.). (2000). *Serving those in need: A handbook for managing faith-based human services organizations.* San Francisco, CA: Jossey-Bass.

7. Studies have examined the importance of institutionalized social capital networks for job attainment. For example, the frequency of church attendance is one of the strongest predictors of whether inner city black youths will become gainfully employed. The youths' religious beliefs have almost no impact on employment, suggesting that it is the social aspect of church going, not the religious aspect, that is behind these youths' economic success. See Freeman, R. B. & Holzer, H. J. (Eds.). (1986). *The black youth employment crisis.* Chicago: University of Chicago Press.

Chapter 8: Vital Bonds: Social Support, Social Networks, and Health

1. See Bruhn, J. G., & Philips, B. U. (1987). A developmental basis for social support. *Journal of Behavioral Medicine, 10*, 213–229.

2. Progress into understanding the emotional pain induced by social exclusion has been made by the recent neuroimaging study of Eisenberger and her colleagues who tested the hypothesis that the brain bases of social pain are similar to those of physical pain. See Eisenberger, N. I., Lieberman, M. D., & Williams, K. D. (2003). Does rejection hurt? An fMRI study of social exclusion. *Science, 302,* 290–292, also Panksepp, J. (2003). Feeling the pain of social loss. *Science, 302,* 237–239.

3. See Luks, A. with Payre, P. (1991). *The healing power of doing good.* New York: Fawcett Columbine.

4. See, for example, the Grief Pattern Inventory developed by Terry Martin and Ken Doka (2000), *Men don't cry, women do.* Philadelphia: Brunner/Mazel.

Chapter 9: The Social Internet: Cybercommunities

1. For a sampling of different ideas about the definitions and qualities of virtual communities see Porter, D. (Ed.). (1997). *Internet culture.* New York: Routledge; Surratt, C. G. (1998). *Netlife: Internet citizens and their communities.* Commack, NY: Nova Science Publishers; also Watson, N. (1997). Why we argue about virtual community: A case study of the Phish.net fan community (pp. 102–132). In S. G. Jones (1997). *Virtual culture: Identity & communication in*

cybersociety. Thousand Oaks, CA: Sage; Stroll, C. (1995). *Silicon Snake Oil*. New York: Doubleday.

2. A comprehensive national analysis of children's media use was published by the Kaiser Family Foundation in November, 1999. The report pointed out evidence of a "digital divide," that young people's access to and use of computers varies by median income of the community in which they live or go to school, and to a lesser degree by race. Children in low-income areas have much less access to computers at home and are less likely to use a computer on a typical day than children who live in high income areas. Black and Hispanic children are less likely than white children to use a computer. The report also emphasized the finding of the absence of a strong parental role in overseeing children's media behavior. Children's bedrooms are often the place where they engage media, outside the presence of adults. The report stressed the need for parents and children to negotiate ground rules governing the use of all media.

3. See Barber, J. T. & Tait, A. A. (Eds.). (2001). *The information society and the black community*. Westport, CT: Praeger. These authors point out that five million African-Americans are using the Net. Yet, there is a need to produce black information professionals to increase their participation in research and development and continue to increase their computer access.

Chapter 10: Solitary Communities: Disconnecting from the Common Good

1. In Gergen, K. J. (1991). *The saturated self: The dilemmas of identity in contemporary life*. New York: Basic Books.

2. In 2002 62 percent of adult Americans were said to own a cell phone.

3. Berger, P. L., Berger, B., & Hansfried, K. (1973). *The homeless mind: Modernization and consciousness*. New York: Random House.

4. Bok, S. (1978). *Lying: Moral choice in public and private life*. New York: Pantheon Books.

5. See Barlett, D. L. & Steele, J. B. (1996). *America: Who stole the dream?* Kansas City, MO: Andrews & McMeel.

6. Franklin, R. S. (2003). *Domestic migration across regions, divisions, and states: 1995–2000*. United States Census Bureau, United States Department of Commerce, Economics and Statistics Administration, August, 2003.

7. Schachter, J. (2001). *Why people move: Exploring the March 2000 current population survey*. United States Census Bureau, United States Department of Commerce, Current Population Reports, March 1999 to March 2000, May, 2001.

8. See *Public Health Reports*, March/April & May/June, 2000, Volume 115 for a series of articles on The Healthy Communities Movement and the Coalition for Cities and Communities.

References

Adams, R. E. (1992). Is happiness a home in the suburbs? The influence of urban versus suburban neighborhoods on psychological health. *Journal of Community Psychology, 20,* 353–371.

Adelman, A. (1995). Traumatic memory and the intergenerational transmission of Holocaust narratives. *Psychoanalytic Study of the Child, 50,* 343–367.

Aguillar-San J, K. (2001). *Creating ethnic places: Vietnamese American community-building in Orange County and Boston* (Doctoral dissertation, Brown University, 2001). *Dissertation Abstracts International,* 61, 9, Mar, 3783-A.

Ainsworth, M. D. Salter (1979). Infant-mother attachment, *American Psychologist, 34,* 10, 932–937.

Alba, R. D. (1990). *Ethnic identity: The transformation of white America.* New Haven, CT: Yale University Press.

Alba, R. D., Logan, J. R., Stults, B. J., Marzan, G., & Zhang, W. (1999). Immigrant groups in the suburbs: A reexamination of suburbanization and spatial assimilation. *American Sociological Review, 64,* 3, 446–460.

Albrecht, T. L. (1994). Social support and community: A historical account of the rescue networks in Denmark. In B. R. Burleson, T. L. Albrecht, & I. G. Sarason (Eds.), *Communication of social support: Messages, interactions, relationships, and community* (pp. 267–279). Thousand Oaks, CA: Sage.

Alesina, A., & La Ferrara, E. (2002). Who trusts others? *Journal of Public Economics, 85,* 2, 207–234.

Allan, G. (1998). Friendship, sociology and social structure. *Journal of Social & Personal Relationships, 15,* 5, 685.

Anderson, L., Snow, D. A., & Cress, D. (1994). Negotiating the public realm: Stigma management and collective action among the homeless. In D. A. Chekki (Ed.), *Research in community sociology,* Suppl. 1, The community of the streets (pp. 121–143). Greenwich, CT: Jai Press.

Antonucci, T. C., & Jackson, J. S. (1990). The role of reciprocity in social support. In B. R. Sarason, I. G. Sarason, & G. R. Pierce (Eds.), *Social support: An interactional view* (pp. 173–198). New York: John Wiley.

Appelbaum, R. P. (1989). The affordability gap. *Society, 26,* 4, 6–8.

Architectural Record (1997). To gate or not to gate. *Architectural Press Roundup,* April 24, 45.

Argyle, M. & Henderson, M. (1985). *The anatomy of relationships.* London: Heinemann.

Aron, L. Y., & Fitchen, J. M. (1996). Rural homelessness: A synopsis. In J. Baumohl (Ed.), *Homelessness in America* (pp. 81–85). Phoenix, AZ: Oryx Press.

Auerswald, C. L., & Eyre, S. L. (2002). Youth homelessness in San Francisco: A life cycle approach. *Social Science & Medicine*, 54, 1497–1512.

Auletta, K. (1999). *The underclass*. New York: The Overlook Press.

Axelrod, R. (1984). *The evolution of cooperation*. New York: Basic Books.

Bachar, E. (1994). Aggression expression in grandchildren of Holocaust survivors: A comparative study. *Israel Journal of Psychiatry & Related Disciplines, 31*, 1, 41–47.

Bahm, A. J. (1992). *The heart of Confucius*. Berkeley, CA: Asian Humanities Press.

Baker, S. G. (1994). Gender, ethnicity, and homelessness. *American Behavioral Scientist, 37*, 4, 476–504.

Ball-Rokeach, S. J., Yong-Chan, Kim, & Sorin, M. (2001). Storytelling neighborhood: Paths to belonging in diverse urban environments. *Communication Research, 28*, 4, 392–429.

Bane, M., Coffin, B., & Thiemann, R. (Eds.) (2000). *Who will provide? The changing role of religion in American social welfare*. Boulder, CO: Westview Press.

Barata, P. (2000). Social exclusion: A review of the literature. Paper prepared for the Laidlow Foundation, Canadian Council on Social Development. Toronto, Canada.

Barnes, S. (2000). Developing a concept of self in cyberspace communities. In S. B. Gibson & O. O. Oviedo (Eds.), *The emerging cyberculture: Literacy, paradigm, and paradox* (pp. 169–201). Cresskill, NJ: Hampton Press.

Barr, S. (2001). Survey of supervisors finds little movement toward "Managing for Results" (2001, June 10). *The Washington Post*, p. C-2.

Baum, A., Gatchel, R., & Schaeffer, M. (1983). Emotional, behavioral, and physiologic effects of chronic stress at Three Mile Island. *Journal of Consulting and Clinical Psychology, 51*, 656–672.

Baumeister, R. F., & Leary, M. R. (1995). The need to belong: Desire for interpersonal attachments as a fundamental human motivation. *Psychological Bulletin, 117*, 497–529.

Baumgartner, M. P. (1988). *The moral order of a suburb*. New York: Oxford University Press.

Beck, A., & Katcher, A. H. (1983). *Between pets and people: The importance of animal companionship*. New York: G. P. Putnam's Sons.

Belluck, P. Mixed welcome as Somalis settle in Maine. (2002, October 15). *The New York Times*, p. A16.

Belsky, J. (1996). Parent, infant, and social-contextual antecedents of father-son attachment security. *Developmental Psychology, 32*, 5, 905–913.

Bergin, A. E. (1991). Values and religious issues in psychotherapy and mental health. *American Psychologist*, 46, 394–403.

Berkman, L. F. (1985). The relationship of social networks and social support to morbidity and mortality. In S. Cohen & S. L. Syme (Eds.), *Social support and health* (pp. 241–262). New York: Academic Press.

Berkman, L. F. (2000). Social support, social networks, social cohesion and health. *Social Work in Health Care*, 31, 3–14.

Berkman, L. F., Leo-Summers, L., & Horwitz, R. I. (1992). Emotional support and survival after myocardial infarction. *Annals of Internal Medicine*, 117, 1003–1009.

Berkman, L. F., & Syme, S. L. (1979). Social networks, host resistance, and mortality: A nine-year follow-up study of Alameda County residents. *American Journal of Epidemiology, 109*, 2, 186–204.

Bernard, J. (1973). *The sociology of community*. Glenview, IL: Scott, Foresman, and Co.

Bianchi, S. M. (1999). Feminization and juvenilization of poverty: Trends, relative risks, causes, and consequences. *Annual Review of Sociology*, 25, 307–333.

Blakely, E. J., & Snyder, M. G. (1997). *Fortress America: Gated communities in the United States.* Washington, DC: Brookings Institution Press & Cambridge, MA: Lincoln Institute of Land Policy.

Boissevain, J. (1974). *Friends of friends.* New York: St. Martins Press.

Bok, S. (1978). *Lying: Moral choice in public and private life.* New York: Vintage.

Bolger, N., & Kelleher, S. (1993). Daily life in relationships. In S. Duck (Ed.), *Social context and relationships* (pp. 100–108). Thousand Oaks, CA: Sage.

Bolin, R., & Bolton, P. (1986). *Race, religion, and ethnicity in disaster recovery.* Boulder, CO: University of Colorado Institute of Behavioral Science, Program on Environment and Behavior, Monograph No. 42.

Bolland, J. M. (2003). Hopelessness and risk behavior among adolescents living in high-poverty inner-city neighborhoods. *Journal of Adolescence, 26,* 2, 145–158.

Bonner, K. (1998). Reflexivity, sociology and the rural-urban destruction in Marx, Tönnies, and Weber. *The Canadian Review of Sociology & Anthropology, 35,* 2, 165–189.

Bouvier, L. F. (1992). *Peaceful invasions: Immigration and changing America.* Lantham, MD: University Press of America.

Bowlby, J. (1982a). *Attachment and loss,* 2nd ed., Vol. 1, Attachment. New York: Basic Books.

Bowlby, J. (1982b). Attachment and loss: Retrospect and Prospect, *American Journal of Orthopsychiatry, 52,* 4, 664–678.

Braumgart, R., Julie, C., Courtney, S., & Garwood, M. M. (1999). Mother and father-infant attachment: Families in context. *Journal of Family Psychology, 13,* 4, 535–553.

Brehony, K. A. (2003). *Living a connected life: Creating and maintaining relationships that last.* New York: Henry Holt & Co.

Brint, S. (2001). Gemeinschaft revisited: A critique and reconstruction of the community concept. *Sociological Theory, 19,* 1, 1–23.

Brown, B. B., & Perkins, D. D. (1992). Disruptions in place attachments. In I. Altman & S. M. Low (Eds.), *Place attachment* (pp. 279–304). New York: Plenum.

Browne, R. B., & Neal, A. G. (2001). Introduction In R. B. Browne and A. G. Neal (Eds.), *Ordinary reactions to extraordinary events* (pp. 1–20). Bowling Green, OH: Bowling Green State University Popular Press.

Bruhn, J. G. (1991). People need people: Perspectives on the meaning and measurement of social support. *Integrative Physiological and Behavioral Science, 26,* 4, 325–329.

Bruhn, J. G., Brandt, E. N., & Shackelford, M. (1966). Incidence of treated mental illness in three Pennsylvania communities. *American Journal of Public Health, 56,* 871–883.

Bruhn, J. G., Chander, B., Miller, M. C., Wolf, S., & Lynn, T. N. (1966). Social aspects of coronary heart disease in two adjacent, ethnically different communities. *American Journal of Public Health, 56,* 1493–1506.

Bruhn, J. G., & Murray, J. L. (1985). "Playing the dozens": Its history and psychological significance. *Psychological Reports, 56,* 483–494.

Bruhn, J. G., Philips, B. U., & Wolf, S. (1972). Social readjustment and illness patterns: Comparisons between first, second and third generation Italian-Americans living in the same community. *Journal of Psychosomatic Research, 16,* 387–394.

Bruhn, J. G., Philips, B. U., & Wolf, S. (1982). Lessons from Roseto 20 years later: A community study of heart disease. *Southern Medical Journal, 75,* 575–580.

Bruhn, J. G., & Wolf, S. (1979). *The Roseto story: An anatomy of health.* Norman, OK: University of Oklahoma Press.

Bruhn, J. G., Wolf, S., Lynn, T. N., Bird, H. B., Chander, B. (1968). Social aspects of coronary heart disease in a Pennsylvania German community. *Social Science & Medicine, 2,* 201–212.

Brummett, B. D., Barefoot, J. C., Siegler, I. C., Clapp-Channing, N. E., Lytle, B. L., Bosworth, H. B., Williams, R. B., & Mark, D. B. (2001). Characteristics of socially isolated patients with coronary artery disease who are at elevated risk for mortality. *Psychosomatic Medicine*, 63, 267–272.

Burgess, M. (2003). A nuclear 9/11: Imminent or inflated threat? Center for Defense Information, *Nuclear Issues*, January 28.

Burt, M. (1992). *Over the edge: The growth of homelessness in the 1980s*. New York: Russell Sage Foundation.

Burt, M., Aron, L. Y., & Lee, E. (2001). *Helping America's homeless: Emergency shelter or affordable housing?* Washington, DC: Urban Institute Press.

Butler, R. (1969). Ageism: Another form of bigotry. *Gerontologist*, 9, 243–246.

Byrd, R. C. (1988). Positive therapeutic effects of intercessory prayer in a coronary care unit population. *Southern Medical Journal*, 81, 826–829.

Caldeira, T. P. R. (1999). Fortified enclaves: The new urban segregation. In S. M. Low (Ed.), *Theorizing the city: The new urban anthropology reader* (pp. 83–107). New Brunswick, NJ: Rutgers University Press.

Campbell, K. E., & Lee, B. A. (1990). Gender differences in urban neighboring. *The Sociological Quarterly*, 31, 495–512.

Carr, L. (1932). Disasters and the sequence-pattern concept of social change. *American Journal of Sociology*, 38, 207–215.

Cassel, J., Patrick, R., & Jenkins, D. (1960). Epidemiological analysis of the health implications of cultural change: A conceptual model. *Annals of the New York Academy of Science*, 84, 938–949.

Cerf, V. (1994). Guidelines for conduct on and use of Internet. www.isoc.org.

Chavez, S., & Quinn, J. Garages: Immigrants in, cars out (1987, May 24). *Los Angeles Times*, pp. 1, 18.

Citrin, T. (1998). Topics for our times: Public health-community or commodity? Reflections on healthy communities. *American Journal of Public Health*, 88, 3, 351–352.

Clark, W. A. V. (1998). *The California cauldron: Immigration and the fortunes of local communities*. New York: Guilford Press.

Cohen, C. I., & Sokolovsky, J. (1989). *Old men of the bowery: Strategies for survival among the homeless*. New York: The Guilford Press.

Cohen, C. I., Teresi, J., & Holmes, D. (1985). Social networks, stress, and physical health: A longitudinal study of an inner-city elderly population. *Journal of Gerontology*, 40, 478–486.

Cohen, L., & Swift, S. (1993). A public health approach to the violence epidemic in the United States. *Environment & Urbanization*, 5, 50–66.

Cohen, S., & Syme, S. L. (Eds.). (1985). *Social support and health*. New York: Academic Press.

Cole, J. (2000). *Surveying the digital future*. Los Angeles, CA: UCLA Center for Communication Policy (www.ccp.ucla.edu).

Coleman, A., & Rebach, H. M. (2001). Poverty, social welfare, and public policy. In H. M. Rebach & J. G. Bruhn (Eds.), *Handbook of clinical sociology*, 2nd ed. (pp. 353–392). New York: Kluwer Academic/Plenum Publishers.

Coleman, J. S. (1994). *Foundations of social theory*. Cambridge, MA: Belknap Press.

Colombo, M., Mosso, C., & DePiccoli, N. (2001). Sense of community and participation in urban contexts. *Journal of Community & Applied Social Psychology*, 11, 457–464.

Community Associations Institute (2003). Alexandria, VA.

Comstock, G. W., & Partridge, K. B. (1972). Church attendance and health. *Journal of Chronic Disease*, 25, 665–672.

Corin, E. (1995). The cultural frame: Context and meaning in the construction of health. In B. A. Amick, III, S. Levine, A. R. Tarlov, & D. C. Walsh (Eds.), *Society & Health* (pp. 272–304). New York: Oxford University Press.

Cornell, S. (1996). The variable ties that bind: Content and circumstance in ethnic processes. *Ethnic and Racial Studies, 19,* 2, 265–289.

Cose, E. (1992). *A nation of strangers.* New York: William Morrow & Co.

Cotter, D. A. (2002). Poor people in poor places: Local opportunity structures and household poverty. *Rural Sociology, 67,* 4, 534–555.

Cozzarelli, C., Wilkinson, A. V., & Tagler, M. J. (2001). Attitudes toward the poor and attributions for poverty. *Journal of Social Issues, 57,* 2, 207–227.

Crandall, C. S. (1994). Prejudice against fat people: Ideology and self-interest. *Journal of Personality and Social Psychology, 66,* 882–894.

Craven, P., & Wellman, B. (1973). The network city. *Sociological Inquiry, 43,* 57–88.

Cutler, D. M., & Glaeser, E. L. (1997). Are ghettos good or bad? *The Quarterly Journal of Economics, 112* (August), 827–872.

Dahl, R. A. (1961). *Who governs? Democracy and power in an American city.* New Haven, CT: Yale University Press.

Daniel, Y. (Ed.). (1998). *International Handbook of multigenerational legacies of trauma.* New York: Plenum.

Darling, N., & Steinberg, L. (1997). Community influences on adolescent achievement and deviance. In J. Brooks-Gunn, G. J. Duncan, & J. L. Aber (Eds.), *Neighborhood poverty,* Vol. 2 (pp. 120–131). New York: Russell Sage Foundation.

Davidson, L., & Baum, A. (1986). Chronic stress and post-traumatic stress disorder. *Journal of Consulting and Clinical Psychology, 54,* 303–308.

Davidson, W. B., & Cotler, P. R. (1989). Sense of community and political participation. *Journal of Community Psychology, 17,* 119–125.

Demaris, A., & Yang, R. (1994). Race, alienation, and interpersonal mistrust. *Sociological Spectrum, 14,* 327–349.

Di Maggio, P. Hargittai, E., Neuman, W. R., & Robinson, J. P. (2001). Social implications of the Internet. *Annual Review of Sociology, 27,* 307–336.

Diamond, E. (2000). *And I will dwell in their midst: Orthodox Jews in suburbia.* Chapel Hill, NC: University of North Carolina Press.

Dossey, L. (1993). *Healing words: The power of prayer and the practice of medicine.* San Francisco, CA: Harper Collins.

Drabek, T. E., & Key, W. H. (1984). *Conquering disaster: Family recovery and long-term consequences.* New York: Irvington Publishers, Inc.

Drake, St. Clair, & Clayton, H. R. (1945). *Black metropolis: A study of negro life in a northern city.* New York: Harcourt Brace.

Du Bois, C. (1974). The gratuitous act: An introduction to the comparative study of friendship patterns. In E. Leyton (Ed.), *The compact: Selected dimensions of friendship* (pp. 15–32). Newfoundland, Canada: University of Newfoundland Press.

Dubos, R. (1968). *So human an animal.* New York: Charles Schribner's Sons.

Dukro, P. N., & Magaletta, P. R. (1994). The effect of prayer on physical health—experimental evidence. *Journal of Religion & Health, 33,* 211–219.

Dunlop, C., & Kling, R. (1996). Social relationships in electronic communities. In R. Kling (Ed.), *Computerization and controversy: Value conflicts and social choices,* 2nd ed., (pp. 322–329). New York: Academic Press.

Durkheim, E. [1897] (1951). *Suicide: A study in sociology* (G. Simpson, Ed. & J. A. Spaulding and G. Simpson, Trans.). Glencoe, IL: Free Press.

Durkheim, E. [1893] (1964). *The division of labor in society.* New York: Free Press; originally published in 1893.

Dworkin, J. (1974). Global trends in natural disasters 1947–1973. Natural Hazards Research, Working Paper No. 26. Toronto: University of Toronto.

Ebaugh, H. R. (2000). Fictive kin as social capital in new immigrant communities. *Sociological Perspectives*, 43(2), 189–210.

Egolf, B., Lasker, J., Wolf, S., & Potvin, L. (1992). The Roseto effect: A 50-year comparison of mortality rates. *American Journal of Public Health*, 82, 1089–1092.

Eliot, T. S. (1949). *Notes toward the definition of culture*. New York: Harcourt, Brace, & Co.

Ellen, I. G. (2000). A new white flight? The dynamics of neighborhood change in the 1980s. In N. Foner, R. G. Rumbaut, & S. J. Gold (Eds.), *Immigration research for a new century: Multidisciplinary perspectives* (pp. 423–441). New York: Russell Sage Foundation.

Engels, F. [1844] (1958). *The condition of the working class in England* (W. O. Henderson & W. H. Chaloner, Eds. & Trans.). Stanford, CA: Stanford University Press.

Erickson, E. H. (1963). *Childhood and society* (2nd ed.). New York: W. W. Norton & Co.

Erikson, K. T. (1976a). *Everything in its path: Destruction of community in the Buffalo Creek Flood*. New York: Simon & Schuster.

Erikson, K. T. (1976b). Loss of community at Buffalo Creek. *American Journal of Psychiatry*, 133, 3, 302–305.

Erikson, K. T. (1994). *A new species of trouble: Explorations in disaster, trauma, and community*. New York: W. W. Norton.

Etzioni, A. (1993). *The spirit of community: The reinvention of American society*. New York: Simon & Schuster.

Etzioni, A. (1996a). The responsive community: A communitarian perspective. *American Sociological Review*, 61, 1–11.

Etzioni, A. (1996b). *The new golden rule: Community and morality in a democratic society*. New York: Basic Books.

Eveland, J. D., & Bikson, T. K. (1988). Work group structures and computer support: A field experiment. *ACM Transactions on Office Information Systems*, 6, 354–379.

Fadiman, A. (1997). *The spirit catches you and you fall down*. New York: Farrar, Straus & Giroux.

Fehr, B. (1996). *Friendship processes*. Thousand Oaks, CA: Sage.

Field, J., Schuller, T., & Baron, S. (2000). Social capital and human capital revisited. In S. Baron, J. Field, & T. Schuller, *Social capital: Critical perspectives* (pp. 243–263). New York: Oxford University Press.

Figley, C. R. (1985). From victim to survivor: Social responsibility in the wake of catastrophe. In C. R. Figley (Ed.), *Trauma and its wake: The study and treatment of post-traumatic stress disorder* (pp. 398–415). New York: Brunner/Mazel.

First, R. J., & Rife, J. C. (1994). Homelessness in rural areas: Causes, patterns, and trends. *Social Work*, 39, 1, 97–109.

Fischer, C. S. (1982). *To dwell among friends: Personal networks in town and city*. Chicago, IL: University of Chicago Press.

Fischer, D. H. (1994). *Paul Revere's ride*. New York: Oxford University Press.

Fiske, M., & Chiriboga, D. A. (1990). *Change and continuity in adult life*. San Francisco, CA: Jossey-Bass.

Fix, M., & Passel, J. S. (1994). *Immigration and immigrants: Setting the record straight*. Washington, DC: The Urban Institute.

Fixico, D. L. (2000). *The urban indian experience in America*. Albuquerque, NM: University of New Mexico Press.

Flannery, D. J., & Singer, M. I. (1999). Exposure to violence and victimization at school. *Choices Briefs*, No. 4 in *Choices in preventing youth violence*. Teachers College, New York: Columbia University.

Foley, M. W. (2001). Religious institutions as agents for civic incorporation: A preliminary report on research on religion and new immigrants. Paper presented at the 97th Annual meeting of the American Political Science Association, August 30 to September 2, 2001, San Francisco, CA.

Forrest, R., & Kearns, A. (1999). *Joined-up places? Social cohesion and neighborhood regeneration.* York, England: York Publishing Services for Joseph Rowntree Trust.

Forrest, R., & Kearns, A. (2001). Social cohesion, social capital and the neighborhood. *Urban Studies, 38,* 12, 2125.

Fosburg, L. B., & Dennis, D. L. (1999). *Practical lessons: The 1998 national symposium on homelessness research.* U.S. Department of Housing and Urban Development and U.S. Department of Health and Human Services, August.

Fox, N. A., Kimmerly, N. L., & Schafer, W. D. (1991). Attachment to mother/attachment to father: A meta-analysis. *Child Development, 62,* 1, 210–225.

Foxman, A. H. (2002). Remarks. Conference on "Psychology of Terror: Tackling the terrorist threat." Jerusalem, Israel, May 26.

Frasure-Smith, N., Lespérance, F., Gravel, G., Masson, A., Juneau, M., Talajic, M., & Bourassa, M. G. (2000). Social support, depression, and mortality during the first year after myocardial infarction. *Circulation, 101,* 1919–1924.

Frazier, E. F. (1937). *The negro family in Chicago.* Chicago, IL: University of Chicago Press.

Frosch, C. A., Mangelsdorf, S. C., & McHale, J. L. (2000). Marital behavior and the security of preschooler parent attachment relationships. *Journal of Family Psychology, 14,* 1, 144–161.

Fukuyama, F. (1995). *Trust: The social virtues and the creation of prosperity.* New York: The Free Press.

Fukuyama, F. (1999). *The great disruption.* New York: The Free Press.

Fuller, R. C. (2001). *Spiritual, but not religious: Understanding unchurched America.* New York, NY: Oxford University Press.

Furstenberg, F. F. (1993). How families manage risk and opportunity in dangerous neighborhoods. In W. J. Wilson (Ed.), *Sociology and the public agenda* (pp. 231–258). Newbury Park, CA: Sage.

Galston, W. A. (2000). Does the Internet strengthen community? *National Civic Review, 89,* 193–202.

Gans, H. J. (1962). *The urban villagers.* New York: Free Press.

Gansberg, M. 37 who saw murder didn't call the police (1964, March 27). *The New York Times,* p. 1.

Gardner, C. B. (1994). A family among strangers: Kinship claims among gay men in public places. In D. A. Chekki (Ed.), *The community of the streets* (pp. 95–118). Greenwich, CT: Jai Press.

Gareis, E. (1995). *Intercultural friendship: A qualitative study.* Lanham, MD: University Press of America.

Geertsen, R. (1997). Social attachments, group structures, and health behavior. In D. S. Gochman (Ed.), *Handbook of health behavior research,* Vol. 1 (pp. 267–288). New York: Plenum.

Geis, K. J., & Ross, C. E. (1998). A new look at urban alienation: the effect of neighborhood disorder on perceived powerlessness. *Social Psychology Quarterly, 61,* 232–246.

Gellner, E. (1996). *The psychoanalytic movement.* Chicago, IL: Northwestern University Press.

Giel, R. (1990). Psychosocial processes in disasters. *International Journal of Mental Health, 19,* 1, 7–20.

Gilkey, L. (1994). The Christian congregation as a religious community. In J. P. Wind & J. W. Levis (Eds.), *American Congregations,* Vol. 2 (pp. 100–132). Chicago, IL: University of Chicago Press.

Ginexi, E. M., Weihs, K., Simmens, S. J., & Hoyt, D. R. (2000). Natural disaster and depression: A prospective investigation of reactions to the 1993 Midwest floods. *American Journal of Community Psychology, 28*, 4, 495–518.

Gist, R., & Lubin, B. (Eds.). *Response to disaster: Psychosocial, community and ecological approaches.* London: Brunner/Mazel.

Glantz, M. D., & Johnson, J. L. (Eds.). (1999). *Resilience and development: Positive life adaptations.* New York: Kluwer Academic/Plenum Publishers.

Glassner, B. (1999). *The culture of fear.* New York: Basic Books.

Glazer, N. (2000). On beyond the melting pot, 35 years after. *International Migration Review, 34*, 270–276.

Glazer, N., & Moynihan, D. P. (1963). *Beyond the melting pot.* Cambridge, MA: The M.I.T. Press.

Glenn, C. L. (2000). *The ambiguous embrace: Government and faith-based schools and social agencies.* Princeton, NJ: Princeton University Press.

Gleser, G. C., Green, B. L., & Winget, C. (1981). *Prolonged psychosocial effects of disaster: A study of Buffalo Creek.* New York: Academic Press.

Godfrey, B. J. (1988). *Neighborhoods in transition: The making of San Francisco's ethnic and nonconformist communities.* Berkeley, CA: University of California Press.

Goffman, E. (1961). *Asylums: Essays on the social situation of mental patients and other inmates.* New York: Anchor Books.

Gold, S. J. (1994). Patterns of economic cooperation among Israeli immigrants in Los Angeles. *International Migration Review, 28*, 1, 114–131.

Golec, J. A. (1983). A contextual approach to the social psychological study of disaster recovery. *International Journal of Mass Emergencies and Disasters, 1*, 2, 255–276.

Goleman, G. (1995). *Emotional intelligence.* New York: Bantam Books.

Gonzalez, M. (2001). The development context: What is the impact of HIV/AIDS? The Joint United Nations Programme on HIV/AIDS (UNAIDS), New York, NY.

Gottdiener, M. (1994). *The new urban sociology.* New York: McGraw Hill.

Gottlieb, B. H. (1981). Preventive interventions involving social networks. In B. H. Gottlieb (Ed.), *Social networks and social support* (pp. 201–232). Beverly Hills: Sage.

Gottlieb, B. H. (1985). Social support and community mental health. In S. Cohen & S. L. Syme (Eds.), *Social support and health* (pp. 303–326). New York: Academic Press.

Granovetter, M. S. (1973). The strength of weak ties. *American Journal of Sociology, 78*, 6, 1360–1380.

Haines, V. A., Hurlbert, J. S., & Beggs, J. J. (1996). Exploring the determinants of support provision: Provider characteristics, personal networks, community contexts, and support following life events. *Journal of Health and Social Behavior, 37*, 252–264.

Hall, E. T. (1966). *The hidden dimension.* Garden City, NY: Doubleday.

Hammer, M. (1983). "Core" and "extended" social networks in relation to health and illness. *Social Science & Medicine, 17*, 405–411.

Hampton, K., & Wellman, B. (2000). Examining community in the digital neighborhood: Early results from Canada's wired suburb. In T. Ishida & K. Isbister (Eds.), *Digital cities: Experiences, technologies, and future perspectives* (pp. 475–492). Heidelberg, Germany: Springer-Verlag.

Hancock, T. (2000). Healthy communities must also be sustainable communities. *Public Health Reports, 115*, 153–156.

Handy, C. (1994). *The age of paradox.* Boston, MA: Harvard Business School Press.

Harris, F. R., & Curtis, L. A. (Eds.). (1998). *Locked in the poorhouse: Cities, race, and poverty in the U.S.* Lanham, MD: Rowman & Littlefield.

Harrison, L. E. The cultural roots of poverty (1999, July 13). *The Wall Street Journal*, p. A22.

Harshman, E. F., Fisher, J. E., Gilliespie, W. B., Gilsinan, J. F., & Yeager, F. C. (1998). Gated communities in cyberspace: The creation of defensible space holds the key to commerce on the Internet. *Issues in Ethics*, 9, 3, 1.

Helgeson, V. S. (1991). The effects of masculinity and social support on recovery from myocardial infarction. *Psychosomatic Medicine*, 53, 621–633.

Heller, K., Price, R. H. & Hogg, J. R. (1990). The role of social support in community and clinical interventions. In B. R. Sarason, I. G. Sarason, & G. R. Pierce (Eds.), *Social support: An interactional view* (pp. 482–507). New York: John Wiley.

Helm, H., Hays, J. C., Flint, E., Koenig, H. G., & Blazer, D. G. (2000). Effects of private religious activity on mortality of elderly disabled and nondisabled adults. *Journal of Gerontology (Medical Sciences)*, 55A, M400–405.

Henderson, D. A. (1998). Bioterrorism as a public health threat. *Emerging Infectious Diseases*, 4, 3, 488–492.

Hermann, W. (2001). Brewing up a cup of community. (2001, March 1) *Arizona Republic*, B1.

Hesselbein, F. (1998). The dream that lies before us. In F. Hesselbein, M. Goldsmith, R. Beckhard, & R. F. Schubert (Eds.), *The community of the future* (pp. 177–182). San Francisco, CA: Jossey-Bass.

Hewitt, K. & Sheehan, L. (1969). A pilot survey of global natural disasters of the past twenty years. Natural Hazards Research, Working Paper No. 11. Toronto: University of Toronto.

Hiltz, S. R. & Turoff, M. (1993). *The network nation: Human communication via computer* (Rev. Ed.). Cambridge, MA: M.I.T. Press.

Hirsch, B. J. (1981). Social networks and the coping process: Creating personal communities. In B. H. Gottlieb (Ed.), *Social networks and social support* (pp. 149–170). Beverly Hills: Sage.

Hobfoll, S. E. (1998). *Stress, culture, and community: The psychology and philosophy of stress*. New York: Plenum.

Hobfoll, S. E., & Stephens, M. P. (1990). Social support during extreme stress: Consequences and intervention. In B. R. Sarason, I. G. Sarason, & G. R. Pierce (Eds.), *Social support: An interactional view* (pp. 454–481). New York: John Wiley.

Hollenbach, D. (1999). The common good and urban poverty. *America, 180*, 20, 8–11.

Hollingshead, A. B. (1949). *Elmtown's youth: The impact of social classes on adolescents*. New York: John Wiley.

Hollingshead, A. B., & Redlich, F. C. (1958). *Social class and mental illness: A community study*. New York: John Wiley.

Hostetler, J. (1997). *Amish society*. Baltimore, MD: The Johns Hopkins University Press.

House, J. S., Robbins, C., & Metzner, H. L. (1982). The association of social relationships and activities with mortality: Prospective evidence from the Tecumseh community health study. *American Journal of Epidemiology*, 116, 123–140.

Howard, P. K. (1994). *The death of common sense*. New York: Warner Books.

Howard, P. K. (2001). *The collapse of the common good*. New York: Ballantine Books.

Howard, P. E. N., Rainie, L., & Jones, S. (2001). Days and nights on the Internet: The impact of a diffusing technology. *American Behavioral Scientist*, 45, 383–404.

Hummon, D. M. (1992). Community attachment: Local sentiment and sense of place. In I. Altman & S. M. Low (Eds.), *Place attachment* (pp. 253–278). New York: Plenum.

Hunt, G. P., & Satterlee, S. (1986). The pub, the village and the people. *Human Organization*, 45, 1, 62–74.

Hunter, F. (1953). *Community power structure: A study of decision-makers*. Garden City, NY: Anchor Books.

Isaacs, W. (1999). *Dialogue and the art of thinking together*. New York: Currency.

Iscoe, I. (1974). Community psychology and the competent community. *American Psychologist*, 29, 607–613.

Janowitz, M. (1967). *The community press in an urban setting: The social elements of urbanism* (2nd ed.). Chicago, IL: University of Chicago Press.

Jaquith, J. (1999). Religion creates foundation for community. (1999, November 7). *The Topeka Capital-Journal*, p. 1.

Jarvenpaa, S. L., Knoll, K., & Leidner, D. E. (1998). Is anybody out there? Antecedents to trust in global virtual teams. *Journal of Management Information Systems, 14,* 29–64.

Jarvenpaa, S. L., & Leidner, D. E. (1999). Communication and trust in global virtual teams. *Organization Science, 10,* 791–815.

Jason, L. A. (1997). *Community building: Values for a sustainable future.* Westport, CT: Praeger.

Jeffres, L. W. (2002). *Urban communication systems: Neighborhoods and the search for community.* Cresskill, NJ: Hampton Press, Inc.

Jencks, C. (1994). *The homeless.* Cambridge, MA: Harvard University Press.

Jensen, E. A neighborly place to move. (2002, February 8). *Arizona Republic,* A1.

Jerrome, D. (1984). Good company: The sociological implications of friendship. *Sociological Review, 32,* 696–718.

Johnson, B. D. (1973). *Marijuana users and drug subcultures.* New York: Wiley Interscience.

Jones, M. A. (1960). *American immigration.* Chicago, IL: University of Chicago Press.

Jones, M. A. (1992). *American immigration* (2nd ed.). Chicago, IL: University of Chicago Press.

Jones, S. G. (1995). Understanding community in the information age. In S. G. Jones (Ed.), *Cybersociety: Computer-mediated communication and community* (pp. 10–35). Thousand Oaks, CA: Sage.

Jones, S. G. (1997). The Internet and its social landscape. In S. G. Jones (Ed.), *Virtual culture: Identity and communication in cybersociety* (pp. 7–35). Thousand Oaks, CA: Sage.

Junn, J. (2000). Participation in liberal democracy: The political assimilation of immigrants and ethnic minorities in the United States. In N. Foner, R. G. Rumbaut, & S. J. Gold (Eds.), *Immigration Research for a new century: Multidisciplinary perspectives* (pp. 187–214). New York: Russell Sage Foundation.

Kalish, R. A. (1979). The new ageism and the failure models: A polemic. *Gerontologist, 19,* 398–402.

Kandel, D. B., Yamaguchi, K., & Chen, K. (1992). Stages of progression in drug involvement from adolescence to adulthood: Further evidence for the gateway theory. *Journal of Studies on Alcohol, 53,* 447–457.

Kaniasty, K., & Norris, F. H. (1995). In search of altruistic community: Patterns of social support mobilization following Hurricane Hugo. *American Journal of Community Psychology, 23,* 4, 447–477.

Kark, J. D., Carmel, S., Sinnreich, R., Goldberger, N., & Friedlander, Y. (1996a). Psychosocial factors among members of religious and secular kibbutzim. *Israeli Journal of Medical Science, 32,* 185–194.

Kark, J. D., Shemi, G., Friedlander, Y., Martin, O., Manor, O., & Blondheim, S. H. (1996b). Does religious observance promote health? Mortality in secular vs. religious kibbutzim in Israel. *American Journal of Public Health, 86,* 341–346.

Kates, R. W., & Clark, W. C. (1996). Environmental surprise: Expecting the unexpected? *Environment, 38,* 6–7.

Katz, J. E., & Aspden, P. (1997). A nation of strangers? *Communications of the ACM, 40,* 81–86.

Katz, J. E., & Rice, R. E. (2002). Syntopia: Access, civic involvement, and social interaction on the Net. In B. Wellman & C. Haythornthwaite (Eds.), *The Internet in everyday life* (pp. 114–138). Malden, MA: Blackwell.

Kawachi, I., & Berkman, L. F. (2001). Social ties and mental health. *Journal of Urban Health, 78,* 458–467.

Kelly, J. A., Laurence, J. S., Smith, S., Hood, H. V., & Cook, D. J. (1987). Stigmatization of AIDS patients by physicians. *American Journal of Public Health, 77*, 789–791.

Kerns, K. A., & Barth, J. M. (1995). Attachment and play: Convergence across components of parent-child relationships and their relations to peer competence. *Journal of Social and Personal Relationships, 12*, 2, 243–260.

Kesler, J. T. (2000). The healthy community movement: Counterintuitive next steps. *National Civic Review, 89*, 3, 271–284.

Kesler, J. T., & O'Connor, D. (2001). The American communities movement. *National Civic Review, 90*, 4, 295–305.

Kestnbaum, M., Robinson, J. P., Neustadtl, A., & Alvarez, A. (2002). Information technology and social time displacement. *IT & Society, 1*, 21–37.

Kivisto, P. (Ed.). (1989). *The ethnic enigma: The salience of ethnicity for European-origin groups.* Philadelphia, PA: Balch Institute Press.

Kleinman, A. (1995). *Writing at the margins: Discourse between anthropology and medicine.* Berkeley, CA: University of California Press.

Knight, J. (2001). Social norms and the rule of law: Fostering trust in a socially diverse society. In K. S. Cook (Ed.), *Trust in Society.* Vol. 2 in the Russell Sage Foundation Series on Trust (pp. 354–373). New York: Russell Sage Foundation.

Koenig, H. G. (1999). *The healing power of faith.* New York, NY: Simon & Schuster.

Koenig, H. G., & Cohen, H. J. (Eds.). (2002). *The link between religion and health: Psychoneuroimmunology and the faith factor.* New York, NY: Oxford University Press.

Koenig, H. G., Kvale, J. N., & Ferrel, C. (1988). Religion and well-being in later life. *The Gerontologist, 28*, 18–28.

Koenig, H. G., Cohen, H. J., Blazer, D. G., Pieper, C., Meador, K. G., Shelp, F., Goli, V., & DiPasquale, R. (1992). Religious coping and depression among elderly, hospitalized medically ill men. *American Journal of Psychiatry, 149*, 1693–1700.

Koenig, H. G., George, L. K., Meador, K. G., Blazer, D. G., & Ford, S. M. (1994). Religious practices and alcoholism in a Southern adult population. *Hospital and Community Psychiatry, 45*, 225–231.

Koenig, H. G., McCullough, M. E., & Larson, D. B. (2001). *Handbook of religion and health.* New York, NY: Oxford University Press.

Komito, L. (1998). The Net as a foraging society: Flexible communities. *Information Society, 14*, 97–107.

Koplewicz, H. S., Vogel, J. M., Solanto, M. V., Morrissey, R. F., Alonso, C. M., Abikoff, H., Gallagher, R., & Novick, R. M. (2002). Child and parent response to the 1993 World Trade Center bombing. *Journal of Traumatic Stress, 15*, 1, 77–85.

Kosmin, B. A., & Lachman, S. P. (1993). *One nation under God: Religion in contemporary society.* New York, NY: Harmony Books.

Kraut, R., Patterson, M., Lundmark, V., Kiesler, S., Mukopadhyay, T., & Scherlis, W. (1998). Internet paradox: A social technology that reduces social involvement and psychological well-being? *American Psychologist, 53*, 1017–1031.

Kraybill, D. (1997). *The riddle of Amish culture.* Baltimore, MD: The Johns Hopkins University Press.

Ladd, E. C. (1999). *The Ladd report.* New York: The Free Press.

Ladd, J. (1989). Computers and moral responsibility: A framework for ethical analysis. In C. C. Gould (Ed.), *The information Web: Ethical and social implications of computer networking* (pp. 207–227). Boulder, CO: Westview Press.

Lasker, J. N., Egolf, B. P., & Wolf, S. (1994). Community social change and mortality. *Social Science & Medicine, 39*, 53–62.

Lazarus, R. S., & Folkman, S. (1984). *Stress, appraisal, and coping.* New York: Springer.

Lears, J. No there there (1997, December 28). *The New York Times Book Review*, p. 9.

Lee, B. A., Campbell, K. E., & Miller, O. (1991). Racial differences in urban neighboring. *Sociological Forum, 6,* 3, 525.

Lefebvre, H. (1991). *The production of space.* Oxford: Blackwell.

LeVay, S., & Nonas, E. (1995). *City of friends: A portrait of the gay and lesbian community in America.* Cambridge, MA: M.I.T. Press.

Levin, H. (1980). The struggle for community can create community. In A. Gallaher & H. Padfield (Eds.), *The dying community* (pp. 257–277). Albuquerque: University of New Mexico Press.

Levin, J. (2001). *God, faith and health: Exploring the spirituality-healing connection.* New York, NY: John Wiley & Sons.

Levin, J. S., & Vanderpool, H. Y. (1987). Is frequent religious attendance really conducive to better health? Toward an epidemiology of religion. *Social Science & Medicine, 24,* 589–600.

Levitt, M. (1996). To be or not to be a community: The dilemma of Israelis in New York City. Paper presented at the American Sociological Association Annual Meeting, August 16–20, 1996.

Lewicki, R. J., & Wiethoff, C. (2000). Trust, trust development, and trust repair. In M. Deutsch & P. T. Coleman (Eds.), *The handbook of conflict resolution: Theory and practice* (pp. 86–107). San Francisco, CA: Jossey-Bass.

Liebow, E. (1967). *Talley's corner: A Study of Negro street corner men.* Boston, MA: Little, Brown & Co.

Liebow, E. (1993). *Tell them who I am: The lives of homeless women.* New York: Penguin Books.

Lifton, R. J. (1982). *Death in life: Survivors of Hiroshima.* New York: Basic Books.

Light, I. (1972). *Ethnic enterprise in America: Business and welfare among Chinese, Japanese, and Blacks.* Berkeley, CA: University of California Press.

Lin, N. (1999). Social networks and status attainment. *Annual Review of Sociology, 25,* 467–487.

Lin, N. (2001). *Social capital: A theory of social structure and action.* New York: Cambridge University Press.

Linenthal, E. T. (2001). *The unfinished bombing: Oklahoma City in American memory.* New York: Oxford University Press.

Link, B. G., Phelan, J. C., Stueve, A., Moore, R. E., Bresnahan, M., & Struening, E. L. (1996). Public attitudes and beliefs about homeless people. In J. Baumohl (Ed.), *Homelessness in America* (pp. 143–148). Phoenix, AZ: Oryx Press.

Lipnack, J., & Stamps, J. (1997). *Virtual teams: Reaching across space, time and organizations with technology.* New York: John Wiley.

Loewy, E. H. (1993). *Freedom and community: The ethics of interdependence.* Albany: State University of New York Press.

Logan, J., & Molotch, H. (1988). *Urban fortunes: The political economy of place.* Berkeley, CA: University of California Press.

Logan, J. R., Alba, R. D., & Zhang, W. (2002). Immigrant enclaves and ethnic communities in New York and Los Angeles. *American Sociological Review, 67,* 299–322.

Logue, J. N., Melick, M. E., & Struening, E. L. (1981). A study of health and mental health status following a major national disaster. *Research in Community and Mental Health, 2,* 217–274.

Lorenz, K. (1965). *Evolution and modification of behavior.* Chicago: University of Chicago Press.

Low, S. M. (Ed.). (1999). *Theorizing the city: The new urban anthropology reader.* New Brunswick, NJ: Rutgers University Press.

Low, S. M. (2001). The edge and the center: Gated communities and the discourse of urban fear. *American Anthropologist, 103,* 45–58.

Luhmann, N. (1995). Soziale systeme-grundriss einer allgemeinen theorie. Frankfurt am Main: Suhrkamp Verlag.

Lynch, J. J. (2000). *A cry unheard: New insights into the medical consequences of loneliness.* Baltimore, MD: Bancroft Press.

Lynd, R. S., & Lynd, H. M. (1929). *Middletown: A study in contemporary American culture.* New York: Harcourt Brace.

Macionis, J. J., & Parrillo, V. N. (2001). *Cities and urban life* (2nd ed.). Upper Saddle River, NJ: Prentice Hall.

Mallet, G. Has diversity gone too far? (1995, March 15). *The Globe and Mail*, Section D.

Mark, V. H., & Mark, J. P. (1999). *Reversing memory loss.* New York, NY: Houghton Mifflin.

Marris, P. (1982). Attachment and society. In C. M. Parkes & J. Stevenson-Hinde (Eds.), *The place of attachment in human behavior* (pp. 185–201). New York: Basic Books.

Marty, M. E. (1967). The spirit's holy errand: The search for a spiritual style in secular America. *Daedalus*, 96, 99–115.

Marx, K., & Engels, F. [1848] (1972). Manifesto of the communist party. In R. C. Tucker (Ed.), *The Marx-Engel reader* (pp. 331–362). New York: Norton.

Massey, D. S., & Espenosa, K. E. (1997). What's driving Mexico-US migration? A theoretical, empirical, and policy analysis. *American Journal of Sociology*, 102, 4, 939–999.

Masuda, M., & Holmes, T. H. (1978). Life events: perceptions and frequencies. *Psychosomatic Medicine*, 40, 236–261.

Matthews, D. A., McCullough, M. E., Larson, D. B., Koenig, H. G., Swyers, J. P., & Milano, M. G. (1998). Religious commitment and health status. *Archives of Family Medicine*, 7, 118–124.

McCarthy, A. M. (1998). Paternal characteristics associated with disturbed father-daughter attachment and separation among women with eating disorder symptoms (Doctoral dissertation, California School of Professional Psychology, Los Angeles, 1998). *Dissertation Abstracts International, 59-04B*, AA 19831030, p. 1861.

McGarvey, E. L., Kryzhanovskaya, L. A., Koopman, C., Waite, D., & Canterbury, R. J. (1999). Incarcerated adolescents' distress and suicidality in relation to bonding types. *Crisis, 20*, 4, 164–170.

McGuire, L., Kiecolt-Glaser, J., & Glaser, R. (2002). Depressive symptoms and lymphocyte proliferation in older adults. *Journal of Abnormal Psychology*, 111, 192–197.

McIntosh, J. (Ed.). (1987). *Nathaniel Hawthorne's Tales.* NY: W. W. Norton, p. 84. First published in the *New England Magazine*, June, 1835 and in *Twice-told Tales*, 2nd ed., 1842.

McIntyre, A. (1984). *After virtues: A study in moral theory* (2nd ed.). Notre Dame, IN: University of Notre Dame Press.

McKenzie, E. (1994). *Privatopia: Homeowner associations and the rise of residential private government.* New Haven, CT: Yale University Press.

McLaughlin, M. L., Osborne, K. K., & Smith, C. B. (1995). Standards of conduct on Usenet. In S. G. Jones (Ed.), *Cybersociety: Computer-mediated communication and community* (pp. 90–111). Thousand Oaks, CA: Sage.

McLeod, J. D., & Shanahan, M. J. (1993). Poverty, parenting, and children's mental health. *American Sociological Review*, 58, 351–366.

McMillan, W. D., & Chavis, M. D. (1986). Sense of community: A definition and theory. *Journal of Community Psychology*, 14, 6–22.

Melamed, B. G., & Bush, J. P. (1985). Family factors in children with acute illness. In D. C. Turk & R. D. Kerns, (Eds.), *Health, illness, and families: A life-span perspective* (pp. 183–219). New York: John Wiley & Sons.

Merry, S. E. (1993). Mending walls and building fences: Constructing the private neighborhood. *Journal of Legal Pluralism and Unofficial Law*, 33, 71–90.

Messick, D. M., & Kramer, R. M. (2001). Trust as a form of shallow morality. In K. S. Cook, (Ed.), *Trust in society*. Vol. 2 in the Russell Sage Foundation Series on Trust (pp. 89–117). New York: Russell Sage Foundation.

Meyerson, D., Weick, K. E., & Kramer, R. M. (1996). Swift trust and temporary groups. In R. M. Kramer & T. R. Tyler (Eds.), *Trust in organizations: Frontiers of theory and research* (pp. 166–195). Beverly Hills, CA: Sage.

Milgram, N., Sarason, B. R., Schönpflug, U., Jackson, A., & Schwarzer, C. (1995). Catalyzing community support. In S. E. Hobfoll & M. W. de Vries (Eds.), *Extreme stress and communities: Impact and intervention* (pp. 473–488). Dordrecht: Kluwer.

Milgram, S. (1970). The experience of living in cities. *Science, 167,* (March 13), 1461–1468.

Milgram, S., Greenwald, J., Kessler, S., McKenna, W., & Waters, J. (1972). A psychological map of New York City. *American Scientist, 60,* (March/April), 194–200.

Milgram, S., & Hollander, P. (1964). The murder they heard. *The Nation, 198,* 25, 602–605.

Mills, C. Wright (1956). *The power elite.* New York: Oxford University Press.

Miringhoff, M., & Miringhoff, M. (1999). *The social health of the nation: How America is really doing.* New York: Oxford University Press.

Misztal, B. A. (1996). *Trust in modern societies: The search for the bases of social order.* Cambridge: Polity Press.

Miyares, I. M. (1997). Changing perceptions of space and place as measures of Hmong acculturation. *Professional Geographer, 49,* 2, 214–224.

Moe, R., & Wilkie, C. (1997). *Changing places: Rebuilding community in the age of sprawl.* New York: Henry Holt.

Moen, P., Dempster-McClain, D., & Williams, R. M. (1989). Social integration and longevity: An event history analysis of women's roles and resilience. *American Sociological Review, 54,* 635–647.

Mohr, C. Apathy is puzzle in Queens killing. (1964, March 28). *The New York Times,* p. 21.

Molina, E. (2000). Informal non-kin networks among homeless Latino and African American men. *American Behavioral Scientist, 43,* 4, 663–686.

Moody, H. R., & Carroll, D L. (1997). *The five stages of the soul: Charting spiritual passages.* New York, NY: Doubleday.

Morse, S. W. (1998). Five building blocks for successful communities. In F. Hesselbein, M. Goldsmith, R. Beckhard, & R. F. Schubert (Eds.), *The community of the future* (pp. 229–236). San Francisco, CA: Jossey-Bass.

Mossey, J., & Shapiro, E. (1982). Self-rated health: A predictor of mortality among the elderly. *American Journal of Public Health, 72,* 800–808.

Myers, D. G. (2000). *The American paradox: Spiritual hunger in an age of plenty.* New Haven, CT: Yale University Press.

Nagi, S. Z. (1991). Disability concepts revisited: Implications for prevention. In A. M. Pope & A. R. Tarlov (Eds.), *Disability in America: Toward a national agenda for prevention* (pp. 309–327). Washington, DC: National Academies Press.

Naroll, R. (1983). *The moral order.* Beverly Hills, CA: Sage.

National Institute of Allergy and Infectious Diseases, National Institutes of Health (2002). *HIV/AIDS Statistics. Fact Sheet,* December, 2002.

National Institute of Mental Health (1993). *Decade of the Brain.* U.S. Department of Health and Human Services, Public Health Service, National Institutes of Health, NIH Publication Manual No. 93-3477, January, 1993. Washington, DC, 20402–9328.

National Institute of Mental Health (2000). Office of Communications and Public Liaison. NIH Publication No. 00-4501. Bethesda, MD.

Nee, V., & Sanders, J. (2001). Trust in ethnic ties: Social capital and immigrants. In K. S. Cook (Ed.), *Trust in Society,* Vol. 2 in the Russell Sage Foundation Series on Trust (pp. 374–392). New York: Russell Sage Foundation.

Neumann, W. R., O'Donnell, S. R., & Schneider, S. M. (1996). The Web's next wave: A field study of Internet diffusion and use patterns. Manuscript M.I.T. Media Laboratory.

Newman, K. S. (1999). *No shame in my game: The working poor in the inner city*. New York: Knopf.

Nie, N. H., & Ebring, L. (2000). *Internet and society: A preliminary report*. Stanford, CA: Institute for the Quantitative Study of Society.

North, C. S., Nixon, S. J., Shariat, S., Mallonee, S., McMillen, J. C., Spitznagel, E. L., & Smith, E. M. (1999). Psychiatric disorders among survivors of the Oklahoma City bombing. *Journal of the American Medical Association, 282,* 8, 755–762.

North, C. S., Smith, E. M., & Spitznagel, E. L. (1997). One–year follow-up of survivors of a mass shooting. *American Journal of Psychiatry, 154,* 12, 1696–1702.

Novak, M. (1972). *The rise of the unmeltable ethnics*. New York: Macmillan.

Nunez, R. de Costa. (1996). *The new poverty: Homeless families in America*. New York: Insight Books.

O'Connor, D., & Gates, C. T. (2000). Toward a healthy democracy. *Public Health Reports, 115,* 2 & 3, 157–160.

Oldenberg, R. (1997). *The great good place: Cafes, coffee shops, community centers, beauty parlors, general stores, bars, hangouts, and how they get you through the day*. New York: Marlowe & Co.

Oliver, J. E. (1999). The effects of metropolitan economic segregation on local civic participation. *American Journal of Political Science, 43,* 186–212.

Oliver, M. L. (1988). The urban black community as network: Toward a social network perspective. *The Sociological Quarterly, 29,* 4, 623–645.

Ordway, N. K., Leonard, M. F., & Ingles, T. (1969). Interpersonal factors in failure to thrive. *Southern Medical Bulletin, 57,* 23–28.

Ornstein, R., & Sobel, D. (1987). *The healing brain*. New York: Simon & Schuster.

Orth-Gomer, K., Rosengren, A., & Wilhelmson, L. (1993). Lack of social support and incidence of coronary heart disease in middle-aged Swedish men. *Psychosomatic Medicine, 55,* 37–43.

Owen, M. T., & Cox, M. J. (1997). Marital conflict and the development of infant-parent attachments. *Journal of Family Psychology, 11,* 2, 152–164.

Paddison, R. (2001). Communities in the city. In R. Paddison, *Handbook of urban studies* (pp. 194–205). Thousand Oaks, CA: Sage.

Paffenbarger, R. S., & Asnes, D. P. (1966). Chronic disease in former college students, III: Precursors of suicide in early and middle life. *American Journal of Public Health, 56,* 1026–1036.

Paffenbarger, R. S., King, S. H., & Wing, A. L. (1969). Chronic disease in former college students, IV: Characteristics in youth that predispose to suicide and accidental death in later life. *American Journal of Public Health, 59,* 900–908.

Palinkas, L. A., Downs, M. A., Petterson, J. S., & Russell, J. (1993). Social, cultural, and psychological impacts of the Exxon Valdez oil spill. *Human Organization, 52,* 1, 1–13.

Palinkas, L. A., Petterson, J. S., Russell, J., & Downs, M. A. (1993). Community patterns of psychiatric disorders after the Exxon Valdez oil spill. *American Journal of Psychiatry, 150,* 1517–1523.

Park, R. E. (1936). Human ecology. *American Journal of Sociology, 42,* 1–15.

Park, R. E. (1952). *Human Communities: The city and human ecology*. New York: The Free Press.

Patterson, O. (1999). *Rituals of blood: Consequences of slavery in two American centuries*. Washington, DC: Civitas/Counter Point.

Peck, M. Scott. (1987). *The different drum*. New York: Simon & Schuster.

Pennebaker, J. W., & Harber, K. D. (1993). A social stage model of collective coping: The Loma Prieta earthquake and the Persian Gulf War. *Journal of Social Issues, 49,* 4, 125–145.

Perry, R. W., & Mushkatel, A. H. (1986). *Minority citizens in disasters*. Athens, GA: University of Georgia Press.

Peterson, G. H., Mehl, L. E., & Leiderman, P. H. (1979). The role of some birth-related variables in father attachment. *American Journal of Orthopsychiatry, 49*, 2, 330–338.

Pettigrew, T. (1971). *Racially separate or together?* New York: McGraw Hill.

Philips, B. U., & Bruhn, J. G. (1981). Smoking habits and reported illness in two communities with different systems of social support. *Social Science & Medicine*, 15A, 625–631.

Picou, J. S. (2000). The "talking circle" as sociological practice: Cultural transformation of chronic disaster impacts. *Sociological Practice: A Journal of Clinical and Applied Sociology*, 2, 2, 77–97.

Picou, J. S., Gill, D. A., & Cohen, M. J. (Eds.). (1997). *The Exxon Valdez disaster: Readings on a modern social problem*. Dubuque, IA: Kendall/Hunt.

Pilisuk, M., & Parks, S. H. (1986). *The healing web: Social networks and human survival*. Hanover: University Press of New England.

Portes, A., & Rumbaut, R. G. (1990). *Immigrant America: A portrait*. Berkeley, CA: University of California Press.

Preece, J. (1999). Empathic communities: Balancing emotional and factual communication. *Interacting with Computers*, 12, 63–77.

Preece, J. (2000). *Online communities: Designing usability, supporting sociability*. New York: John Wiley.

Prezza, M., Amici, M., Roberti, T., & Tedeschi, G. (2001). Sense of community referred to the whole town: Its relations with neighboring, loneliness, life satisfaction, and area of residence. *Journal of Community Psychology, 29*, 1, 29–52.

Prezza, M., & Constantine, S. (1998). Sense of community and life satisfaction: Investigation in three different territorial contexts. *Journal of Community and Applied Social Psychology, 8*, 181–194.

Prince-Embury, S., & Rooney, J. (1988). Psychological symptoms of residents in the aftermath of the Three Mile Island nuclear accident and restart. *The Journal of Social Psychology, 128*, 6, 779–790.

Purdy, J. (1999). *For common things*. New York: Vintage Books.

Putnam, R. D. (1995). Bowling alone: America's declining social capital. *Journal of Democracy*, 6, 65–78.

Putnam, R. D. (1996). The strange disappearance of civic America. *The American Prospect, 24*, (Winter), 34–46.

Putnam, R. D. (2000). *Bowling alone: The collapse and revival of American community*. New York: Simon & Schuster.

Putnam, R. D., & Feldstein, L. M. (2003). *Better together: Restoring the American community*. New York: Simon & Schuster.

Pyszczynski, T., Solomon, S., & Greenberg, J. (2003). *In the wake of 9/11: The psychology of terror*. Washington, DC: American Psychological Association.

Quan-Haase, A., & Wellman, B. (with Witte, J. C., & Hampton, K. N.). (2002). Capitalizing on the Net: Social contact, civic engagement, and sense of community. In B. Wellman & C. Haythornthwaite (Eds.), *The Internet in everyday life* (pp. 291–324). Walden, MA: Blackwell.

Quarantelli, E. L. (Ed.). (1985). *What is a disaster: Perspectives on the question*. New York: Routledge.

Quarantelli, E. L. (1993). Community crises: An exploratory comparison of the characteristics and consequences of disasters and riots. *Journal of Contingencies & Crisis Management, 1*, 2, 67–78.

Rasinski, K. A., & Smith, T. W. (2002). *Public response to a national tragedy. Has America recovered from 9/11?* National Opinion Research Center, Chicago, IL: University of Chicago.

Redfield, R. (1941). *The folk culture of the Yucatan*. Chicago, IL: University of Chicago Press.

Reed, D., McGee, D., Yano, K., & Feinleib, M. (1983). Social networks and coronary heart disease among Japanese men in Hawaii. *American Journal of Epidemiology*, *117*, 4, 384–396.

Reynolds, P., & Kaplan, G. A. (1990). Social connections and risk for cancer: Prospective evidence from the Alameda County Study. *Behavioral Medicine*, *16*, 3, 101–110.

Rheingold, H. (1993). *The virtual community: Homesteading on the electronic frontier*. Reading, MA: Addison Wesley.

Rheingold, H. (1994). A slice of life in my virtual community. In L. M. Harasim (Ed.), *Global networks: Computers and international communication* (pp. 57–80). Cambridge, MA: M.I.T. Press.

Rice, R. E., & Barnett, G. (1986). Group communication networks in electronic space: Applying metric multidimensional scaling. In M. McLaughlin (Ed.), *Communication Yearbook*, 9 (pp. 315–338). Beverly Hills, CA: Sage.

Riekse, R. J., & Holstege, H. (1996). *Growing older in America*. New York: McGraw Hill.

Riger, S., & Laurakas, P. J. (1981). Community ties: Patterns of attachment and social interaction in urban neighborhoods. *American Journal of Community Psychology*, *9*, 1, 55–66.

Ringwalt, C., Greene, J., Robertson, M., & McPheeters, M. (1998). The prevalence of home-lessness among adolescents in the United States. *American Journal of Public Health*, *88*, 9, 1325–1329.

Roberts, D. F., Foehr, U. G., Rideout, V. J., & Brodie, M. (1999). *Kids & media @ the new millennium*. A Kaiser Family Foundation Report. Menlo Park, CA.

Robertson, M. J., & Toro, P. A. (1999). Homeless youth: Research, intervention and policy. In L. B. Fosburg & D. L. Dennis (Eds.), *Practical lessons: The 1998 national symposium on homelessness research*. U.S. Department of Housing and Urban Development and U.S. Department of Health and Human Services, August, 1999.

Robin, M., & ten Bensel, R. (1985). Pets and the socialization of children. In M. Sussman (Ed.), *Pets and the family* (pp. 63–78). Binghamton, NY: Haworth Press.

Rodin, M., Downs, M., Petterson, J., & Russell, J. (1997). Community impacts of the Exxon Valdez oil spill. In J. S. Picou, D. A. Gill, & M. J. Cohen (Eds.), *The Exxon Valdez disaster: Readings on a modern social problem* (pp. 193–209). Dubuque, IA: Kendall/Hunt.

Roof, W. C. (1993). *A generation of seekers*. New York, NY: Harper Collins.

Ropers, R. H. (1988). *The invisible homeless: A new urban ecology*. New York: Insight Books.

Rosenheck, R., Leda, C. A., Frisman, L. K., Lam, J., & Chung, A. (1996). Homeless veterans. In J. Baumohl (Ed.), *Homelessness in America* (pp. 97–108). Phoenix, AZ: Oryx Press.

Ross, C. E., & Jang, S. J. (2000). Neighborhood disorder, fear, and mistrust: The buffering role of social ties with neighbors. *American Journal of Community Psychology*, *28*, 4, 401–420.

Ross, C. E., Mirowsky, J., & Pribesh, S. (2001). Powerlessness and the amplification of threat: Neighborhood disadvantage, disorder, and mistrust. *American Sociological Review*, *66*, 568–591.

Rossi, P. H. (1989). *Down and out in America: The origins of homelessness*. Chicago, IL: University of Chicago Press.

Rubin, Z. (1982). Children without friends. In L. A. Peplau & D. Perlman (Eds.), *Loneliness: A sourcebook of current theory, research and therapy* (pp. 255–268). New York: John Wiley.

Rumbaut, R. G. (1997). Paradoxes (and orthodoxies) of assimilation. *Sociological Perspectives*, *40*, 3, 483–511.

Running Wolf, P., & Rickard, J. A. (2003). Talking circles: A Native American approach to experiential learning. *Journal of Multicultural Counseling & Development*, *31*, 39–43.

Runyan, D. K., Hunter, W. M., Socolar, R. R. S., Amaya-Jackson, L., English, D., Landsverk, J., Dubowitz, H., Browne, D. H., Bangdiwala, S. I., & Matthew, R. M. (1998). Children who prosper in unfavorable environments: The relationship to social capital. *Pediatrics*, *101*, (January), 12–18.

Rushkoff, D. (1994). *Cyberia*. San Francisco, CA: Harper San Francisco.

Russek, L., King, S., Russek, S., & Russek, H. (1990). The Harvard mastery of stress study 35 year follow-up: Prognostic significance of patterns of psychophysiological arousal and adaptation. *Psychosomatic Medicine, 52,* 271–285.

Saloojee, A. (2003). *Social inclusion, anti-racism and democratic citizenship*. Toronto: Laidlow Foundation.

Samter, W. (1994). Unsupportive relationships: Deficiencies in the support-giving skills of the lonely person's friends. In B. R. Burleson, T. L. Albrecht, & I. G. Sarason (Eds.), *Communication of social support: Messages, interactions, relationships, and community* (pp. 195–214). Thousand Oaks, CA: Sage.

Samuelson, R. J. Bowling alone is bunk. (1996, April 10). *The Washington Post*, p. A19.

Sandel, M. J. (1998). *Liberalism and the limits of justice* (2nd ed.). New York: Cambridge University Press.

Sanders, J. M. (2002). Ethnic boundaries and identity in plural societies. *Annual Review of Sociology, 28,* 327–357.

Sarason, B. R., Pierce, G. R., & Sarason, I. G. (1990). Social support: The sense of acceptance and the role of relationships. In B. R. Sarason, I. G. Sarason, & G. R. Pierce (Eds.), *Social support: An interactional view* (pp. 97–128). New York: John Wiley & Sons.

Sarason, S. B. (1974). *The psychological sense of community: Prospects for a community psychology*. San Francisco, CA: Jossey-Bass.

Sayenko, Y. (1996). The trace of Chernobyl in consciousness of victims. Paper presented at World Health Organization International Conference, *One decade after Chernobyl: Summing up the consequences of the accident*. Vienna, Austria, April 8–12.

Schaefer, W. Neighborhood gate cuts off traffic. (2001, December 21). *The Cincinnati Enquirer*.

Schnaderman, B. (2000). Designing trust into online experiences. *Communications of the ACM, 43,* 57–59.

Schuler, D. (1996). *New community networks*. New York: ACM Press.

Schuller, T., Baron, S., & Field, J. (2000). Social capital: A review and critique. In S. Baron, J. Field, & T. Schuller, *Social capital: Critical perspectives* (pp. 1–38). New York: Oxford University Press.

Schuster, M. A., Stein, B. D., Jaycox, L. H., Collins, R. L., Marshall, G. N., Elliott, M. N., et al. (2001). A national survey of stress reactions after the September 11, 2001, terrorist attacks. *The New England Journal of Medicine, 345,* 20, 1507–1512.

Schwalbe, M. (1998). *The sociologically examined life*. Mountain View, CA: Mayfield.

Seelye, K. Q. (2003). Right wing Zionist and moralist William J. Bennett a big time gambler. (2003, May 3). *New York Times*.

Selznick, P. (1995). Thinking about community: Ten theses. *Society, 32,* 5, 33–38.

Selznick, P. (2002). *The communitarian persuasion*. Washington, DC: Woodrow Wilson Center Press.

Sethi, S., & Seligman, M. E. P. (1994). The hope of fundamentalists. *Psychological Science, 4,* 256–259.

Shapiro, J. H. (1971). *Communities of the alone: Working with single room occupants in the city*. New York: Association Press.

Sherman, A. L. (2003). Faith in communities: A solid investment. *Society, 40,* 19–27.

Shonkoff, J. P., & Phillips, D. A. (Eds.). (2000). *From neurons to neighborhoods: The science of early childhood development*. Washington, DC: National Academy Press.

Sibley, D. (1995). *Geographies of exclusion*. New York: Routledge.

Simmel, G. [1905] (1964). The metropolis and mental life. In K. Wolff (Ed.), *The sociology of Georg Simmel* (pp. 409–424). New York: Free Press. (Originally published in 1905)

Singer, P. (1995). *How are we to live?* New York: Prometheus Books.

Sitterle, K. A. (1995). Mental health services at the Compassion Center: The Oklahoma City bombing. *National Center for Post-traumatic Stress Disorder Clinical Quarterly, 5,* 4, Fall.

Sitterle, K. A., & Gurwitch, R. H. (1995). The terrorist bombing in Oklahoma City. In E. S. Zinner & M. B. Williams (Eds.), *When a community weeps: Case studies in group survivorship* (pp. 161–189). Philadelphia, PA: Brunner/Mazel.

Skocpol, T. (1997). Building community top-down or bottom-up? *The Brookings Review, 15,* 4, 16–19.

Smith, A. C., & Smith, D. I. (2001). *Emergency and transitional shelter population 2000.* U.S. Department of Commerce, Economics and Statistics Administration, U.S. Census Bureau, October, CENSR/0/-2.

Smith, D. A. (1995). The new urban sociology meets the old. *Urban Affairs Review, 30,* 3, 432–458.

Smith, J. P., & Edmonston, B. (Eds.). (1997). *The new Americans.* Washington, DC: National Academy Press.

Smith, M. A., & Kollock, P. (Eds.). (1999). *Communities in cyberspace.* New York: Routledge.

Snow, D. A., & Anderson, L. (1993). *Down on their luck: A study of homeless street people.* Berkeley, CA: University of California Press.

Snow, D. A., Anderson, L., Quist, T., & Cress, D. (1996). Material survival strategies on the street: Homeless people as bricoleurs. In J. Baumohl (Ed.), *Homelessness in America* (pp. 67–95). Phoenix, AZ: Oryx Press.

Snowdon, D. (2001). *Aging with grace.* New York, NY: Bantam Books.

Snowdon, D. A., Kemper, S. J., Mortimer, J. A., Greiner, L. H., & Wekstein, D. R. (1996). Linguistic ability in early life and cognitive function and Alzheimer's disease in late life: Findings from the Nun Study. *Journal of the American Medical Association, 275,* 528–532.

Sonn, C. C. (2002). Immigrant adaptation: Understanding the process through sense of community. In A. T. Fisher, C. C. Sonn, & B. J. Bishop (Eds.), *Psychological sense of community: Research, applications, and implications* (pp. 205–222). New York: Kluwer Academic/Plenum Publishers.

Sorokin, P. H. (1940). Preface. In F. Tönnies *Fundamental concepts of sociology (Gemeinschaft and Gesellschaft).* Translated and supplemented by C. P. Loomis (pp. v–vii). New York: American Book Co.

Sosa, L. (1998). *Americano dream: How Latinos can achieve success in business and in life.* New York: Penguin Group.

Sowell, T. (1981). *Ethnic America.* New York: Basic Books.

Sproull, L., & Kiesler, S. (1991). *Connections: New ways of working the networked organization.* Cambridge, MA: The M.I.T. Press.

Stark, L. A. (1994). The shelter as "total institution." *American Behavioral Scientist, 37,* 4, 553–562.

Starr, P. (1995). The disengaged. *American Prospect,* Fall, 7–8.

Steffens, L. (1904). *The shame of the cities.* New York: McClure, Phillips.

Stein, M. C., & McCall, G. J. (1994). Home ranges and daily rounds: Uncovering community among urban nomads. In D. A. Chekki (Ed.), *Research in community sociology,* Suppl. 1, The community of the streets (pp. 77–94). Greenwich, CT: Jai Press.

Steinberg, S. (1989). *The ethnic myth.* Boston, MA: Beacon Press.

Stokes, M., & Zeman, D. (1995, September 4). The shame of the city. *Newsweek, 126,* 10, 26.

Storr, A. (1988). *Solitude.* New York: Ballantine Books.

Strauss, J. (2003). Peace of mind still eludes some USS Indianapolis survivors. (2003, April 23). *The Indianapolis Star.*

Strawbridge, W. J., Cohen, R. D., Shema, S. J., & Kaplan, G. A. (1997). Frequent attendance at religious services and mortality over 28 years. *American Journal of Public Health, 87,* 957–961.

Stueve, C. A., & Gerson, K. (1977). Personal relations across the lifecycle. In C. S. Fischer, R. M. Jackson, C. A. Stueve, K. Gerson, L. M. Jones, with M. Baldassare, *Networks and places: Social relations in the urban setting* (pp. 79–98). New York: The Free Press.

Susser, E. S., Struening, E. L., & Conover, S. (1987). Childhood experiences of homeless men. *American Journal of Psychiatry*, 9, 119–135.

Syme, S. L. (1994). The social environment and health. *Daedalus*, Fall, 79–86.

Szasz, T. S. (1964). *The myth of mental illness*. New York: Hoeber-Harper.

Taylor, J. B., Zurcher, L. A., & Key, W. H. (1970). *Tornado: A community response to disaster*. Seattle, WA: University of Washington Press.

Thomas, C. B., & Duszynski, K. R. (1974). Closeness to parents and the family constellation in a prospective study of five disease states: suicide, mental illness, malignant tumor, hypertension, and coronary heart disease, *Johns Hopkins Medical Journal*, 134, 251–270.

Thomas, C. B., & Greenstreet, R. L. (1973). Psychobiological characteristics in youth as predictors of five disease states: Suicide, mental illness, hypertension, coronary heart disease and tumor. *The Johns Hopkins Medical Journal*, 132, 1, 16–43.

Thomas, L. (1974). *The lives of a cell: Notes of a biology watcher*. New York: Bantam Books.

Thomason, B. T., & Campos, P. E. (1997). Health behavior in persons with HIV and AIDS. In D. S. Gochman (Ed.), *Handbook of Health Behavior Research*, Vol. 3, (pp. 163–177). New York: Plenum Press.

Thoits, P. (1983). Multiple identities and psychological well-being. *American Sociological Review*, 48, 174–187.

Tinsley, B. J. (1997). Maternal influences on children's health behavior. In D. S. Gochman (Ed.), *Handbook of Health Behavior Research*, Vol. 1 (pp. 223–240). New York: Plenum.

Tizard, B., & Joseph, A. (1970). Cognitive development of young children in residential care: A study of children aged 24 months. *Journal of Child Psychology & Psychiatry*, 11, 177–186.

Tönnies, F. (1940). *Fundamental concepts of sociology (Gemeinschaft and Gesellschaft)*. Translated and supplemented by C. P. Loomis. New York: American Book Co.

Tönnies, F. [1887]. (1957). *Community & society*. Translated and edited by C. P. Loomis. East Lansing, MI: Michigan State University Press.

Tousley, M. (2003). Personal Communication.

Traugott, M. W. (2002). *How Americans respond (part 2)*. Institute for Social Research. Ann Arbor, MI: University of Michigan.

Turiel, E. (2002). *The culture of morality: Social development, context, and conflict*. New York: Cambridge University Press.

Turkle, S. (1995). *Life on the screen: Identity in the age of the Internet*. New York: Simon & Schuster.

Turkle, S. (1996). Virtuality and its discontents. *The American Prospect*, 24, 50–57.

Turner, R. J., Frankel, B. G., & Levin, D. M. (1983). Social support: Conceptualization, measurement, and implications for mental health. In J. Greeley (Eds.), *Research in community and mental health*, Vol. 3, (pp. 67–111). Greenwich, CT: Jai Press.

Tyler, T. R. (2001). Why do people rely on others? Social identity and the social aspects of trust. In K. S. Cook, (Ed.), *Trust in Society*, Vol. 2 in the Russell Sage Foundation Series on Trust (pp. 285–306). New York: Russell Sage Foundation.

United States National Commission on Terrorism (2000). *Countering the changing threat of international terrorism*. Washington, DC.

United States State Department (2002). Bureau of Population, Refugees, and Migration. Washington, DC.

The Urban Institute (2000). *A new look at homelessness in America*. February 1, Washington, DC.

Uriely, N. (1994). Rhetorical ethnicity of permanent sojourners: The case of Israeli immigrants to the Chicago area. *International Sociology*, 9, 4, 431–446.

Uslander, E. (2000). Social capital and the Net. *Communications of the ACM*, December, 2000.

Vaillant, G. (1978). Natural history of male psychological health: VI. Correlates of successful marriage and fatherhood. *American Journal of Psychiatry, 135*, 6, 653–659.

Van den Berghe, P. L. (1981). *The ethnic phenomenon*. New York: Elsevier.

Verschueren, K., & Marcoen, A. (1999). Representation of self and socioemotional competence in kindergartens: Differential and combined affects of attachment to mother and father. *Child Development, 70*, 1, 183–201.

Vidich, A. J., & Bensman, J. (1958). *Small town in mass society: Class, power and religion in a rural community*. Garden City, NY: Anchor Books.

Waldinger, R. (1996). *Still the promised city?* Cambridge, MA: Harvard University Press.

Wallace, P. (1999). *The psychology of the Internet*. Cambridge, MA: Cambridge University Press.

Wallis, J. (2001). *Faith works: How faith based organizations are changing lives, neighborhoods, and America*. Berkeley, CA: Page Mill Press.

Walther, J. B., Anderson, J. F., & Park, D. W. (1994). Interpersonal effects in computer-mediated instruction: A meta-analysis of social and antisocial communication. *Communication Research, 21*, 460–487.

Walton, J. (1981). The new urban sociology. *International Social Science Journal, 33*, 2, 374–391.

Warner, R. S. (1994). The place of the congregation in the contemporary American religious configuration. In J. P. Wind & J. W. Lewis (Eds.), *American Congregations*, Vol. 2 (pp. 54–99). Chicago, IL: University of Chicago Press.

Warner, W. L., & Lunt, P. S. (1941). *The social life of a modern community*. New Haven, CT: Yale University Press.

Warren, M. R. (2001). *Dry bones rattling: Community building to revitalize American democracy*. Princeton, NJ: Princeton University Press.

Warren, M. R., Thompson, J. P., & Saegert, S. (2001). The role of social capital in combating poverty. In S. Saegert, J. P. Thompson, & M. R. Warren (Eds.), *Social capital in poor communities* (pp. 1–28). New York: Russell Sage Foundation.

Waskul, D., & Douglass, M. (1997). Cyberself: The emergence of self in on-line chat. *The Information Society, 13*, 375–397.

Waters, M. (1990). *Ethnic options*. Berkeley, CA: University of California Press.

Waters, M. C., & Eschbach, K. (1995). Immigration and ethnic and racial inequality in the United States. *Annual Review of Sociology, 21*, 1, 419–446.

Waysman, M., Schwarzwald, J., & Solomon, Z. (2001). Hardiness: An examination of its relationship with positive and negative long term changes following trauma. *Journal of Traumatic Stress, 14*, 3, 531–548.

Webber, M. M. (1970). Order in diversity: Community without propinquity. In R. Gutman & D. Popenoe (Eds.), *Neighborhood, city, and metropolis* (pp. 792–811). New York: Random House.

Weber, A. [1921]. (1966). *The city*. New York: Free Press. (Originally published 1921)

Wellman, B. (1982). Studying personal communities. In P. V. Marsden & N. Lin (Eds.), *Social structure and network analysis* (pp. 61–80). Thousand Oaks, CA: Sage.

Wellman, B. (Ed.). (1999). *Networks in the global village: Life in contemporary communities*. Boulder, CO: Westview Press.

Wellman, B. (2001). Physical place and cyberplace: Changing portals and the rise of personalized networking. *International Journal of Urban and Regional Research, 25*, 227–252.

Wellman, B., & Craven, P. (1973). The network city. *Sociological Inquiry, 43*, 57–88.

Wellman, B., & Gulia, M. (1999). Net-surfers don't ride alone: Virtual communities as communities. In B. Wellman (Ed.), *Networks in the global village: Life in contemporary communities* (pp. 331–366). Boulder, CO: Westview Press.

Wellman B., & Potter, S. (1999). The elements of personal communities. In B. Wellman (Ed.), *Networks in the global village: Life in contemporary communities* (pp. 49–81). Boulder, CO: Westview Press.

Wellman, B., & Wortley, S. (1990). Different strokes from different folks: Community ties and social support. *American Journal of Sociology, 96*, 558–588.

West, J. (1945). *Plainville U.S.A.* New York: Columbia University Press.

Wethington, E., & Kavey, A. (2000). Neighboring as a form of social integration and support. In K. Pillemer, P. Moen, E. Wethington, & N. Glasgow (Eds.), *Social integration in the second half of life* (pp. 190–210). Baltimore, MD: The Johns Hopkins University Press.

Whyte, W. F. (1943/1955). *Street corner society* (Enlarged edition). Chicago, IL: The University of Chicago Press.

Wiener, N. (1950/1954). *The human use of human beings: Cybernetics and society.* New York: Houghton Mifflin, 1950 (Second edition revised, Doubleday Anchor, 1954).

Wilber, K. (1979). *No boundary.* Boston, MA: New Science Library.

Wilcox, R., & Knapp, A. (2000). Building communities that create health. *Public Health Reports, 115*, 2 & 3, 139–143.

Wilkinson, R. (1996). *Unhealthy societies: The afflictions of inequality.* New York: Routledge.

Wilson, E. O. (1975). *Sociobiology: The new synthesis.* Cambridge, MA: The Belnap Press of Harvard University Press.

Wilson, W. J. (1987). *The truly disadvantaged: The inner city, the underclass, and public policy.* Chicago: University of Chicago Press.

Wilson, W. J. (1996). *When work disappears: The world of the new urban poor.* New York: Alfred A. Knopf.

Wirth, L. (1938). Urbanism as a way of life. *American Journal of Sociology, 44*, 1–24.

Wise, J. M. (1997). *Exploring technology and social space.* Thousand Oaks, CA: Sage.

Wituk, S. A., Shepherd, M. D., Warren, M., & Meissen, G. (2002). Factors contributing to the survival of self-help groups. *American Journal of Community Psychology, 30*, 349–366.

Wolf, S. (1992). Predictors of myocardial infarction over a span of 30 years in Roseto, Pennsylvania. *Integrative Physiological & Behavioral Science, 27*, 246–257.

Wolf, S., & Bruhn, J. G. (1993). *The power of clan: The influence of human relationships on heart disease.* New Brunswick, NJ: Transaction Publishers.

Wolfe, A. (2001). *Moral freedom: The impossible idea that defines the way we live now.* New York: W. W. Norton.

The World Almanac and Book of Facts (2003). New York: World Almanac Books, p. 408.

World Health Organization (2002). Joint United Nations Programme on HIV/AIDS (UNAIDS). *AIDS epidemic update,* December, 2002.

Wortman, C. B., & Conway, T. L. (1985). The role of social support in adaptation and recovery from physical illness. In S. Cohen & S. L. Syme (Eds.), *Social support and health* (pp. 281–302). New York: Academic Press.

Wright, J. D. (1989). *Address unknown: The homeless in America.* New York: Aldine de Gruyter.

Wrong, D. H. (1976). *Skeptical sociology.* New York: Columbia University Press.

Wuthnow, R. (1998). *Loose connections: Joining together in America's fragmented communities.* Cambridge, MA: Harvard University Press.

Wuthnow, R., & Evans, J. H. (Eds.). (2002). *The quiet hand of God: Faith based activism and the public role of mainline Protestantism.* Berkeley, CA: University of California Press.

Wuthnow, R. (2000). How religious groups promote forgiving: A national study. *Journal for the Scientific Study of Religion, 39*, 125–140.

Yinger, J. M. (1985). Ethnicity. *Annual Review of Sociology, 11*, 151–180.

Young, F. W. (2001). Review essay: Putnam's challenge to community sociology. *Rural Sociology, 66*, 3, 468–474.

Zhou, M. (1992). *New York's Chinatown: The socioeconomic potential of an urban enclave*. Philadelphia: Temple University Press.

Zinner, E. S., & Williams, M. (Eds.). (1999). *When a community weeps: Case studies in group survivorship*. Philadelphia, PA: Brunner/Mazel.

Zlotnick, C., & Robertson, M. J. (1999). The impact of childhood foster care and other out-of-home placement on homeless women and their children. *Child Abuse and Neglect: The International Journal, 23*, 11, 1057–1069.

Index

285